The Politics of Evidence and Results
in International Development

Praise for the book

'This report from the aid trenches is a brilliant exploration of how power and politics can distort or even wreck a potentially sound idea (measuring impact), and provides valuable advice on how to turn the results agenda into a positive force.'

Duncan Green, Senior Strategic
Adviser, Oxfam GB

'While few would question the value of evidence-informed policy, not enough questions have been asked about the politics of evidence itself. This radical and thought-provoking book challenges the reader to consider how the evidence and results agenda in international development has the potential to dilute efforts to pursue transformational change in favour of incremental, more easily measured but less impactful improvements. Importantly, the authors remind us that the production of evidence isn't a technical process but a deeply political one, where some voices, some ways of counting, are valued more than others.'

Heather Marquette, Director of the Developmental
Leadership Program (DLP) and the Governance
and Social Development Resource Centre (GSDRC),
University of Birmingham

'Approaches to development, and methods to evaluate development results, run the gamut from simple to complex. Across this spectrum of diverse development initiatives and accompanying calls for rigorous evidence of results, there is one constant: politics. Thus has it always been and thus will it inevitably be. The danger is that acknowledging the intrinsically political nature of development evaluation leads to cynicism. This book not only avoids that danger, it offers concrete strategies for generating and using results and evidence that support transformational development. Such development seeks to change power dynamics that sustain inequality, foment injustice, and undermine human rights. Far from avoiding or lamenting politics, this book shows that being sophisticated about political games and playing those games astutely can enhance transformation while meeting accountability demands and learning what works for whom in what ways under what conditions. Political sophistication becomes an asset that makes dealing with power effectively an opportunity not a quagmire. But you have to know how to play the game. This is the instruction manual.'

Michael Quinn Patton, author of
Utilization-Focused Evaluation

'*The Politics of Evidence and Results in International Development* shows that designing development projects that are easily measurable, rather than development projects that address underlying causes, can be counter-productive. Even so, it states that transformational development and the results agenda can be mutually supportive, if you know what and how to do it. This book provides some pointers.'

Marco Segone, Director, Independent
Evaluation Office, UNWomen, and Chair,
United Nations Evaluation Group

'Despite the common sense appeal of the push for improved accountability and focus on results, it is clear that these can and often do lead to reduced transparency and performance. This timely book not only documents how this occurs, in specific and diverse examples, it explains what can and should be done differently.'

Patricia J. Rogers, Professor of Public Sector
Evaluation and Director, BetterEvaluation, RMIT
University, Melbourne, Australia

The Politics of Evidence and Results in International Development
Playing the game to change the rules?

Edited by Rosalind Eyben, Irene Guijt,
Chris Roche and Cathy Shutt

PRACTICAL ACTION
Publishing

Practical Action Publishing Ltd
The Schumacher Centre,
Bourton on Dunsmore, Rugby,
Warwickshire, CV23 9QZ, UK
www.practicalactionpublishing.org

A catalogue record for this book is available from the British Library.
A catalogue record for this book has been requested from the Library of Congress.

ISBN 9781853398858 Hardback
ISBN 9781853398865 Paperback
ISBN 9781780448855 Library Ebook
ISBN 9781780448862 Ebook

Citation: Eyben, R., Guijt, I., Roche, C. and Shutt, C. (eds) (2015) *The Politics of Evidence and Results in International Development: Playing the game to change the rules?* Rugby, UK: Practical Action Publishing, <http://dx.doi.org/10.3362/9781780448855>

Since 1974, Practical Action Publishing has published and disseminated books and information in support of international development work throughout the world. Practical Action Publishing is a trading name of Practical Action Publishing Ltd (Company Reg. No. 1159018), the wholly owned publishing company of Practical Action. Practical Action Publishing trades only in support of its parent charity objectives and any profits are covenanted back to Practical Action (Charity Reg. No. 247257, Group VAT Registration No. 880 9924 76).

Cover design by Mercer Design
Indexed by Liz Fawcett
Typeset by Allzone Digital Services Limited
Printed by Berforts Information Press Ltd, United Kingdom

Contents

Lists of figures, tables, and boxes

Figures

Tables

Boxes

About the editors

Rosalind Eyben is a feminist anthropologist and Emeritus Fellow at the Institute of Development Studies. Previous books include *Relationships for Aid* (Earthscan, 2006), *Feminists in Development Organizations* (Practical Action, 2013), and *International Aid and the Making of a Better World* (Routledge, 2014). She was a Big Push Forward convener.

Irene Guijt is a rural development specialist with 25 years' experience in participatory processes in planning and monitoring and evaluation. She is particularly curious about how to understand what we do not know we need to know that is critical for transformative change. She is a research associate for the Overseas Development Institute on impact evaluation. She is active in global evaluation capacity-building through BetterEvaluation and on theory of change with Hivos. She was a Big Push Forward convener.

Chris Roche was one of the conveners of the Big Push Forward. He is Associate Professor of International Development and Director of the Institute for Human Security and Social Change at La Trobe University. He was previously Director of Development Effectiveness at Oxfam Australia.

Cathy Shutt is an academic with over 20 years' experience within the international development sector. She is particularly interested in how different operations of power help or hinder social change. Cathy combines teaching on politics and power in aid institutions with consultancy work focused on learning for transformation and value for money. She was a Big Push Forward convener.

Acknowledgements

This book is the outcome of an international conference organized by the book's editors in 2013, with Brendan Whitty. The conference was for people who wanted their work in international development to support local, national, and global efforts to transform power relations for greater social justice and the realization of rights within a political context of ever increasing emphasis on certain kinds of tangible results and evidence. Participants were invited to share experiences and strategize about their efforts; most shared rich, varied, and frank cases, a small selection of which have been developed into chapters for the present book. These – and all the other cases discussed at the conference – take us beyond simple generalizations about the results agenda. We are grateful to all those who participated for their efforts and willingness to reflect critically on their own and each other's politics of results and evidence.

We gratefully acknowledge the administrative and communications support received from the Institute of Development Studies in hosting the conference. We also thank the conference's voluntary rapporteurs whose dedication allowed us to capture these discussions: Anna Roche (coordinator), Itil Asmon, Bodile Arensman, Therese Brolin, Rebecca Carter, Kate Newman, Chris Speed, Yang Ting, Josephine Tsui, Paola Velasco, and Mike Wang. We thank Fiona Donohoue and Anna Altmann of the Institute for Human Security and Social Change, La Trobe University for managing the author contracts. Alice Eldridge made a vital contribution by creating and managing the Big Push Forward website from its early beginnings, making it possible for the debate to reach and benefit from the input of many practitioners concerned and curious about the results agenda.

Funders were crucial for the conference and for the entire Big Push Forward initiative that underpinned it, including for the preparation of the present book. For their support, we are grateful to 3ie, Australian National University, Big Lottery, Comic Relief, Hivos, ICCO, In-Develop, La Trobe University, Mercy Corps, Murdoch University, Oxfam America, Oxfam International, Swiss Development Cooperation Agency (SDC), Swedish Development Agency (Sida), and WaterAid, plus grants from two individuals who prefer to remain anonymous.

Finally, the editors would like to thank Clare Tawney and Toby Milner of Practical Action Publishing for their interest and encouragement in making this book a reality.

List of abbreviations and acronyms

ACFID   Australian Council for International Development
AEJ   Arbeitsgemeinschaft der Evangelischen Jugend
BMZ   Federal Ministry for Economic Cooperation and
        Development (Germany)
BPF   Big Push Forward
CBA   cost–benefit analysis
CEO   chief executive officer
CFO   co-financing organization (for Dutch NGOs)
CFP   Co-financing Programme (for Dutch NGOs)
CSO   civil society organization
DAC   Development Assistance Committee
DFID   Department for International Development (United
        Kingdom)
DGIS   Dutch Ministry of Development Cooperation
DIB   development impact bond
DPO   disabled people's organization
GIZ   Deutsche Gesellschaft für Internationale Zusammenarbeit
GPE   Global Partnership for Education
GTZ   Gesellschaft für Technische Zusammenarbeit
HICODEF   Himalayan Community Development Forum
HTMB   hard-to-measure benefits
IBO   Interdepartmental Policy Research (Netherlands)
ICAI   Independent Commission for Aid Impact (United Kingdom)
INGO   international non-governmental organization
LFA   logical framework approachM&E monitoring and evaluation
MBO   management by objectives
MIT   Massachusetts Institute of Technology
NGO   non-governmental organization
NPM   new public management
OBI   Open Budget Initiative
OECD   Organisation for Economic Co-operation and Development
PBR   payment by results
PIM   Participatory Impact Monitoring
PwC   PricewaterhouseCoopers
RCT   randomized control trial
SIDA   Swedish International Development Authority
Sida   Swedish International Development Agency
SiRS   Sida internal Rating System
SMART   simple, measurable, achievable, relevant, time-bound

SROI	social return on investment
ToC	theory of change
UNCRC	United Nations Convention on the Rights of the Child
USAID	United States Agency for International Development
VfM	value for money

Counting Guts

How does one persuade the pains of identity
to fit obediently into assessment charts?
The struggle for change
Tears your stomach apart
Your intestines fall at your feet.
Still, you have to pick them up and count them.
Counting guts is not the problem...
How does one turn them into a stringed quartet?

Last night we turned our back
on a feast of delicacies
and ran into the arms of a writer.
A woman ripe in beauty and age who sixty years ago
had rushed off for a glimpse of the great Tagore,
braving the displeasure of her parents.
The icebergs of history that
melted in our warm embrace –which frameworks can they be bent into?
which indicators can contain them?
what are the measures that will absorb them?
Yet measure we must.

We need to break free of the
python grip of mechanical measures.
As we exercise our assessments and indicators
we must exult at the beauty of
the heated muscles of our brain.
we must learn to capture
the twilights of history which
know no boundaries...

Volga (P. Lalitha Kumari)

Reproduced here with kind permission of the poet. Written based on her participation at the Hivos partner consultation on results assessment in Bangalore, 5 February 2004.

CHAPTER 1
Introduction

Rosalind Eyben and Irene Guijt

Abstract

This chapter introduces the concerns that have guided the Big Push Forward and its culminating conference about the politics of evidence from which originated the case studies in the present book. The book's principal themes that emerge from the case studies are identified and the chapter concludes with a summary outline of the contributing chapters.

Keywords: Big Push Forward, results and evidence, power practices, accountability, transformational development

In June 2014, the board of the Global Partnership for Education (GPE) adopted a new funding model 'to have a positive leveraging effect on the development of national sector-wide policies, strategies and systems' (GPE, 2014: 4). Thirty per cent of the funds were to be used for ex-post payments against pre-determined results. The United Kingdom, Australia, and the United States had pushed for a greater percentage of the allocation to be through payment by results (PBR), but the majority of the board members were reluctant to risk a higher proportion of funding to a bold experiment they did not fully understand – and of which the pilot phase was cancelled. One of those objecting to PBR in principle (a civil society representative) emailed Rosalind Eyben:

> I don't think the Board really understood the implications of this when it approved this new model – and [recipient] countries certainly were not aware of what this means in practice.

Despite some discomfort about where the PBR model was taking them, most board members found it difficult to challenge the proposal. Everyone wants results! Eyben's informant, on the other hand, was keenly aware of how PBR risks instrumentalizing education, apart from its possible perverse effects (see Chapter 2). He feared that judging children's performance against measurable learning outcomes would become the sole yardstick for value, crowding out a transformational approach to education as a process of empowerment.

PBR is one of the mechanisms of a 'results and evidence agenda' that seeks to improve and manage development aid through protocols, procedures, and mechanisms for reporting, tracking, disbursing, appraising, and evaluating its effectiveness and impact. As detailed in Chapter 2, the agenda became influential

http://dx.doi.org/10.3362/9781780448855.001

in the first decade of the present century, with, by around 2010, an increasing number of development practitioners concerned about what they saw to be the agenda's pernicious effects. As in the GPE case, they worried that the results and evidence agenda undermined the potential for development aid to support transformational development and risked reinforcing power relations and structures that reproduce rather than diminish inequality, injustice, and the non-fulfilment of human rights. Concerned practitioners mentioned the time and money wasted in negotiating with funders over the utility and feasibility of imposed protocols and complained of the accountability pressure that forced the generation of 'sausage numbers' (Chapter 3), leaving limited time and energy for adaptive and responsive programming in support of complex change processes. One worried senior official from a United Nations agency rang the authors of this chapter to explain how his agency had negotiated for several months with a government funder:

> They themselves knew it was ridiculous what they were asking for but they said it was political. In the end it comes down to money and for X millions of dollars we had to agree. But we rely on you academics working on the flanks to start a conversation about this.

Where could these and the growing number of other concerned voices discuss the trends, consequences, and options?

The initial impetus for what became the Big Push Forward (BPF) was a conference in May 2010 in the Netherlands about evaluation in complex contexts (Guijt et al., 2011). Although it was borne out of a deep disquiet about how the term 'rigour' had been captured by advocates of certain impact approaches, most participants discussed methodological innovations and challenges with little reference to the shrinking political space within which the methods discussed could be used. Knowing that many practitioners were interested in the politics of how impact and results are defined and assessed, the authors organized a meeting in Britain where more than 70 participants shared their experiences and reaction to the results and evidence agenda. Six months later (April 2011) we launched the BPF to make the results and evidence agenda a legitimate subject for public debate. Our first blog laid out the challenge:

> Hard evidence, rigorous data, conclusive proof, value for money, evidence-based policy are tantalizing terms promising clarity about what works and what should be funded in international development. Yet behind these terms lie definitional tussles, vested interests and contested worldviews. For those who hold the purse strings, certain ways of knowing and assessing impact are considered more legitimate than others. Yet increasingly people are recognizing the need for multiple and mixed methods and approaches to better understand complex change and that these compared to imposed standards are more likely to lead to fair assessments helping us learn how to support a fairer world.[1]

In the two years that followed, development practitioners commented on our blogs and debated the issues at meetings and workshops with us, including in Germany, the Netherlands, Nigeria, Sweden, Switzerland, the United States, and the United Kingdom. In Australia, for example, we contributed to a workshop on evaluation methods for staff of AusAID (now part of the Department of Foreign Affairs and Trade), organized by the Development Leadership Programme. Participants discussed the practical challenges staff faced in juggling methodological and political demands in the messiness of development programming in complex contexts (Roche and Kelly, 2012). In these forums, practitioners spoke of managing these demands in ways that would enable them to pursue approaches more aligned with transformational development. We found that the politically alert were subtly playing the game and changing the rules, with some seeing the results agenda as creating opportunities to support transformational development.

The BPF conveners (joined in mid-2011 by Chris Roche, Cathy Shutt, and Brendan Whitty) were discovering how diverse and context-specific the effects of the results and evidence agenda were. Findings from a BPF survey (Chapter 3), comments on our website and the 'From Poverty to Power' debate (Green, 2013) revealed that the agenda was not necessarily harmful; it could trigger improvements in design and learning, as well as in accountability. Yet, whether on balance the effects were judged as positive or negative for transformational development depended on the perspective of the judge. That, in turn, begged a political question: 'Whose perspective counts?' We realized that such a fundamental question, along with others about the values and ideology of the results and evidence agenda, risked being ignored in a context of 'highly constrained resources, crazy time pressure, and the need to deliver some (any!) results to feed the MEL [monitoring, evaluation, learning] machine' (ibid.).

Furthermore, while accounts about the more negative power dynamics of the agenda were circulating over cups of coffee and glasses of beer, detailed case studies were rare. People were frightened of going public about their experiences of distortions and problems. They feared exposing international aid to an often-sceptical press, or being subjected to ridicule – or worse, putting their jobs or organizations at risk. The BPF conveners, therefore, decided to create an opportunity for practitioners and researchers to reflect critically on these issues in a safe space through a conference held in April 2013. We organized it so as to protect participants' identities, with a strict insistence on 'Chatham House rules'.[2] Even so, some participants were reluctant to present case studies (even verbally) and others unwilling to go public in this book. Power was influencing people to opt out of sharing their experience of the reality of the situation. Even the contributors here have exercised care in their decisions about what to include and what to leave out of their chapters – and about how to portray choices about results and evidence.

To our chagrin, budget constraints prevented the financing of participants' travel and other costs, limiting the range of perspectives present at the conference.[3] Apart from a video link with Ola Abu Alghaib in Ramallah, experiences of grantee organizations in aid-recipient countries were largely absent (as they are in this book). Participants were either development agency staff (bilateral, multilateral, and international non-governmental organization (NGO)) or managers or technical advisers in projects these agencies funded. The others were consultants and researchers, as were the BPF conveners.

The conference was organized around participants' own case studies of the artefacts – the processes, mechanisms, and tools employed by them and their organizations to assess results and to generate and use evidence (Chapter 2). This book contains a selection of these cases, as well as an assessment of the organizational and power dynamics associated with their use. Conference participants examined whether and how one can reconcile messy, unpredictable, and risky pathways of societal transformation with bureaucracy-driven protocols. Participants stressed the importance of conscious engagement in the politics of evidence (Chapter 11), providing positive examples of how they either successfully resisted the unhelpful demands of the results and evidence agenda or used these to good effect to challenge myths, promote methodological advances, and gain theoretical insights.

We chose the conference title 'The Politics of Evidence' from Denzin and Giardina's (2008) volume about why and how academic institutions and policy-making bodies regard evidence from qualitative research as being less robust and rigorous than quantitative research. We broadened the 'politics of evidence' term to encompass both how power works to define what is or is not accepted as robust evidence or determined as a result (in both programming and evaluation), and the resistance and contestation that such power generates.

Power and the politics of evidence

We analyse power both as an asset that individuals and organizations control and also as a process to which we are all subject.[4] When conceptualizing 'power' as an asset, the politics concerns who controls the definition of a result or of evidence and what is acceptable to whom (Morse, 2006). This kind of power operates through the formal institutional arrangements for policy-making and implementation, such as the civil service, the legislature, and local government; certain policy actors, such as ministers and parliamentarians, are visibly powerful. Janet Vähämäki (Chapter 8) uses this perspective on power to examine 30 years of recurrent struggle over results-based management between Swedish ministers and the staff of the Swedish International Development Agency (Sida). Power as an asset can also be less formal. Private individuals and organizations, such as philanthropic foundations or academic think tanks, influence meaning and value in development. The financial or intellectual capital they deploy gives them legitimacy in articulating and promoting (or interrogating) the discourse. In 2012, the BPF (itself exercising some modest power in this manner) undertook a preliminary power analysis of the results and evidence agenda from this perspective, as summarized in Chapter 2.

Power as an asset can be related to the idea of 'power over', when A (with more power) controls how B (with less power) behaves. The international aid system is often portrayed as a power chain – official aid agencies at the top, international NGOs and recipient governments in the middle, and local community organizations at the bottom. Yet many rules and procedures cannot be clearly attributed to specific decisions made by identifiable actors. Much of the results and evidence agenda is an effect of more diffuse power dynamics. Even when someone 'in charge' makes a decision, they may be unaware of – or indeed unable to prevent – what actually happens, since this is an outcome of multiple interactions by myriads of interconnected actors. Those in authority – chief executives and government ministers – are as much subjects of power as the most junior staff member; and multilateral aid agencies as much as grassroots organizations.

This kind of invisible power is at work in all our relationships – each time we walk into a room, make a suggestion, or participate in a workshop. It is the process of socializing and embedding that shapes what we think, say, and do. An example from the present book is how societal norms render children marginalized and their voices disregarded (Chapter 9). Participatory and visual evaluation methodologies designed to elicit children's perspectives and knowledge fail to influence adult decisions, unless there are complementary efforts to change the social norms. Because it shapes habitual patterns of relations, this kind of power is rarely noticed – and therefore remains unchallenged. 'Power relations were never discussed during the term of the project: nobody brought it up,' observe Bernward Causemann and Eberhard Gohl (Chapter 10). Only by becoming aware of such power can anyone seek to change inequities in the relationship, an act of conscious agency.

Both of these approaches to power are drawn upon in *Power and Organizations*, which identifies 'significant and subtle power practices' (Clegg et al., 2006: 176) at work in institutional life. We find six approaches particularly relevant to the international development sector. Awareness of these can help people understand the nature of their experience with the results and evidence agenda:

- locking members inside and keeping outsiders out and systematically misrepresenting other realities;
- the division of labour into complex chains of power, enabling those at the top to maintain a distance from the effects of power;
- staff staying obedient through a ceaseless round of activities with little time for reflection;
- delegation to intermediaries, obliging them to implement decisions that have been made higher up the system;
- making those who are the subjects of power complicit in its exercise;
- applying instrumental and value-free science.

Reference is made to these power practices in the thematic analysis that follows.

Principal themes

The case studies in this book take up two substantive issues of concern to those interested in transformational development, namely the impact of the evidence and results agenda on the ability to pursue rights-based approaches and whether the growing emphasis on upward accountability is trumping mutual learning. Perspectives on these issues are informed by personal values and professional formation, and influenced by the position – or positionality – of individuals in an organization or of an organization within the aid system. These interact to affect people's judgement as to whether, on balance, the effects of the results and evidence agenda are positive or negative and to influence how people respond to the changes induced by that agenda. The dynamics of perspective and of push and response are thus examined first, followed by a discussion of how these play out with respect to the substantive issues of rights/results and learning/accountability.

Position and perspective

We launched the BPF to 'push back' against the bureaucracy-driven protocols we believed were shrinking the possibilities of development organizations supporting messy, unpredictable, and risky pathways of societal transformation. Not everyone shared our initial views! The survey of practitioners conducted prior to the conference (Chapter 3) suggests that whether the agenda's effects are experienced as largely positive or negative depends on a person's organizational role and on their organization's location in the aid nexus. BPF conveners fell into that category of development professionals, mainly academics and consultants, with the most negative views of the results and evidence agenda. In contrast, people with monitoring and evaluation (M&E) responsibilities had more positive experiences than, for example, programme officers, and senior staff were more positive than technical advisers or those in middle management. The importance of position and perspective is also evident in Chapter 5, where Chris Roche looks at the arguments between managers responsible for finance and fundraising, who want standardized, organization-wide performance measures, and those in programming and advocacy, who seek a variety of forms of assessment and reporting depending on the context and activity.

However, the survey was far from comprehensive. Very few recipient governments and national NGOs responded, with even fewer responses from smaller civil society organizations in the South. Abu Alghaib's experience in leading a network of disabled people's organizations (DPOs) and her research findings into the experience of other DPOs in the region (Chapter 7) indicate that such organizations have been impacted negatively by the results agenda. Her case study of what happened to her own organization after winning a grant from a multilateral agency is a devastating account of the impunity and arrogance of a bureaucratic machine that 'makes those who are subjects of power complicit in its exercise' (Clegg et al., 2006: 179). In the end, writes Abu Alghaib, 'the organization became a stranger in its own project'.

Although Abu Alghaib had no access to the internal workings of the bureaucratic machine that had triggered such effects, other chapters written from an inside perspective show such bureaucracy to be more heterogeneous than might appear when viewed from the end link of the chain. Vähämäki's account of the evolution of the results agenda in Sida tells how staff were aware of the possible negative effects of what they were asking from grantees. In the 1970s, Sida field offices were already complaining: 'Talks and observations on how results valuation affect the Kenyans has given me goose bumps' (Chapter 8).

As Roche discusses (Chapter 5), it is difficult to imagine what the world might look like if one were positioned differently. Causemann and Gohl (Chapter 10) observe that Southern NGO staff had little understanding of the realities and needs of the German NGOs, intermediaries in the funding chain:

> They had hardly ever travelled to Germany to meet NGO staff there, and as such did not have an opportunity to experience the realities of a donor desk officer ... Donor desk officers told us they lacked the time for such explanation, but we did not see that they recognized the need, not appreciating how hard it was for Southern NGOs to put donor requirements in context.

Two practices of power are at work in the above example: maintaining a distance between the designated exercisers and subjects of power, and ensuring NGO obedience to power through 'a ceaseless round of activity with little room for reflection' (Clegg et al., 2006: 178).

Another subtle power practice is to delegate to intermediaries decisions that have been made higher up the system (ibid.: 177). Intermediary organizations, for example a UN agency or a Northern development NGO, as well as individuals in middle-management positions, can have a 'squeezed middle' experience (Chapter 2) when they are aware of the potential negative effects of what is asked of them. These individuals are responsible for reporting results while at the same time trying to protect the front line from the perceived excessive demands of those higher up the chain. Marjan van Es and Irene Guijt (Chapter 6) discuss how the programme officers in a Dutch NGO, Hivos, were 'balancing between insisting on justified requirements for accountability while maintaining a flexible attitude to enable responsive programming by partners'. Intermediaries are potential brokers because their position provides them with more than one perspective; this enables them to adopt creative responses to this particular power practice, and these are examined in this book's conclusion (Chapter 11.)

The dynamics of pressure and response

Some of the chapters usefully take a historical perspective on pressure from and reactions to the results and evidence agenda, illustrating the dynamics of thinking and practice. Vähämäki analyses her case with reference to the literature on management reform cycles in public sector bodies that highlights politicians' desire to control by institutionalizing new management technologies. These technologies inevitably fail to meet expectations, yet subsequent governments ignore history and try again. Her case study – an account of top-down pressure and of staff resistance – appears to support the theory that every 'failure allows the surge of new optimism for yet another round of reforms' (Chapter 8). Rosalind Eyben (Chapter 2) notes how 'performance measurement systems' operate in a near-continual cycle of reform, but rather than history just repeating itself, each failure results in the introduction of more stringent and controlling practices, echoing Vähämäki's account of the most recent phase in Sida. Vähämäki cites senior managers' belief that this time – at last – the reforms might trigger their intended effects. One reason she cites for this situation is that long-serving staff have retired – or, as Rosalind Eyben discovered when participating in a BPF-initiated public meeting in Stockholm, they have resigned because of their unhappiness with the new organizational culture of compliance and silence (driven by the results agenda) – to be replaced by new staff who share management's vision of a results-oriented Sida.

Describing the experience of Hivos, van Es and Guijt note that: 'Although the need for more systematic and better quality result information of partners for organizational learning was internally felt and discussed ... there was little external pressure to change existing M&E practices' (Chapter 6). But from the early 2000s, growing internal and external pressures triggered a creative process of improving the organization's and its partners' M&E capacities in ways that sought to stay faithful to Hivos' transformational objectives and partnership values. Some partners were critical of the new request for indicators, despite Hivos giving them the freedom to choose, asking 'why social change investments and agencies are being so closely scrutinized for effectiveness and impact, when private sector actors are not similarly held to account' (Chapter 6).

Causemann and Gohl tell a similar story of how in the early 2000s a network of German NGOs came under increasing pressure from the German government and the European Union to improve their reporting of results. Moreover, 'NGOs themselves, many of whom financed themselves by public donations or by foundation funds rather than through government funding, also believed that the public expected enhanced accountability on the outcomes and impacts achieved with a results-based mindset' (Chapter 10). A group of NGOs took the initiative in designing an approach 'before the government imposed more restrictive requirements'.

In contrast to these historical analyses that take us up to the present day, Cathy Shutt focuses on the current dynamics of push and response in the UK. She examines how a network of individuals from foundations and development NGOs – as well as the Department for International Development (DFID) itself – responded to DFID's emphasis on value for money (VFM) from 2010 onwards by simultaneously adapting their practice to respond to the VFM discourse while keeping open the space for continued

DFID funding of transformational development that many believed was under threat (Chapter 4). Ex-post VFM analyses provided grant-makers with opportunities for learning:

> The main reason an outstanding programme that began with a few women getting together to reflect on their lives led to a successful political and social movement anticipated to provide economic empowerment for several thousands living in their community was the extreme flexibility the grant-maker allowed the women in their use of funds.

This is in striking contrast to the stringent requirements placed on the women's DPO that Abu Alghaib describes in an account of the organization's response to the promotion of the results agenda (Chapter 7).

As further discussed in the book's conclusion, collectively the case studies reveal a wide variance in organizational responses to the demands of the results and evidence agenda. We now turn to discuss how this diversity of positionality and organizational dynamics with respect to the results and evidence agenda plays out with respect to the challenge of pursuing rights-based approaches, and when and how upward accountability trumps organizational learning.

Rights and results

Rights-based, transformational approaches (where 'how' matters as much as 'what') and transactional results-based management (focused on the 'what') may be uncomfortable bedfellows (Hulme, 2010). The number of agencies, particularly international NGOs, using rights language has continued to increase, but the contradiction between rights-based approaches and their political and process approach to intangible goals such as empowerment and the increasing popularity of results-based management has become very apparent. It is harder to manage support for transformational approaches when one is required to report tangible, easy-to-measure changes, as discussed, for example, by van Es and Guijt (Chapter 6) with respect to the experience of Hivos, a Dutch NGO committed to transformational development.

Like Hivos, the BPF conveners understand transformational development as involving processes of political change that secure a greater realization of rights and social justice. We understand poverty as a product of structured relationships of unequal power, and, as David Mosse puts it, 'the consequence of normal economic and political relations' (2007:6). Hence, from this perspective, transformation is a process that changes the status quo. However, because the international development sector is part of 'normal economic and social relations', when it seeks to support transformational development it encounters fundamental contradictions concerning its legitimacy of action, its practice of power, and its lines of accountability, all of which are recurrent themes in the politics of evidence and results, as explored in this volume's chapters. It is only by addressing these contradictions that the sector has the potential to make a modest contribution to processes of transformational change. A transformational approach is thus about both means – how and with whom the sector behaves – and values. In Table 4.1 in Chapter 4, Shutt contrasts aid as transactional (value-free, technical, focusing on the 'what') with aid that supports transformational change. In the same chapter (Table 4.2), she demonstrates how a managerial concept such as the practice of VFM can be adapted to serve transformational change, provided its users are conscious of their values and of the power relations at play. And in Chapter 5, Roche explores how the meaning and practice of accountability – another central theme in current international development practice – change when associated with a transformational development approach.

We equate a transformational with a rights-based approach, and we understand this approach as providing a normative framework (human rights) that not only guides development practice but also – and importantly – is one in which:

> People are placed at the centre of development processes, no longer seen as beneficiaries of development projects with needs, but as active citizens with rights and entitlements. As a result, aid can be seen as contributing to the transformation of state–society relations [that empower] all citizens to claim their rights ... Politics and power relations are thus put at the centre of programming analysis and interventions rather than seen as negative 'risk' factors attached to projects. (Piron, 2005: 22–3)

Not everyone at the Politics of Evidence conference agreed with us. In conference evaluation feedback, one participant criticized 'transformational development' for being highly normative, with assumptions about what aid could or could not achieve. Rather, the participant wrote, the purpose of aid is to support local development 'which may or may not be transformative depending on the context and need'. We believe, however, that when aid is indifferent to the power relations of the process, is regarded as objectively technical (non-normative), and concentrates on outcomes, then by default it risks contributing to the maintenance of inequitable power relations that prevent greater social justice. For this reason, we fear that the results agenda may have a negative effect when framed in terms of efficiency and effectiveness – a power practice that applies 'instrumental and value-free science' (Clegg et al., 2006: 177) that is common to transactional approaches that treat rights as a measurable project outcome (Ackerman, 2005).

In Chapter 2, Eyben discusses how, in 1997, the New Labour government in the UK introduced the discourse of technical, value-free 'evidence' to escape accusations that its policies were driven by old-fashioned socialist ideology. In Sweden (Chapter 8), results-based approaches were promoted by both centre-right and centre-left governments. Historically, the results and evidence agenda can be seen as part of the 'new public management' paradigm, modelled on corporate sector practices designed to maximize shareholder profit and eschewing any explicit ideological commitment (which, of course, does not preclude such practices being informed by tacit values and ideology).

Even a development agency still subscribing to a normative human rights framework may prejudice transformational development if it focuses solely on outcomes and ignores process. Abu Alghaib's chapter (Chapter 7) provides such a case of a funder focused on the delivery of rights outcomes. The funder undermined the grantee's rights-based approach that was one of recognizing and respecting the situation of marginalized groups and providing space and time for them to gradually build their self-confidence as a precursor to claiming their rights. By assuming and requiring that the small and doubly marginalized network of women's DPOs should be capable of organizing themselves into national advocacy networks within a two-year funding period, the donor agency was adopting a transactional results-based approach despite framing its support in terms of realizing rights. Similarly, Oxfam Australia (Chapter 5) risked undermining its commitment to a rights-based approach through its head office's desire for transformational change in impossibly short time frames.

Johnson (Chapter 9) also shows how talking about 'rights' does not necessarily imply a rights-based approach. In revisiting projects she had evaluated some 10 years earlier, she found that, while everyone agreed on the importance of children's rights, participatory evaluation approaches enabling children's voices to be heard were under threat. NGO staff were under pressure to deliver a certain kind of evidence they described as 'hard', in contrast to the 'soft' children's evidence from participatory visual methods. Vähämäki (Chapter 8) noticed that even the mere reference to transformational development (let alone support for transformative processes) was disappearing. Sida staff feel that the increasing emphasis on results and reporting systems has made them lose sight of the agency's purpose. 'Results, transparency, and accountability' have become the primary reform objectives, prioritized above content themes such as gender and poverty reduction.

Shutt, on the other hand, describes how some British development NGOs are managing to square this circle. These NGOs initially believed that DFID's VFM requirements threatened transformational development projects:

> And, even though there was no evidence to imply long-term social change programmes were receiving less money, some working on such initiatives were frustrated that the focus on quantitative metrics denied adequate discussion of qualitative dimensions of value.

Yet, enabled by their relationships with 'politically savvy DFID staff equally frustrated with DFID's focus on economy and efficiency', over time the NGOs are succeeding in interpreting VFM in ways consistent with transformational development. Nevertheless, only some grantees have succeeded in playing the game to change the rules. The particularly difficult challenge for those engaged in transformational development is to avoid diluting their efforts and ideas of what counts as evidence of change.

Learning and accountability

While there is no doubt that the results and evidence agenda is a veritable battlefield between 'accountability' and 'learning', the issue is more nuanced than the stereotypical frustration about upward accountability always trumping learning (Wallace and Porter, 2013).

As a positive, accountability pressures can stimulate deep organizational discussions on core values and what success looks like, along with heightened appreciation of the contribution of M&E as an organizational practice. Half of the 153 respondents in the BPF survey reported that the push for results had led to some or considerable improvement in their organization's ability to learn (Chapter 3). The head of Oxfam Great Britain's M&E unit commented that 'five years ago [we] struggled to get the ear of senior managers (let alone ministers). But the results agenda has increased the stakes ... encouraging organizations not only to increase investment, but also to listen to the findings coming from our own data gathering and analysis' (Richmond, 2013). The Hivos experience echoes this (Chapter 6). Until external pressures accelerated the search for improvements, Hivos' existing M&E practice with partners contributed little to their learning about social change, knowledge sharing, or building new theory and practice. In response to growing demands, the M&E unit at Hivos developed a theory of change (ToC) approach that encourages partners to be explicit, self-critical, and adaptive. In the UK, the VFM debate has also stimulated internal debate and learning around what is valued and how to represent that (Chapter 3).

Perhaps the clue lies in how accountability is defined (Guijt, 2010). If accountability is relational – being answerable to others within a relationship of power (Goetz and Jenkins, 2005), it requires clarity about 'who has the power to call for an account and who is obligated to give an explanation for their actions' (Newell and Bellour, 2002: 2). For transformational development, in which the 'how' is as important as the 'what', being accountable to oneself is essential to understand what one has undertaken, to explain strategic decisions and the ToC, and, of course, to show how money was spent. This form of 'strategic accountability' seeks to answer the question: 'Did we act as effectively as possible with the means we had?' In this sense, accountability is intrinsically about commitment to one's ideas and strategies (Fry, 1995).

Roche (Chapter 5) recounts how the accountability debate opened up space in Oxfam Australia to explore, in particular, more bottom-up processes of feedback. There has been a lot of experimentation in recent times (Guijt, 2014); however, these experiments have often lacked adequate political or power analysis in their design (Fox, 2014). Several chapters allude to this perspective on accountability in which learning plays a critical role in ensuring that organizations are not mere 'delivery agents' but rather 'drivers of change' (Reeler, 2007). Van Es and Guijt explain how Hivos pursued ToC as one learning mechanism to strengthen the strategic accountability of partners and Hivos alike (Chapter 6). Shutt cites a similar example in Chapter 4 using a VFM perspective: 'The HIV/Aids Alliance, one of the earliest adopters, found that comparisons across their portfolio raised questions about sustainability that they could integrate in future planning.' Johnson refers to the way in which deep listening to children can remind decision-makers about what they need to be accountable for – and to whom (Chapter 9).

But tensions remain. And there is a constant need to ask who is learning and for what. Being held accountable means having 'respond-ability', according to Ebrahim (2005). This becomes impossible when organizations are viewed by funders as 'merely ... contractors for implementing the ideas of others' (Chapter 7). Interestingly, even when couched in terms of 'more critical thinking to get better results', some Hivos partner organizations still perceived ToC as 'a donor-driven invention' for upward accountability. This was aggravated in the first years of ToC use, as Southern partners of Hivos noted that while *they* were required to use a ToC to enhance reflective learning, Hivos itself had not done so. Abu Alghaib's survey of 25 DPOs found that only five of these Southern NGOs considered that M&E approaches helped promote organizational learning. And although German NGOs valued regular reporting as an indication that 'something meaningful was happening on the ground' (Chapter 10), reports 'did not contribute to anyone's learning or conceptual development with respect to impact assessment', as reports were not read and were written only to meet accountability requirements. Rigid protocols for reporting back to donors are choking the space to learn and adapt, aggravated by budget pressures.

Consultants hired by Sida observed that the new reporting requirements had not enabled Sida staff to think more 'but rather less' (Chapter 8). Eventually, the push for upward accountability – which generated specific results matrices – created such dire difficulties for those grantees who had to provide the data that reporting became solely the responsibility of Sida staff, a death blow to the original intention of mutual learning. Currently, grantees are not involved – upward accountability trumped learning in this case. The drive is more 'to appear transparent and communicate results than to actually work for results in practice', a Sida director told Vähämäki. A possible irony of the drive for accountability is that, in detaching itself from any reality other than Swedish politics, Sida may have secured what some of its staff have been seeking for the last 30 years: that is, allowing its grantees considerable flexibility to carry out their work free from interference.

Overall, while the results agenda in theory opens up space for bottom-up, people-centred accountability (Melamed, 2011), the narratives in this book are not optimistic about the possibility of leveraging accountability for learning. The particular interpretation of accountability as an upward, financial 'holding to account' on promises obstructs learning but also fails in its raison d'être of communicating to citizens and politicians what has been achieved with taxpayers' money. We need to understand better what makes it possible for what Whitty notes (Chapter 3) is the potential of accountability: 'encouraging a more disciplined reflection on programming that will achieve results, strengthen knowledge management, curb the tendency to "over claim" and improve broader learning processes'.

Structure of the book

Earlier versions of Chapters 2 and 3 were written as framing papers for discussion at the conference. Updated with insights from the conference, they provide crucial context for the nuanced experiences of the results agenda discussed in the case study chapters, which analyse the politics of results and evidence in a variety of organizational contexts and sets of relationships. Two of the cases included in the book are from the UK, with one each from Australia, Germany, the Netherlands, Palestine, and Sweden. They illuminate different sets of relationships in the aid chain, including those between a network of grass-roots organizations and a multilateral agency, within a government agency, between a government agency and its own country's development NGOs, and within and between Northern NGOs and their Southern partners.

Following this introduction, Chapter 2 aims to alert the reader to the way in which power informs the apparently technical and value-free language of efficiency and effectiveness. Rosalind Eyben starts with the tools and protocols – the 'artefacts' – that are the concrete expression of the results and evidence discourses and analyses their diffuse power effects. 'Through a mutually constituted process of production, consumption, and resistance, artefacts evolve and mutate, beyond the control of any individual or organization.' She then traces the interlinked genealogies of the discourses of 'results' and 'evidence' in public sector management and looks at how and why they have become so influential in the international development sector. Armed with these insights, practitioner readers should be better placed to analyse and confront power that works invisibly, normalizing inappropriate means of designing and assessing the kinds of programmes that have multiple pathways of change and a transformational development objective. At the same time, any such power analysis requires reflexivity, a self-awareness to avoid disempowering others.

The other framing chapter (Chapter 3) is Brendan Whitty's analysis of the findings from the crowdsourcing survey. At the Politics of Evidence conference, he brought home the extent to which opinions differ on the pros and cons of the results agenda. His chapter offers insights from over 100 experiences of people's responses to results artefacts, noting how respondents' positive or negative experiences are shaped by their positionality (as discussed above) and – as part of that positionality – by their specific relationship to the production and use of numbers: people in senior management were most positive about how simplification and reporting against common formats provide a useful big picture. Respondents' perspectives are also shaped by their experience of how results-oriented reforms have been implemented in their own part of the sector and by their own organization's capacities for and history of monitoring, evaluation, and reporting. Whitty provides an organizational typology that can particularly help funders engage more productively and sensitively with grantees with low administrative capacity to translate their 'nuanced contexts and programming to standardized administrative formats'. He points out the grave error of funders supporting only those who are good at showing what they can do. Failure to demonstrate this because of limited administrative capacity 'does not necessarily indicate poor work'.

The next three chapters deal with key concepts: VFM, accountability, and ToCs. In Chapter 4, Cathy Shutt makes use of her recent experience in advising variously positioned British development organizations in order to address readers who want to engage politically with the increasingly dominant VFM concept. A useful table summarizes the differences between transformational and transactional development as these relate to VFM, and the chapter helps the reader further by unpacking the different technical elements of assessing VFM. Shutt then discusses the tactics she has observed being deployed to reduce the negative effects of VFM and identifies the possibilities for making the concept more supportive of transformational development. She argues that, positively, VFM can offer power-aware practitioners opportunities to increase accountability to citizens and to each other, and it also has the potential to influence links between VFM and what is valued in development.

In Chapter 5, Chris Roche critiques the upward accountability that is informed by principal–agent theory (as discussed in Chapter 2). Drawing on his experience of working for Oxfam Australia, he describes how Oxfam attempted to adopt an alternative approach that recognized multiple accountabilities and had a particular emphasis on 'bottom-up' or downward accountability. Describing the findings of an independent review into Oxfam's implementation of this alternative approach, Roche looks at how staff positionality has influenced diverse perceptions of how well the organization has been doing, thus making it difficult to secure organization-wide agreement for a single performance framework. To achieve this, we suggest, the organization would need to engage in a strategic conversation about accountability – a conversation that explicitly took account of internal power relations, as well as relations between Oxfam Australia and those with whom it interacts. And this is when the Australian government is ratcheting up the results agenda, cutting aid budgets drastically, and reducing development NGOs' room for manoeuvre. Roche suggests that a greater focus on understanding and sharing the practice of effective relational accountability and its benefits might be an important way forward.

Chapter 6 is also written from a practitioner perspective, and from inside another development NGO. Marjan van Es and Irene Guijt provide a historical account of how, rather than letting itself be pushed around by its principal funder (the Dutch government), Hivos has sought to stay faithful to its transformative development vision by taking the initiative. It responded to the results agenda by elaborating its own approach to ToC as a means of strengthening its strategic accountability: 'Although compliance drained time and energy from staff and further reduced the M&E unit's space to shape processes for Hivos' own results information and learning needs, the unit continued to promote programme quality and critical thinking.' Hivos refrained from using rigid ToC protocols, instead issuing a clear policy statement. Yet staff have now asked for guidelines to ensure a high-quality ToC that, for Hivos, includes political analysis. We wonder whether this raises an interesting contradiction for agencies such as

Hivos. Should critical reflexive practice for social change be mandatory? What is the risk of a thought process becoming a mechanical artefact?

The need to appreciate that large international development agencies are internal political battlefields is a headline in our reading of Chapter 7. Ola Abu Alghaib describes what happened to a grass-roots disabled women's network that, from a position at the end of the aid chain, perceived such an agency as a black box rather than an organization with which they could engage politically. After they succeeded in obtaining funding from a multilateral development organization, 'Women Advance' (a pseudonym), she and her colleagues, like Rosario León, cited in Chapter 2, found themselves obliged to revise and revise again results matrices that bore no relationship to what they were trying to do. 'In effect, staff felt that it had become a project designed by consultants based on a methodology prescribed by Women Advance's staff.' Abu Alghaib tracks her own learning journey from this encounter, including her research into the experience of other DPOs in the Middle East and North Africa. Echoing Whitty's point about effective organizations with low administrative capacity to manage the results agenda, she concludes that such organizations should collectively resist the donor pressure that makes them strangers to their own projects.

In the next chapter, another insider (turned researcher), this time in a government agency, Sida, uses a longer time frame to chronicle the organizational dynamics of push and response. In Chapter 8, Janet Vähämäki reveals a diversity of power relationships and perspectives over a period of 40 years with ministers, senior management, and other staff promoting and resisting the results agenda. For readers wanting to influence a bilateral agency, the chapter demonstrates the importance of undertaking an organizational power analysis, bearing in mind the fact that it is only too easy to assume that such agencies are homogeneous monoliths. In this amazing account, Vähämäki shows us something very different.

While Chapter 7 emphasizes the UN Convention of the Rights of Persons with Disabilities and how donors subscribing to the convention are in practice ignoring the DPOs' principle of 'nothing about us without us', Chapter 9 is about another convention – the Rights of the Child – and looks at how that convention's focus on children's participation is often neglected in programme evaluations. Vicky Johnson analyses how managers and programme leaders ignored children's evidence she had compiled through participatory visual methods and describes how she negotiated the politics of evidence, her tactics, and the resistance she generated. She stresses the need to include people with decision-making power over strategies and budgets in participatory processes to ensure that children's voices are heard. Johnson offers her experience-based framework for others using similar evaluation approaches to elevate marginalized voices.

The final case study concerns a key power practice of the results agenda: project reporting. In Chapter 10, Causemann and Gohl reflect on their experience as 'squeezed middle' project managers employed in a multi-country initiative run by German NGOs and their Southern partners. The co-authors analyse why their Southern partners resisted submitting regular written reports to the German NGOs. Bearing in mind that reports rarely enhance the learning of either the grantee or the funder (the latter often not even reading them), they look at possible strategies for easier and improved reporting, as well as alternatives to reporting. Causemann and Gohl argue that, rather than using formal written reports, it is better to undertake critical analysis and reflection in a process of dialogue.

Lastly, in Chapter 11, Irene Guijt takes a forward-looking perspective, recognizing that the results and evidence agenda is here to stay for some time. Drawing on the book's case studies and the BPF conference report, she looks at how those working in international development can deal with the politics of evidence, in ways that do not compromise the space for supporting transformational development.

References

Ackerman, J.M. (2005) *Human Rights and Social Accountability, Social Development Paper* 86, Washington: World Bank <http://portals.wi.wur.nl/files/docs/gouvernance/HumanRightsandSocial0AccountabilityFINAL.pdf>.

Clegg, S. and Haugaard, M. (2009) *Handbook of Power*, London: Sage.

Clegg, S., Courpasson, D. and Phillips, N. (2006) *Power and Organizations*, London: Sage.

Denzin, N.K. and Giardina, M.D. (eds) (2008) *Qualitative Inquiry and the Politics of Evidence*, Walnut Creek: Left Coast Press.

Ebrahim, A. (2005) 'Accountability myopia: losing sight of organizational learning', *Nonprofit and Voluntary Sector Quarterly* 34(1): 56–87.

Fox, J. (2014) 'Social accountability: what does the evidence really say?', keynote speech at the Global Partners Forum of the Global Partnership for Social Accountability, 14–15 May 2014.

Fry, R.E. (1995) 'Accountability in organizational life: problem or opportunity for non-profits?', *Non-profit Management and Leadership* 6: 181–95.

Goetz, A.M. and Jenkins, R. (2005) *Reinventing Accountability: Making Democracy Work for Human Development*, Basingstoke: Palgrave Macmillan.

GPE (2014) 'Report of the country grants and performance committee part 1: operational framework for requirements and incentives in the funding model of the global partnership for education and results- based financing pilot', BOD/2014/05–DOC 03, May 2014, Washington DC: Global Partnership for Education (GPE).

Green, D. (2013) 'So what do I take away from the great evidence debate? Final thoughts (for now)', in From Poverty to Power [blog] <http://oxfamblogs.org/fp2p/so-what-do-i-take-away-from-the-great-evidence-debate-final-thoughts-for-now/>.

Guijt, I. (2010) 'Exploding the myth of incompatibility between accountability and learning', in J. Ubels, N.-A. Acquaye-Baddoo and A. Fowler (eds), *Capacity Development in Practice*, London and Washington DC: Earthscan.

Guijt, I. (2014) 'Feedback loops – new buzzword, old practice?' in Better Evaluation [blog] <http://betterevaluation.org/blog/feedback_loops_new_buzzword_old_practice>.

Guijt, I., Brouwers, J., Kusters, C., Prins, E. and Zeynalova, B. (2011). Evaluation Revisited: Improving the Quality of Evaluative Practice by Embracing Complexity, Conference Report, Wageningen: Centre for Development Innovation, Wageningen University and Research Centre <http://edepot.wur.nl/169284>.

Hulme, D. (2010) 'Lessons from the making of the MDGS: human development meets results-based management in an unfair world', *IDS Bulletin* 41(1): 15–25.

Melamed, C. (2011) 'If not results, then what? The risks of not having a results agenda' in From Poverty to Power [blog] <http://oxfamblogs.org/fp2p/if-not-results-then-what-the-risks-of-not-having-a-results-agenda/>.

Morse, J.M. (2006) 'The politics of evidence', *Qualitative Health Research* 16(3): 395–404.

Mosse, D. (2007) *Power and the Durability of Poverty: A Critical Exploration of the Links Between Culture, Marginality and Chronic Poverty*. CPRC Working Paper 107, Manchester: Chronic Poverty Research Centre.

Newell, P. and Bellour, S. (2002) *Mapping Accountability: Origins, Contexts and Implications for Development*, IDS Working Paper 168, Brighton: Institute of Development Studies.

Piron, L.H. (2005) 'Rights-based approaches and bilateral aid agencies: more than a metaphor?', *IDS Bulletin* 36(1): 19–30.

Reeler, D. (2007) 'A three-fold theory of social change and implications for practice, planning, monitoring and evaluation', Cape Town: Community Development Resource Association <http://www.cdra.org.za/threefold-theory-of-social-change.html>.

Richmond, J. (2013) 'Theory's fine but what about practice?' in From Poverty to Power [blog] <http://oxfamblogs.org/fp2p/theorys-fine-but-what-about-practice-oxfams-mel-boss-on-the-evidence-agenda/>.

Roche, C. and Kelly, L. (2012) *The Evaluation of Politics and the Politics of Evaluation*, DLP Background Paper 11, Birmingham: Developmental Leadership Program, University of Birmingham <http://www.gsdrc.org/go/display&type=Document&id=4340>.

Wallace, T. and Porter, F. with Ralph Bowman (eds) (2013) *Aid, NGOs and the Realities of Women's Lives: A Perfect Storm*, Rugby: Practical Action.

Notes

1. <http://bigpushforward.net/archives/502>.
2. Chatham House rules require participants to protect the anonymity of those contributing to discussions by not disclosing to a wider public which particular person said what.
3. The difficult process of raising finance was an intriguing illustration of the politics of the results and evidence agenda. Was it because most funders viewed the debate that we had triggered as regressive and unhelpful? Or was it because they feared being associated with controversy and how this might affect their standing with DFID/AusAID or others?
4. We deliberately avoid an over-academic discussion of concepts of power. Readers interested in going deeper into the complexity of the concept are recommended Clegg and Haugaard (2009).

CHAPTER 2

Uncovering the politics of evidence and results

Rosalind Eyben

Abstract

The chapter starts with the tools and protocols – the artefacts – that are the concrete expression of the results and evidence discourses. I then look at the origins and history of the discourses themselves as these have evolved in public sector management, discuss how and why these are increasingly influential in the international development sector, and consider the possibilities for pushback.

Keywords: results and evidence discourses, techniques of power, international development, evidence-based policy, payment by results

> The results-based framework within which we operated existed in the context of complex power relationships ... Sometimes we found ourselves talking openly and finding support from among the donors, while at other times we had to conceal our true objectives and ensure that the results-based, logical framework outputs were achieved ... We found ourselves adopting a language and a set of tools – technical activity reports, expenditure reports and products – quite distinct from the work we were actually doing. (Rosario Leon)[1]

I do not concur with the view that progressively minded practitioners are naive to imagine that they can work from within the development sector to help make a better world. The sector's complexity and diversity offer many opportunities for supporting transformation (Eyben, 2014). Such opportunities have been seized to good effect in the past and may still be seized today – provided we remain aware of how power operates within the sector, including through the results and evidence discourse that is the focus of the present chapter. By revealing this discourse as just one way of imagining how the world works, this chapter aims to encourage development practitioners to expand the political space for the flexible and creative support of locally generated and transformative change. And when I refer to political, I do not mean politics in the limited sense of party politics but rather politics as that which shapes and orders society, and, importantly, is always subject to contestation and resistance (Mouffe, 2005).

I bring this understanding of politics to examine how development projects and programmes are increasingly planned, appraised, implemented,

http://dx.doi.org/10.3362/9781780448855.002

and evaluated within a 'results' and 'evidence' discourse that uses a particular meaning of 'evidence' – i.e. what works to solve a problem – as the basis for delivering and reporting quantifiable 'results'. Results and evidence discourses shape working practices through different 'artefacts' – tools and protocols – that the development sector uses and abuses. The chapter starts by examining our experience of these. Logical framework analysis ('logframes'), key performance indicators, and randomized control trials influence daily work in much of the development sector, particularly but not exclusively in English-speaking official and non-governmental agencies as well as in multilateral organizations and global funds. I then look at the history of the discourses – 'results' and evidence' – that generate such artefacts. I explore their family resemblance, look at their material effects on development practices and institutions, and enquire into the context and drivers of their influence.

Results and evidence artefacts

A personal experience provoked my investigation of these artefacts as 'techniques of power' (Foucault, 1980: 155). As a researcher at the Institute of Development Studies, I was asked to revise one of our programme's logframes to comply with our funder's new guidance. This included quantifying the policies our programme aimed to influence or help create, which thus required our programme to understand 'policy' as a bounded, quantifiable entity. With funding from this programme I had just published a paper exploring policy as a relational, contested, and never-finished process (Eyben, 2008). Policy was not a thing that could be counted. I emailed to that effect the official with whom our programme dealt. The reply was: 'Please complete the matrix in accordance with the guidance.' So I invented a spurious number. I had complied! But I was angry at being forced to make a mockery of our programme's approach and even angrier at my inability to direct that anger at a particular individual or department. The official requiring that we conform was only following instructions; it was hard to locate and therefore challenge the power over us. Indeed, I knew that many staff in that funding agency were aware that the new logframe requirement distorted what programmes like this one were trying to do. Like me, they felt powerless.

Yet it is not that simple. As well as compliance, power produces resistance. That experience helped create a network of individuals and organizations, the Big Push Forward, that challenged the results discourse and its artefacts. 'A first and necessary step,' writes Bronwyn Davies, 'in counteracting the force of any discourse is to recognise ... its capacity to become hegemonic, to saturate our very consciousness, so that it becomes the ... world we see and interact with, and the common sense interpretations we put on it' (Davies 2003 102). This chapter draws on Foucault's archaeological approach (Burrell, 1999) to consider how, through a mutually constituted process of production, consumption, and resistance, results and evidence artefacts evolve and mutate, beyond the control of any one individual or organization. I start by itemizing those artefacts commonly used in the sector.

Results artefacts are used for implementation, monitoring, and reporting on changes during and on completion of the project. These include:

- baseline data
- progress reviews
- performance measurement indicators
- logical framework analysis
- risk registers
- theories of change (ToCs – as versions of logframes)
- results reporting.

Evidence artefacts are not so widely used but are popular with, among others, the Department for International Development (DFID), USAID, the World Bank, and the Gates Foundation to find out 'what works best' and to deliver 'value for money' (VFM). Evidence artefacts are used to select the most appropriate 'intervention', to appraise proposals against different options, and to evaluate longer-term effectiveness and impact. These include:

- randomized control trials
- systematic reviews
- cost-effectiveness analysis
- option appraisal
- social return on investment
- business cases
- impact evaluation.

Artefacts, and users' experiences of them, may change over time. As an employee of DFID in the late 1980s, I was an early advocate of the logical framework. I had previously made its acquaintance when consulting for USAID, and had found it useful. A logframe, I argued, requires you to state a purpose – for example, increased incomes of landless families – and then to work out what a project can do to achieve that purpose. British projects at that time did the opposite: an available technology or resource was identified accompanied by a half-hearted effort to justify its use for improving the world. I also appreciated the logframe's assumptions column, which was used then to identify the dynamic social and political environment of aid projects, introducing uncertainty and iterative project-planning processes. Have other routes to improving landless people's incomes become apparent during project implementation? Has an unforeseen event occurred that requires a quite different response than that initially planned? Even then, however, some organizations were using the logframe mechanically rather than creatively. Today it is a rigid tool that constrains responsive planning, demanding ever more precise and predetermined 'results' with SMART indicators. As a consequence, a new artefact, the ToC, has become popular because, like the logframe used to do, it poses questions about assumptions and conditions.

A struggle has been taking place within DFID and other agencies about whether ToC should be a mandatory requirement, making it another micro-technology of power that requires obedience rather than independent and, above all, critical thought (see Chapter 6; Vogel, 2012).

The logframe–ToC dynamic illustrates Power's argument (2004) about 'performance measurement systems' that operate in a near-continual cycle of reform. Such reforms can make artefacts more controlling, as happened with logframes, but refinement may mean a dilution of excessive control, as with systematic reviews, some of whose designers are showing signs of greater flexibility in the definition of evidence.

The disciplining effect of artefacts

Results and evidence artefacts can be useful. But in contexts of inequitable power relations they can be abused, as in an incident that an education programme officer working in the head office of a large development agency told me about. At a meeting called by the agency's director general to determine whether to finance an education programme in a certain country, the director general asked the programme officer to provide the unit cost of educating a girl through primary school. He accused her of sloppiness when she replied that the prevailing civil conflict made it impossible to provide him with a figure. She looked desperately round the table for colleagues' support. Silent, they stared into their laps. Why had they not come to her defence, she asked them after they had left the director general's office. 'You should not have refused him the figures,' they replied. 'Next time, just make up a number.' Yet, should each time subordinates fabricate numbers, they would reconfirm the director general's belief that cost–benefit analysis (see Chapter 4) is *always* feasible and suitable and therefore always to be used:

> People find no reason to change their assumption that the action is possible and suitable ... They have no reason to question the principle behind the action, consequently, on the contrary, they have the 'experience' of a 'successful' attempt, which helps to reinforce their hope. They have avoided learning and have succeeded in preserving their faith in a principle. (Brunsson, 2006: 157)

The director general was as much a subject of the power of the artefact as his subordinates.

Artefacts are often so much part of the organizational furniture that they become independent of the authority that had initially required their use. Auto-surveillance creates a disciplined practitioner. A grant-receiving organization may be more exigent and controlling in how these artefacts are used than ever envisaged by those artefacts' originators. An international non-governmental organization (INGO) participant at a Big Push Forward meeting in New York in 2012 recounted how a conversation she had had with their donors allowed her INGO to provide grants to their local partners without the requirement for logframes or other quantifiable output-oriented mandatory procedures. Yet, when she visited her local partners to invite qualitative stories of change, they provided lists of quantified results. Had they internalized what they believed was expected of them?[2]

Whether individuals internalize the results discourse and voluntarily use its artefacts depends on personality, seniority, experience, capacity for reflexivity, and relative autonomy, as well as the institutional culture of the person's organization. Two grant recipients, equally dependent on the same donor, may respond differently to an artefact's power. Nevertheless, there is a 'squeezed middle' of programme officers (those responsible for managing grants, including in-country programmes with local partners) who try to protect front-line practitioners and partner organizations from the artefacts' exigencies. Cynical compliance may sometimes be accompanied by secret resistance: people carry on working according to their own professional judgement, while reporting up the system in accordance with the artefact's requirements. Yet compliance and resistance consume valuable energy and enthusiasm, diverting attention from the purpose of the job itself (see Chapter 8).

The effect on transformational agendas

Projects that emphasize measureable outcomes tend to drive out projects that produce immeasurable ones.

> That crowding out of less measurable activities has in turn led to a greater emphasis on service delivery instead of institution building and policy reform as the predominant programmatic approach to development. (Natsios, 2010: 61)

Yet there are few detailed examples about whether and how this happens. Apart from the cases in the present volume, little has been published so far on the local effects of results and evidence artefacts. However, one such rare study – of women's rights organizations (Mukhopadhyay and Eyben, 2011) – found that donor emphasis on management systems and reporting had a positive effect on organizational strengthening and effectiveness, especially when accompanied by a sense of partnership and trust within a long-term donor–grantee relationship. On the other hand, the study also found that when short-term and fluctuating project-related funding combined with the pooling of donor funds and a distancing of relations between funder and grantee, these artefacts worked to discourage grantees from designing strategies with social transformational outcomes.

I suggest that the artefacts have perverse effects when power determines which and whose knowledge counts, and when hierarchical ways of working limit communications and dialogue, constraining an organization's leadership in discussing with its donors what is sensible and feasible. I now turn to examining the history of the discourses that have generated these artefacts.

'Results' and 'evidence' discourses: their origins and affinity

Acknowledging the historical genesis of a discourse within a *particular* context and intellectual tradition is important for challenging its normalcy and the relevance of its artefacts for *all* times and purposes. To this end, I look at the origins and affinities of 'results' and 'evidence' discourses in public sector management, examining how and why they have generated resistance.

A history of 'results'

The epistemology of 'results-based management' can be traced back to the late eighteenth-century expansion of capitalism. Western Europe industrialized at home, colonized the rest of the world for its raw materials – and invented classical economics. This last included the theory of the principal (who invests) and the agent (who manages or implements). Principal–agent theory assumes that individuals are goal-oriented in pursuit of their own interests. It follows that agents will pursue the principal's goals only when they judge them to be also in their own interests. Hence, incentives are required to make the principal's goals interesting for the agent. Carrots (e.g. bonuses) and sticks (e.g. threats of dismissal) are so normal in modern management that we easily forget how principal–agent theory is just one among many theories explaining social reality and human behaviour.

As the public sector expanded in the nineteenth century, principal–agent theory fuelled an anxiety that without incentives public officials would not deliver 'VFM'. The British government accordingly introduced 'payment by results' (PBR) into the elementary school system: teachers' pay was based on the measurable results (learning outcomes) achieved by their pupils. But the increased administration costs of verifying the results and the damage this approach did to children's education led to PBR being discredited and abolished by the end of the century (Madaus et al., 1987). Half a century later, 'results' re-emerged in the public sector through the language of 'management by objectives' (MBO) and was popularized in social democratic Sweden, which had a big public sector (Sundström, 2006). MBO was also introduced in the United States during the Democratic administration's large-scale anti-poverty programmes, with artefacts such as cost–benefit analysis (CBA) and risk assessment (Espeland, 1997).

By the 1990s, 'objectives' had evolved into 'results'. Again, the impetus came from a United States Democratic administration adopting accounting methods from the private sector (Gray and Jenkins, 1995). 'Results' was part of a broader shift, commonly known as 'new public management' (NPM), that had emerged in the 1970s. Other elements of NPM include the linking of resource allocation to performance; competition between providers of services; greater discipline and parsimony in resource use; and more general adoption of what are represented as private sector management practices (Hood, 1991). Today, NPM prevails in most Organisation for Economic Co-operation and

Development (OECD) countries and is exported to aid-receiving countries through development agencies and international institutions such as the World Bank. Critics have argued that performance indicators, when used for control, 'are unreliable: they do not measure performance itself, distort what is measured, influence practice towards what is being measured and cause unmeasured parts to get neglected' (Elton, 2004: 121). Nevertheless, in spite of, or perhaps because of, the criticism, more radical approaches are being adopted for tackling the principal–agent problem, including the reintroduction of PBR; this is popular in those OECD countries where NPM was first adopted and where less rigorous systems have been tried and judged wanting. In the United States, PBR has returned again to schools. Reporting on one such scheme, the *Economist* commented: 'You are transferring from a system where the agents are (to a degree) public-spirited individuals to one that motivates agents to be self-interested.'[3]

A more radical version of PBR is the government transfer of responsibility to the market for securing social policy objectives. With 'social impact bonds', the market invests in projects (such as reducing the number of long-term unemployed) that are implemented by private sector contractors. If the project achieves the predetermined results, the government calculates the proportion of savings made to the welfare budget through private sector contracting rather than public sector provision and provides a return to the bondholders accordingly. The intended service users or beneficiaries – citizens – are generally not invited to contribute to the design or monitoring of such projects (Whitfield, 2012).

Evidence-based approaches

'Evidence' and 'results' have a common intellectual heritage of 'methodological individualism' that economics shares with medicine; in this they differ from the holistic social sciences, which are concerned with relations between people and the culture and history that shape them. As discussed, 'results' can be traced back to utilitarian efficiency concerns; the origins of 'evidence' of what works lie in the field of medicine, developed in Canada, whence it spread to the UK and the USA (Solomon, 2011). Randomized control trials (RCTs) were cited as the 'gold standard' for judging whether a treatment works (Sackett et al., 1996). Yet, even within medicine, the leap from evidence-based clinical practice into evidence-based health policy was subjected to challenge. An article in the *British Medical Journal* argued that policy was shaped by institutional arrangements, values, and beliefs as well as by a variety of different sources of information (Black, 2001). Meanwhile, 'evidence' moved out from health to other fields of policy and practice, such as education.

Evidence-based policy, uncontaminated by politics, may be a consequence of the Cold War's end and the disappearance of ideological battles between left and right. In the UK, the 1997 New Labour government was keen to demonstrate that its decisions would be driven by technical, unbiased evidence rather than by socialist ideas (Solesbury, 2002). But critics questioned the evidence-based approach's linear cause-and-effect thinking and its dismissal of values (Biesta, 2007). It was argued that evidence-based approaches were unhelpful at the community level where multiple perspectives come into play and there is no shared agreement about the problem (Harrison, 2000).

The famous 'evidence' pyramid – that puts RCTs at the top and local practitioner knowledge at the bottom – has also been critiqued for its causal claims (Cartwright, 2007) and for its control, categorization, and containment that do not take into account potentially significant but uncontrollable influences on practice, such as trust-based relationships between front-line workers and their clients.[4] Evidence of 'what works' can also be critiqued for its naïve positivism that conveniently deflects the distributive question of 'works for who?' Nevertheless, by 2013, 'evidence' had become central to UK social policy practice. The government announced the creation of a 'What Works' team in the Cabinet Office, mandated to take the 'evidence culture' of the health sector into 'other areas of social policy: crime reduction, active and independent aging, early intervention, educational attainment and local economic growth'.[5]

As with results, there is pushback here too, primarily from academics and evaluation specialists challenging the narrow understanding of evidence the UK government is promoting and the implications of this for domestic policy practice.[6] A sign of their success is that alternatives are still current, and publicly funded economic and social policy research continues to support a variety of methodological approaches to evidence.

Conclusion to this section

'Evidence' and 'results' as a set of predetermined, concrete, measurable outcomes make social policy practice an analogue of drug trials. The social distance of the unemployed, offenders, and children renders them unknowable to those in power, making these the most likely to be the targets of PBR interventions or of RCTs. Such people become subjects who require treatment through 'interventions' rather than citizens with a political voice. Power can silence challenges to the technical framing of the problem, foreclosing discussion of the structural causes and consequences of the social problems these interventions seek to tackle.

The disciplines that generated 'results' and 'evidence', neoclassical economics and clinical medicine, share a common epistemology that categorizes, counts, and measures people as individual entities. This contrasts with a way of knowing, to which I subscribe, that primarily sees people as part of society, people whose lives are shaped by the actions of others. With the first mindset, *her* poverty is never a function of *my* wealth, whereas in the second the possibility of a relationship between *her* poverty and *my* wealth is considered and explored. This applies also to global inequalities and the role or otherwise of development cooperation in reducing these, and this should be borne in mind as I look at how results and evidence discourses have played out in the development sector.

Results and evidence in development

Statistics have been instruments of progressive change. Reformers and campaigners have used numbers to reveal social injustices and to inform socially progressive policy. But statistics have also been used for repressive purposes, for categorizing and controlling deviant populations suicides, prostitutes, and criminals, among others – people different from us. This may explain why bureaucratic quantification was most fully developed and applied in the colonies, where entire populations were different from the colonizing power (Anderson, 2006). It may also explain why the development sector has proven such fertile ground for the results and evidence discourse.

Development results

Following the 2002 Monterrey Conference on Financing for Development, 'results' spread widely through the international development sector. In 2003, the Joint Venture on Managing for Development Results was set up by the OECD Development Assistance Committee (DAC) and 'results' was one of the five pillars of the Paris Declaration on Aid Effectiveness (2005). Most DAC members have since developed results-based management (RBM) strategies. In Switzerland, for example, a primer on RBM introduced a revised logframe with a 'results chain [that] clearly shows the plausible, causal relationships among the elements' (Batliner et al., 2011: 5); it stresses the importance of baselines and key performance indicators. The Dutch government revised its co-financing agreement with its big INGOs, obliging them to produce a single global logframe with aggregate data based on work undertaken by multiple partners across the world (see Chapter 6). DFID revised its logframe to include mandatory baseline numbers. Then, with a change of government and the introduction of a new artefact – the 'business case' DFID revised yet again its logframe to incorporate a results chain.[7]

From the examples used by these agencies when promoting the results agenda, health and education interventions appear most amenable to measurement. In 2011, DFID announced the results it aimed to deliver by 2015. These included 'to secure schooling for 11 million children – more than we educate in the UK but at 2.5% of the cost'.[8] Possibly because of criticism (including from the Big Push Forward) about DFID's self-representation as the only actor (where were the partner governments in this narrative?), DFID's language changed the following year from 'securing' to 'supporting children to go to primary school'.[9] Meanwhile, PBR[10] entered the development sector in 2008 when the World Bank's Health Results Innovation Trust Fund was established, funded by the governments of Norway and the United Kingdom.[11] The Washington-based think tank Center for Global Development has actively promoted PBR or 'cash on delivery' and Anglo-Saxon governments have been its most enthusiastic proponents, for example in the Global Partnership for Education cited in Chapter 1. Pushed by an enthusiastic minister, DFID published in 2014 a PBR strategy paper.[12] Officials privately expressed their reservations and economists debated theoretically the suitable conditions for PBR (Barder et al., 2014) but without considering what happens in practice. For example, whereas PBR should in theory be accompanied by reduced requirements for financial reporting, DFID continues to demand high levels of financial tracking from its grantees.[13] Findings from the German Development Institute's research into government-to-government PBR grants confirm that donors have difficulties in shifting to the hands-off position that the philosophy of PBR requires. Furthermore, pressure to disburse makes donors cautious about overcommitting to PBR – what do they do with their money if the results are not achieved? – and thus PBR often comprises a relatively small proportion of larger interventions.[14]

'Social impact bonds' have also appeared in the sector as 'development impact bonds' (DIBs).[15] A DIB scoping study of family planning, commissioned by DFID in 2012, stressed that 'the feasibility of a DIB approach depends on creating a compelling value case for both outcome funders and investors'.[16] There is only one mention of the views on value of the recipient governments, and no mention at all of the beneficiaries in the countries concerned. DFID launched its first DIB (in 2014) in a more bounded field, tapping into private sector investors to purchase drugs to tackle bovine sleeping sickness.[17] Meanwhile, inspired by the private sector's venture capital model, the American, British, Swedish, and Australian governments have promoted 'social impact investing', which has materialized in the Global Innovations Fund, designed by the Center for Global Development and launched in New York in September 2014.[18]

Large accountancy companies with contracts from USAID and DFID have heavily influenced results-based programming. Broader private sector interest includes US-based philanthro-capitalists, such as the Gates Foundation, as well as corporate sector actors in public–private sector partnerships, such as Coca-Cola's 5by20 programme for women's economic empowerment, co-financed by DFID. Global public–private partnerships are an increasingly significant funding model in the education and health sectors. Yet the speed at which the agenda is driven forward means that there are few, if any, evaluations of either the process or the outcomes of such partnerships. However, Gideon and Porter (2014) have examined the influence of two global public–private partnerships on understandings and approaches to women's health at national and local levels. They conclude that gender equality in health is significantly undermined by these global partnerships' results-based approaches that decontextualize women's health from the political and social context that shapes their lives. The authors warn that this may lead to policy-makers forgetting that women's health is fundamentally linked to women's empowerment and rights.

Development evidence

At the start of the new millennium, donor focus on poverty reduction strategies stimulated an interest in governance and the complex politics of development – and this interest continues to this day (Booth and Unsworth, 2014). However, to contradict this trend, there emerged technical best-practice interventions based on rigorous objective evidence. This marks the revival of a long-standing approach to development that speaks to the sector's 'need to overlook its internal involvement in the places and problems it analyses and present itself instead as an external intelligence that stands outside the objects it describes' (Mitchell, 1995: 130).

A relatively small group of institutional actors and academics have promoted evidence-based approaches in development. According to Robert Picciotto (former director of the World Bank's Evaluation Department), a stalemate in the battle between macro-economists Sachs and Easterly about aid effectiveness provided the opportunity for a group of young micro-economists at the Massachusetts Institute of Technology (MIT) to shift this debate to a clinical examination of specific development interventions (Picciotto, 2012: 215).

MIT's *Poor Economics* (Banerjee et al., 2011) was named one of the top books of the year by *The Economist*, the *Financial Times*, and Goldman Sachs. Enthusiastic support and very substantial funding from large foundations have generated great momentum behind this evidence-based movement. The Gates Foundation was instrumental in setting up 3ie and is its biggest annual donor. 3ie funds impact evaluations and systematic reviews. According to 3ie, high-quality impact evaluations measure the net change in those outcomes within a particular group, or groups, of people that are attributable to a specific programme. This narrows the OECD definition of 'impact': 'the positive and negative changes produced by a development intervention, directly or indirectly, intended or unintended'.[19] Increasingly, impact evaluation is associated with experimental and quasi-experimental methods. USAID evaluation policy states:

> Impact evaluations in which comparisons are made between beneficiaries that are randomly assigned to either a treatment or a control group provide the strongest evidence of a relationship between the intervention under study and the outcome measured.[20]

Evidence-based approaches in development have not as yet spread as widely as has the pressure to demonstrate 'results'. Nevertheless, even in countries such as France – where there is a strong tradition of the philosophy of ideas, compared with the atheoretical empiricism of English-speaking countries – evidence-based approaches are now discussed in the development literature (Labrousse, 2010). Their penetration into developing countries is triggering similar debates as in the countries where 'evidence' originated. In South Africa:

> Designing 'good' pro-poor policy is not something that can be guaranteed by focusing on generic, technical 'best practice' skills: rather, it requires a clear focus on the substantive issues at hand, and the concrete institutional, fragile and contested political nature of the South African state. (Du Toit, 2012: 10)

There has also been a negative reaction among mainstream development evaluators; this is typified by Picciotto (cited above), who concludes that the bubble is bound to burst because evidence-based approaches are appropriate only for 'relatively simple interventions, the effects of which are realized in a short period of time' (Picciotto, 2012: 227). MIT and DFID have both publicly stated at conferences that only a small proportion of portfolios are amenable to experimental and quasi-experimental approaches. However, from what I have seen of its practice, DFID business cases continue to draw primarily on narrowly defined evidence.

The drivers of the results and evidence agenda and the countervailing trends

The increasing dominance of results and evidence artefacts coincides with – and may be a consequence of – the changing aid funding landscape. A greater variety of providers are financing development, permitting recipient countries to be less dependent on traditional OECD donors. This section considers the implications of such change for what OECD donors prefer to fund; it then examines three other trends among these donors: the political pressures to be seen to be in control in a world of uncertainty and surprises; the politics of accountability; and the sector's internal dynamics.

The changing landscape of international aid

The current popularity of results and evidence approaches coincides with the emergence of non-traditional forms of aid, including South–South cooperation, that are based on principles of mutual self-interest and the absence of conditionality (Greenhill et al., 2013; Gore, 2013). Recipient governments' ability to choose among diverse providers has meant a decline in OECD donors' ability to influence recipients' macro-level policies. It has contributed to donors' disenchantment with general budget support that is conditional on political changes in favour of more transparent and accountable governance; in any case, such conditions have been difficult to enforce. An emerging trend is ex-post conditionality that is not, as previously, linked to broad political reforms but to technical sector-based indicators such as an increase in the numbers of girls attending secondary school. In theory, PBR through contracts between donor and recipient government is de-politicizing the aid relationship in a changing global landscape in which OECD donors are less influential. Nevertheless, this kind of ex-post conditional sector support represents only a small proportion of aid funding; a more common response to the changing environment has been a switch to tightly controlled projects intended to achieve one specific result (Klingbiel and Janus, 2014). At the same time, South–South cooperation's different approach is creating space for criticism. A United Nations document published before the Mexico Global

Partnership conference (April 2014) noted that the current enthusiasm of some DAC actors for results orientation is 'considered narrow and inadequate by others who have developed their own approaches (i.e. South–South Cooperation) to delivering effective assistance to the poor'.[21]

The need to be seen to be in control

The rights-based approaches of the 1990s – and the recognition by some development agencies of the messiness of political voice and shifts in power relations associated with development processes have been challenged by the results and evidence discourse, which is about controlling and ring-fencing the lives of people in poverty. A desire to be seen to be in control, symptomatic of a refusal to engage with complexity in a dynamic and uncertain world, has created both elaborate performance measurement systems and an emphasis on quick deliverables – typified by bed nets to tackle malaria in the absence of support to strengthen the health system.[22] Researchers design RCTs to discover 'what works', but their popularity with some donor governments may be due to their utility in attributing interventions to donor financing – important for the politics of accountability – which has coincided with the resurgence in popularity of branding, for example with British and Australian aid. To paraphrase Mark Duffield (2002), this is a performance of the will to govern directed towards domestic audiences, who are increasingly sceptical about international aid.

Many mainstream development managers – and evaluators – are conscious that this *is* a performance; in practice they are more flexible than the public face of their agency might indicate.[23] Sensible conversations with donors are sometimes possible and always worth trying. Evaluators are more aware of alternatives, enabling organizations to learn about how to support social change in complex and dynamic contexts.[24] Nevertheless, much bureaucratic practice has not yet shifted, is often contradictory and – without challenge – may never change sufficiently to create the space for appropriate methodological choices in support of processes of social transformation.

The urge for control may become a pathological condition in the face of two uncomfortable realities. The first is that aid is increasingly likely to be funnelled to countries where chronic poverty is sustained by unstable political environments (Kharas and Rogerson, 2012). For global security reasons, rich country governments may wish to be seen as being in control in such places, but it is here that results and evidence artefacts are most likely to be irrelevant, possibly undermining the drive to reinforce results and evidence discourses by donors such as Denmark, whose aid emphasizes security and development (Stepputat, 2012). There is an opportunity here to point to the contradiction between exercising control over bounded problems and the challenges of working in highly emergent and fragile contexts.

Value for money and the politics of accountability

VFM is a normative idea conventionally concerned with achieving maximum economy, efficiency, and effectiveness of resources (see Chapter 4). With the increasing need to demonstrate that aid budgets are delivering VFM during a period of austerity, 'results' and 'evidence' become part of the politics of accountability. Pressure is exerted, not so much by taxpayers as by parliaments claiming to respond not only to taxpayers' concerns about corruption and the misuse of funds but more broadly to whether aid is delivering the best possible VFM. The Institute for Fiscal Studies, a British think tank, commented:

> Because the spending occurs elsewhere in the world, there is a relative lack of public [meaning the UK public] scrutiny of the budget's effectiveness – voters can't experience the effectiveness of aid spending in the way they can experience their local school, hospital or police force. This argues for an even greater degree of transparency and clarity about spending decisions and effectiveness than is seen in the rest of public spending.[25]

Results and evidence artefacts seem attractive in proving effectiveness to an audience that has little inside knowledge of the multi-stakeholder dynamics of even the simplest project. The drive for de-politicization manifested in the evidence discourse is linked to the privileging of accounting performance, which is viewed as technical and objective. McSweeney (1994) notes the fantasy that, because accounting calculations can identify the absolute truth, they are able to transcend party-political distinctions. Self-evidently, once a particular discipline gains a discursive foothold in public sector policy and practice, it seeks to strengthen its position therein, generating a path dependency which means that its influence becomes ever more dominant. Large accountancy firms are involved in developing management tools and approaches. They are also responsible for the selection of performance indicators for some programmes and for their monitoring and evaluation; such programmes include NGO challenge funds such as the Dutch government's MDG3 fund and DFID's Girls Education Challenge programme (for which PricewaterhouseCoopers has overall management responsibility), the latter with a PBR pilot. In USAID, an increasing number of senior staff are no longer development professionals but management and compliance experts 'such as accountants, lawyers, auditors, and procurement officers' (Natsios, 2010: 50).

The increasing influence of accountancy companies connects to a belief that the public (and voluntary) sector will become more efficient and effective by imitating the private sector: for example, by adopting explicit standards and measures of performance, control of outputs, competition, and so on. Private sector foundations and companies established to encourage charitable giving – particularly in the United States have been instrumental in promoting the results agenda and its spurious homology with bottom-line profits. Nevertheless, at least outside the United States, there is an opportunity to push back as more is learned about the effects of SMART performance indicators as targets. Their distortive effect for example, the police focusing on easy-to-solve crimes and hospitals treating easy-to-cure illnesses is well known to the public in donor countries (see Chapter 5). More could be done to draw attention to how this plays out in aid funding, including forming coalitions for change with domestic policy actors. Some official donor agencies – for example, the Swiss and the French – are aware of the perverse effects, and, with a change in government in Sweden in late 2014, it appeared that one of its earliest protagonists was shifting away from 'results' as quantifiable deliverables (see Chapter 8).

The sector's internal dynamics

The results and evidence agenda is technical and self-declaredly apolitical. De-politicization has helped official agencies and NGOs preserve their access to funds despite changes in the domestic political climate, at least in the UK. There, in the latter years of the Labour government, officials elaborated an approach to results and evidence that distanced DFID from its early years under the radical minister Clare Short. Her commitment to cross-government policy coherence for global poverty reduction was quietly dropped (as it was in Sweden) and the emphasis she placed on *not* distinguishing the British contribution from the collective effort was replaced with the brand of 'UK Aid'. The results and evidence agenda was designed to protect the aid budget in a time of austerity and has been adopted and further emphasized by the 2010–15 centre-right government, which committed to increasing rather than cutting the aid budget, a commitment that other departments have scrutinized jealously. This, combined with intense parliamentary and media interest, has obliged DFID to further exaggerate its claims to deliver VFM. In the longer term, as traditional aid agencies – both official and non-governmental – face increased competition both from private foundations and individual charitable giving through direct person-to-person cash transfers (Kharas and Rogerson, 2012), they might feel impelled to demonstrate that they can deliver VFM equal to the claims made by these new forms of aid. However, in the process, they disregard what the sector has learned about the importance of local ownership and sustainability.

As already mentioned, a major driver of the results agenda is the competition for resources between official aid agencies and other government spending departments. The same driver is at work between multilateral agencies as well as between INGOs, all competing for donor resources. Competition makes organizations willing to comply with funders' management and monitoring requirements, including proposing projects that can easily be measured. On the other hand, even among United Nations agencies that have come under intense pressure from some donor governments to be results-oriented, creative adaptation is maintaining or reclaiming transformative meanings of development. The United Nations Office of the High Commissioner for Human Rights, for example, has appropriated the language of RBM to improve its evaluation and planning capabilities while firmly rejecting the transactional approach to development that normally accompanies this.[26]

Conclusion

I have sought to disentangle the historical threads and origins of RBM and evidence-based policy and programming, identifying who uses these approaches today, how and in which contexts. I have looked at how results and evidence have entered the development sector and their influence on the sector's priorities and practices. Finally, I have briefly touched on the drivers of the results and evidence discourses in the sector. Armed with these insights, practitioners should be better placed to challenge the power that works invisibly to normalize inappropriate means for designing and assessing development programmes involved with multiple pathways of change. The current rapid proliferation of artefacts may indicate a dominant discourse under challenge in times of uncertainty and rapid change. The greater efforts to exert control through an increase in mandatory procedures and overlapping protocols, and the disagreements over what VFM or a ToC actually is (see Chapters 4 and 6), arguably create more room for transformational interpretation. Moreover, the high transaction costs in using such artefacts generate a likelihood for greater pushback from within aid agencies.

The opportunities for individual and collective agency are manifold: the doctrines of evidence and results are challenged not only by academics (as evidenced by the substantial body of literature on which this chapter draws) but also by many development practitioners who are finding room for manoeuvre to push back and create the space for alternative framings. These successes need to be reflected upon and shared. Poverty reduction is not a technical problem but requires significant social change that must be both political and locally led. This in turn implies a need for self-awareness to avoid disempowering others. It requires the undertaking of power analyses with development practitioners factored in. It means engaging with a wider and more diverse group of policy actors in the state, civil society, and private sector, whenever possible, supporting debate, locally driven problem solving, and independent research.

References

Anderson, B. (2006) *Imagined Communities: Reflections on the Origin and Spread of Nationalism*, London: Verso.

Banerjee, A., Banerjee, A.V. and Duflo, E. (2011) *Poor Economics*, New York NY: Public Affairs.

Barder, O., Perakis, R., Savedoff, W. and Talbot, T. (2014) 'Twelve principles of payment by results in the real world' in Center for Global Development [blog] <http://www.cgdev.org/blog/12-principles-payment-results-pbr-real-world-0>.

Batliner, R., Felber, R. and Günther, I. (2011) 'A primer on results-based management' in SECO Economic Cooperation and Development <http://www.seco-cooperation.admin.ch/themen/01100/index.html>.

Biesta, G. (2007) 'Why "what works" won't work: evidence-based practice and the democratic deficit in educational research', *Educational Theory* 57(1): 1–22.

Black, N. (2001) 'Evidence based policy: proceed with care', *British Medical Journal* 323(7307): 275–9.

Booth, D. and Unsworth, S. (2014) *Politically Smart, Locally Led Development*, Discussion Paper, London: Overseas Development Institute (ODI).

Brunsson, N. (2006) *Mechanisms of Hope: Maintaining the Dream of the Rational Organization*, Copenhagen: Copenhagen Business School.

Burrell, G. (1999) 'Normal science, paradigms, metaphors, discourses and genealogies of analysis', in S. Clegg and C. Hardy (eds) *Studying Organizations*, pp. 388–404, London: Sage.

Cartwright, N. (2007) 'Are RCTs the gold standard?', *BioSocieties* 2: 11–20.

Davies, B. (2003) 'Death to critique and dissent? The policies and practices of new managerialism and of "evidence-based practice"', *Gender and Education* 15(1): 91–103.

DFID (2013) *Annual Report 2012–2013*, London: Department for International Development (DFID).

Du Toit, A. (2012) 'Making sense of "evidence": notes on the discursive politics of research and pro-poor policy making', PLAAS Working Paper 2, Bellville: Institute for Poverty, Land and Agrarian Studies (PLAAS), University of the Western Cape.

Duffield, M. (2002) 'Social reconstruction and the radicalization of development: aid as a relation of global liberal governance', *Development and Change* 33(5): 1049–71.

Elton, L. (2004) 'Goodhart's law and performance indicators in higher education', *Evaluation and Research in Education* 18(1–2): 20–128.

Espeland, W.N. (1997) 'Authority by the numbers: Porter on quantification, discretion, and the legitimation of expertise', *Law and Social Inquiry* 22(4) 1107–33.

Eyben, R. (2008) 'Conceptualising policy practices in researching pathways of women's empowerment', Pathways of Women's Empowerment Working Paper 1, Brighton: Institute of Development Studies.

Eyben, R. (2014) *International Aid and the Making of a Better World*, London and New York NY: Routledge.

Foucault, M. (1980) *Power/Knowledge: Selected Interviews and Other Writings, 1972–1977*, New York NY: Vintage.

Gideon, J. and F. Porter (2014) 'Unpacking women's health in public–private partnerships: a return to instrumentalism in development policy and practice?', WIDER Working Paper 2014/009, Helsinki: UNU-WIDER.

Gore, C. (2013) 'The new development cooperation landscape: actors, approaches, architecture', *Journal of International Development* 25(6): 769–86.

Gray, A. and Jenkins, B. (1995) 'From public administration to public management: reassessing a revolution?', *Public Administration* 73: 75–99.

Greenhill, R., Prizzon, A. and Rogerson, A. (2013) 'The age of choice: developing countries in the new aid landscape', ODI Working Paper 364, London: Overseas Development Institute (ODI).

Harrison, T. (2000) 'Urban policy: addressing wicked problems', in S. Nutley, H. Davies and P. Smith (eds), *What Works?: Evidence-based Policy and Practice in Public Services*, Bristol: The Policy Press.

Hood, C. (1991) 'A public management for all seasons', *Public Administration* 69: 3–19.

Keijzer, N. and Janus, H. (2014) 'Linking results-based aid and capacity development support: conceptual and practical challenges', GDI Discussion Paper, Bonn: German Development Institute (GDI).

Kharas, H. and Rogerson, A. (2012) 'Horizon 2025: creative destruction in the aid industry', ODI Research Report, London: Overseas Development Institute (ODI).

Klingebiel, S. and Janus, H. (2014) 'Results-based aid: potential and limits of an innovative modality in development cooperation', *International Development Policy* [Online], 5.2 | 2014, <http://poldev.revues.org/ 1746;> [accessed 09 May 2015]. <http.dx.doi.org/ 10.4000/poldev.1746>.

Labrousse, A. (2010) 'Nouvelle économie du développement et essais cliniques randomisés: une mise en perspective d'un outil de preuve et de gouvernement', *Revue de la Régulation: Capitalisme, Institutions, Pouvoirs 7*.

Madaus, G.F., Ryan, J.P., Kellaghan, T. and Airasian, P.W. (1987) 'Payment by results: an analysis of a nineteenth-century performance-contracting programme', *The Irish Journal of Education/Iris Eireannach an Oideachais* (21)2: 80–91.

McSweeney, B. (1994) 'Management by accounting', in A. Hopwood and P. Miller (eds), *Accounting as Social and Institutional Practice*, Cambridge: Cambridge University Press.

Mitchell, T. (1995) 'The object of development: America's Egypt', in J. Crush (ed.), *The Power of Development*, London: Routledge.

Mouffe, C. (2005) *The Return of the Political*, London: Verso.

Mukhopadhyay, M. and Eyben, R. (2011) *Rights and Resources. The Effects of External Financing on Organising for Women's Rights*, Brighton: Institute of Development Studies <http://www.pathwaysofempowerment.org/archive_resources/rights-and-resources-the-effects-of-financing-on-organising-for-women-s-rights>.

Natsios, A. (2010) 'The clash of the counter-bureaucracy' in Center for Global Development [online essay] <http://www.cgdev.org/content/publications/detail/1424271>.

Picciotto, R. (2012) 'Experimentalism and development evaluation: will the bubble burst?', *Evaluation* 18(2): 213–29.

Power, M. (1999) *The Audit Society: Rituals of Verification*, Oxford: Oxford University Press.

Power, M. (2004) 'Counting, control and calculation: reflections on measuring and management', *Human Relations* 57(6): 765–83.

Sackett, D.L., Rosenberg, W.M., Gray, J.M., Haynes, R.B. and Richardson, W.S. (1996) 'Evidence-based medicine', *British Medical Journal* 313(7050): 170.

Solesbury, W. (2002) 'The ascendancy of evidence', *Planning Theory and Practice* 3(1): 90–6.

Solomon, M. (2011) 'Just a paradigm: evidence-based medicine meets philosophy of science', *European Journal of Philosophy of Science* 1(3): 451–66.

Stepputat, F. (2012) 'Knowledge production in the security–development nexus: an ethnographic reflection', *Security Dialogue* 43(5): 439–55.

Sundström, G. (2006) 'Management by results: its origin and development in the case of the Swedish state', *International Public Management Journal* 94.

Vogel, I. (2012) Review of the Use of 'Theory of Change' in International Development: Review Report, London: Department for International Development <http://r4d.dfid.gov.uk/pdf/outputs/mis_spc/DFID_ToC_Review_VogelV7.pdf>.

Whitfield, D. (2012) 'The payments-by-result road to marketisation', in A. Silvestri (ed.), *Critical Reflections: Social and Criminal Justice in the First Year of Coalition Government*, London: Centre for Crime and Justice Studies.

About the author

Rosalind Eyben is a feminist anthropologist and Emeritus Fellow at the Institute of Development Studies. Previous books include *Relationships for Aid* (Earthscan, 2006), *Feminists in Development Organizations* (Practical Action, 2013), and *International Aid and the Making of a Better World* (Routledge, 2014). She was a Big Push Forward convener.

Notes

1. <http://www.thebrokeronline.eu/Series/Stories-from-Aidland/The-ghost-in-the-aid-machine> [accessed 15 December 2014].
2. On the other hand, the grantee may have used the logframe because its other funders required its use; there would have been an opportunity cost to developing an alternative reporting method (see also Chapter 6).
3. <http://www.economist.com/blogs/freeexchange/2012/08/teacher-incentives> [accessed 15 December 2014].
4. A point made by Simon Cohn in a paper given at an ESRC seminar 'Trials on Trial', University of Essex, March 2014.
5. <https://www.gov.uk/government/uploads/system/uploads/attachment_data/file/136227/What_Works_publication.pdf> [accessed 15 December 2014].
6. See, for example, <http://www.spacesofevidence.net/> [accessed 15 December 2014].
7. <https://www.dfid.gov.uk/Documents/publications1/how-to-guid-rev-log-fmwk.pdf> [accessed 15 December 2014].
8. <https://www.gov.uk/government/news/the-future-of-uk-aid> [accessed 15 December 2014].
9. <http://webarchive.nationalarchives.gov.uk/20130102161318/http://www.dfid.gov.uk/Documents/publications1/departmental-report/2012/Annual-report-accounts-2011-12.pdf> [accessed 15 December 2014].
10. PBR is just one of the terms used to describe the linking of disbursement to ex-ante results. See Keijzer and Janus (2014).
11. <https://www.rbfhealth.org/> [accessed 15 December 2014].
12. <https://www.gov.uk/government/publications/dfids-strategy-for-payment-by-results-sharpening-incentives-to-perform/payment-by-results-strategy-sharpening-incentives-to-perform> [accessed 15 December 2014].
13. 'How a shift to more institutional donors using contracts and payment by results may affect ActionAid UK', unpublished report prepared for Action Aid by MANGO, 2014.
14. Presentation made by Niell Keijzer and Heiner Janus at a seminar in Paris organized by the French Agency for Development, 26 November 2014.

15. For different views on these, see <www.theguardian.com/global-development-professionals-network/2014/jan/02/development-impact-bonds-success-network> and <http://oxfamblogs.org/fp2p/development-impact-bonds-and-impact-investing-genuine-impact-or-snake-oil/> [both accessed 15 December 2014].

16. <https://www.gov.uk/government/uploads/system/uploads/attachment_data/file/67321/Family-Planning-Dev-Impact-Bonds-Scoping.pdf> [accessed 15 December 2014].

17. <https://www.gov.uk/government/news/uk-development-bonds-will-combat-global-poverty> [accessed 15 December 2014].

18. <http://www.cgdev.org/blog/unga-dispatch-launch-new-global-innovation-fund> [accessed 15 December 2014].

19. <www.oecd.org/development/evaluation/daccriteriaforevaluating developmentassistance.htm> [accessed 15 December 2014].

20. <http://www.usaid.gov/sites/default/files/documents/1868/USAIDEvaluationPolicy.pdf> [accessed 15 December 2014].

21. UN DESA, 'Accountable and effective development cooperation in a post-2015 era. Background Study 1. Quality of development cooperation: accountability, impact and results', United Nations Department of Economic and Social Affairs (UN DESA) and the German Federal Ministry for Economic Cooperation and Development (BMZ), April 2014.

22. See, for example, <http://icai.independent.gov.uk/wp-content/uploads/2014/03/ICAI-Child-Mortality-FINAL-120714.pdf> [accessed 15 December 2014].

23. See <http://devpolicy.org/pushing-forward-for-more-accountability-and-less-theatre/> [accessed 15 December 2014].

24. See <http://www.ode.ausaid.gov.au/publications/documents/impact-evaluation-discussion-paper.pdf>, <https://www.dfid.gov.uk/Documents/publications1/design-method-impact-eval.pdf>, and also <http://www.betterevaluation.org> [all accessed 15 December 2014].

25. See p. 161 at <http://www.ifs.org.uk/budgets/gb2012/12chap7.pdf> [accessed 15 December 2014].

26. Personal communication from Teresa Albero, 24 October 2014.

CHAPTER 3

Mapping the results landscape: insights from a crowdsourcing survey

Brendan S. Whitty[1]

Abstract

This chapter explores how development workers in different positions in the 'aid chain' respond to the tightening results-reporting requirements. A crowdsourcing survey found that, while the results agenda was viewed more positively than not, its influence was seen as deeply ambiguous. Respondents' contrasts in perspective are identified with respect to key facets of development work that the results agenda has influenced. Four factors are proposed that may influence these perspectives: the position of the respondent, their role, the organizational context, and the process of change management through which reporting requirements were introduced.

Keywords: results-based-management, development practice, audit controls, monitoring and evaluation, aid chain

The results agenda emerged to improve the effectiveness and accountability of the development sector.[2] Much less is known about how the increasingly prevalent results-focused management and audit controls into development programming have been translated into practice. This chapter asks: how do development workers in different positions in the 'aid chain' respond to the tightening requirements? It presents responses to an online 'crowdsourcing' survey run by the Big Push Forward (Whitty, 2013) that sought to capture experiences from the sector of this agenda. The Big Push Forward conveners[3] launched the survey after noting an absence of the lived voice of those expected to make the results agenda happen. The survey provided an opportunity for people within the sector to present their experiences of implementing the intentions of the results agenda.

The results agenda for international development is part of a growing audit culture within the public sector (see Power, 1997; Shore and Wright, 2000; Strathern, 2000). Quantification and the focus on 'value for money' (see Chapter 4) are ways to manage and hold public spending to account, thereby seeking to increase efficiency and reduce waste. As conveners, we suspected that, as with other public sectors subjected to similar reforms, this tightening of results accountability and control would create underlying frustrations. We noted that the introduction of 'new public management' and other audit controls had

http://dx.doi.org/10.3362/9781780448855.003

resulted in professional bodies responding with a range of strategies, ranging from resistance to subversion (Power, 1997; Alvesson and Wilmott, 2002; Bezes et al., 2012; Thomas and Davies, 2005). We wondered if the results agenda would lead to a reduction in space for learning and a narrowing of the values, goals, and world views of development agency head offices.

This chapter offers insights from over 100 experiences received about people's responses to results-focused management artefacts (see Chapter 2). I start by describing the crowdsourcing survey as a research instrument. Then I identify five key areas characterized by patterns of contrasting interpretations, some positive and some negative. Drawing further on the survey, I try to explain the patterns of contrasts by referencing four factors with apparent explanatory value. I close by offering some final reflections.

The survey and the respondents

The Big Push Forward conveners launched the survey on 31 October 2012 using Survey Monkey. It was closed for entries four months later, on 1 March 2013. We advertised it by email and through the internet, primarily using Big Push Forward contacts, social media tools, and via the Big Push Forward website. We asked: 1) basic information about the organization and the respondents role; 2) five multiple-choice questions eliciting ratings relating to the effects of the results agenda; and 3) specific stories, prompted by the questions: 'What happened due to the results agenda?' and 'What were your experiences?' All questions were optional.

We received responses to parts one and two from 153 respondents, 65 of whom also provided at least one story. Of these, 32 provided two stories and 11 provided three – giving us 108 distinct experiences. The experiences varied from long and detailed discussions of the context and effects of the experience to one-sentence observations. As the stories are self-selecting, they are neither representative nor comprehensive in their coverage of the sector. For example, in terms of functional responsibilities, over half the respondents had some form of monitoring and evaluation (M&E) function (55 per cent), far more than programme implementation (20 per cent). Over half worked in NGOs (44 per cent from international NGOs, and 8 per cent from national NGOs), while 21 per cent were consultants. Far fewer implementers and programme staff responded and there were no responses from the 'ultimate beneficiaries'. There were also very few from smaller civil society organizations at the 'end' of the aid chain or from governments receiving aid.

This distribution of respondents creates limitations in whose views are captured, and on the inferences we can make. The survey was run on a shoestring budget, making it impossible to canvas development workers closer to the field. Moreover, of the 153 respondents, 41 per cent were subscribers to the Big Push Forward website, perhaps making them more likely to be critical of the results agenda. Given these limitations, the following analysis can do no more than provide some insights into the results agenda beyond its intentions. Filling this gap provides an important addition to the debate.

Patterns of contrasting interpretations

Respondents overwhelmingly agree that the sharpening focus on results has generated change within the development sector. Over half the respondents thought that there had been *significant or greater change* in their daily work (56 per cent) and a further 24 per cent thought that there had been *some change*. When asked about change at the organizational level, 62 per cent of respondents thought that there was *significant discussion or change* in their organization. Perspectives were generally more positive than negative: 42 per cent of responders identified 'some' or a 'great' improvement in their ability to achieve their mission, while 22 per cent reported 'some' or 'great' negative impact. Looking at the averages suggests that the results agenda has – overall – been a success. However, the picture is complicated by the significant number of respondents who identified mixed effects (i.e. both positive and negative) for mission achievement and learning (33 per cent and 29 per cent respectively).

The stories confirm this ambiguous picture. Tonally, they range from expressions of frustration, through careful attempts to present both sides of the story and efforts to frame tensions, to stories of unambiguous gain. The following analysis draws out the patterns that emerged when analysing the experiences, and presents them in the form of five key dualities or 'contrasts' that emerged.

Contrast 1: Accountability versus learning-oriented systems

The experiences tell very different stories about how organizations have reformed their internal systems to accommodate the requirements of the results agenda. Some stories suggest that the results agenda has helped to build the strength and focus on M&E systems overall. These respondents argue that their organizations have improved learning and reporting on results:

> [There was] significantly more attention given to M&E, more consideration of what people should be measuring, and how. More consideration on what the programme actually wanted to achieve – increased clarity on what was realistic, strengthening the logic of the programme.

> [I]t is too early to say if it will work but I think that encouraging folk to think strategically, measure and monitor, report to a single template, that these are good things. We want to provide evidence, but that can be both qualitative as well as quantitative.

These respondents interpreted the results agenda as encouraging a more disciplined reflection on programming that will achieve results, strengthen knowledge management, curb the tendency to 'overclaim', and improve broader learning processes. The quantitative part of the survey seems to confirm this: half (50 per cent) reported 'some' or 'great' improvements in their organization's ability to learn, while only 12 per cent reported a negative impact.

Other respondents painted a less rosy picture. One story spoke of the value colleagues placed on having a space to think creatively within a participatory

M&E system, rather than one defined by the management hierarchy. The story concluded with the following comment:

> I have ... learned that 'accountability trumps learning' and in trying to design an M&E system that can do both you will kill off learning unless really careful to make space for it.

Several experiences noted that results frameworks required knowledge management systems geared to the information needs of funders. The space for an organization to engage in additional forms of knowledge management will be bounded by pragmatic considerations:

> There is no desire to engage with the results agenda to influence organizational learning. Logic models have been developed recently for programmes but again this is only due to a donor requesting these and they do not feed into programme or organizational learning. The results agenda is only seen as another opportunity to access funding without any appreciation of the wider issues and benefits.

Although several respondents acknowledged that their organizations would like to create the space to learn and adapt, they observed that budget pressures constrain available resources and this space is likely to be choked by reporting requirements. Describing one delicate process of collaborative learning, a respondent noted that the requirement to stop and articulate specific results derailed the entire process. From a starting point of confidence that learning and results would be possible, it became apparent that the act of recording some of the progress made would undermine the process of learning. She[4] describes a colleague articulating:

> [a] concern that we only have this beautiful sharing of experience and continual transparency of evolving experience because we have not objectified any of it ... 'So,' says our researcher, 'you don't think it's possible, after all, for a learning-oriented M&E system to meet accountability requirements in a results-driven era?' I am stumped.

The experiences convey conflicting views on whether the results agenda has enabled or closed organizations' space for systematic and institutionalized learning.

Contrast 2: Useful versus meaningless management information

Many experiences spoke about collecting quantitative data intended for managing resources and accountability: in particular, systematic information on costs and benefits. The second contrasting pattern concerns interpretations of the value of this data. Several respondents indicated that the pressure to articulate results systematically (see Contrast 1) had encouraged the generation of useful forms of knowledge in organizations:

> [T]his requirement has helped bring greater discipline to our focus on VFM [value for money] as Programme Managers and then we have

supported our CSO Partners to make sure they are focussing on and controlling their cost drivers and how they provide value.

Some experiences talked about the need for information on value for money and costs to make informed decisions on effectiveness, and said that this information had not been collected previously. For some, the results agenda had prompted them to draw on a wider set of evidence to justify interventions, resulting in more disciplined programming.

As with the first contrast, others presented a more ambiguous picture. One respondent suggested that, while collecting useful management information is possible, it often comes at a cost. This case noted the ability of evaluations to either answer questions of power and politics with regard to an advocacy campaign or understand the value for money of an intervention. It cannot do both:

> [W]e produced a mid-term review of a global campaign for an INGO. This was basically a strategic analysis ... which, according to feedback, was useful to the campaign managers. But the entire questioning at the Senior Management Team was along the lines of, what in this report helps us make the decision whether to allocate funds to the campaign or not?

This seems to confirm a core issue under Contrast 1: working with inevitably constrained resources may mean that M&E systems focusing on one kind of issue exclude the ability to address other issues.

Some of the experiences were more unambiguously negative. The most frequently highlighted problem was frustration about needing to report against commonly defined indicators. Several stories expressed concerns that standardized and simplified reporting data were reductionist, or questioned the utility of reporting against centralized indicators that did not capture the programme or organization being assessed. One worried that standardized reporting on 'beneficiaries reached' through different mass media channels, such as radio, would be extremely hard to count and lead to arbitrary decisions that would detract from the value of the information. Another noted that value for money accounting requirements resulted in a 'complicated, burdensome process of coding and recoding that is practically impossible to follow, and... encourages creative accounting and creative accountability'. Another described the process of reporting against obligatory targets across the operations of an international agency as being 'of little value to program improvement, and a not very credible approach to meeting upwards accountability requirements' due to the lack of fit of the standard indicators to the project's objectives. Another questioned the value of the reporting to its likely users:

> The Results Framework...has partly become a focus on quan[ti]tative numbers ... Unfortunately, [our donors] themselves do not know what they mean by indirect beneficiaries and how we are meant to count these. The numbers are very rubbery and they dont [*sic*] mind that we seem to be only making a guesstimate of the nu[m]bers.

Others expressed worries about the reductionist nature of some value for money metrics, for example:

> [W]e are concerned that the vfm metrics we produce will come to dominate the decision about the value of a particular grant. We have been constantly making the case these metrics cannot be used in isolation but as a part of a broader set of piec[e]s of data.

The respondent from this last quote goes on to explain that their donors were open-minded about moving beyond their narrow value for money metric. However: 'We are not sure whether the debates are going in a direction which will allow space for reasoned judgement.'

Contrast 3: Revealing versus obscuring causal relationships

Contrasts 1 and 2 discussed perceptions about the quality and utility of data generated as a result of the tightening of requirements. The third and fourth contrasts speak more explicitly to the influence that the results agenda has on planning and implementation. Many experiences identified the development and refinement of a 'theory of change' as central to their planning, reporting, and learning. Implementing a theory of change requires the articulation of a set of interlinked causal chains, justified and supported to varying degrees with evidence, which underpin project design and its subsequent evaluation (cf. Chapter 6). The following quotes are typical of the positive views about the utility of theory of change for programme design:

> [T]he process of writing the theory of change has been very positive and has inspired our Country Programmes to think about using 'theory of change' methodologies for specific projects and country strategies. Developing a Theory of Change has been one part of our ongoing journey to better understand what we do and why we do it.

> We now realise we need to embark on a significant piece of research to examine any sort of causal link between the above dimensions and what we call accountability. Let alone examining what other people (i.e. our partners and the communities with whom we work) might call accountability. I think on the whole this has been a positive internal discussion to have had and position to have come to.

For these respondents, this particular manifestation of the results agenda has encouraged agencies to articulate in a more disciplined fashion the links between their work and the changes they want to bring about, which supports them in planning and learning. However, as one respondent observed, what is important is not the artefact itself – be it an impact pathway or a theory of change – but rather how the artefact is used and to what purpose. He went on to say that the results agenda:

> has created space and motivation for greater use of theory of change which if done properly could lead to a more responsive ... research agenda, with greater emphasis on reflection and learning. If ToC is used

[as] 'log-frames on steroids' then the effect could be opposite. We are right in the middle of this debate and it could go either way.

A couple of stories from donor and grantee perspectives showed the potential of theory of change for negotiation. One story commended a donor who responded to a well-articulated and clearly justified theory of change, by reconsidering their own understanding of how change happens and by funding the grantee's alternative strategy. Another respondent reflected on two quite different donors:

> [P]rocesses such as creating theories of change, for example, was more encouraged by [donor X] and there was flexibility in how to measure outcomes and impact in discussion with programme managers. Other donors could be more faceless and systems and procedures would determine that projects submitted for funding would need to be more focused on service delivery with clear indicators of output/outcome for monitoring and evaluation systems.

Views were positive where the organizations had interpreted the results agenda to allow a flexible articulation of results generated through a well-considered and evidence-based theory of change. They were negative when donors demanded reporting against standard indicators underpinned by a generic theory of change, or using theories of change to lock programming into specific targets without flexibility.

Contrast 4: Increased realism in planning versus lack of ambition or focus on the easily measurable

Many stories observed that the results agenda had shifted what donors' signalled would be considered acceptable in proposals and in reporting towards the measurable. The stories indicated a contrast in whether this stance led to a positive increase in discipline in planning and reporting processes, or to a risk-averse focus on the easily measurable and easily planned. According to the following quote, it does both:

> We deliver technical assistance projects for government reform ... We are increasingly under pressure to 'link payments to outputs' ... – this means we have to think very carefully about the level of risk surrounding delivery of the outputs ... this has forced us to analyse what is definitely achievable and what is not so certain, and to develop more robust strategies for achieving the former. Overall I think this has created more realistic proposals ... On the negative side, we are perhaps less ambitious than in the past.

As noted in all three earlier contrasts, some experiences indicate that the results agenda has contributed to greater discipline in planning and claiming results. Conversely, others suggested that the results agenda has also created an aversion to programming that seeks difficult-to-measure but potentially transformative changes. The following piece of hearsay encapsulates this view:

> A high level manager in an organisation funding organisations in the 'Global South' told me they would only support projects that would produce quick tangible outcomes in the future.

Whether the change induced by the results agenda is considered to be positive discipline or negative risk-aversion, the focus on measurable indicators has implications for preferred forms of development:

> [B]y using indicators that are easily measurable, attention is given to activities that will contribute to 'achieving the indicator' instead of activities that really matter but that are more difficult to measure.

> We were developing our operational plan for the division (a regional division). Issues were very dumbed down and certain issues not selected because they were considered to be too hard to measure, and not 'speaking to' or contributing to 'corporate results reporting requirements'. I see this as a negative impact of the results agenda.

Some argued that the results agenda was reducing the number of donors they felt were interested in funding more political, complex, and risky interventions. This issue relates to ongoing debates about the purpose of development, as, on the one hand, transformative change that seeks deep-seated but uncertain and risky pro-marginalized political, social, or cultural shifts; and, on the other, transactional change that looks for outcomes linked to inputs through shorter impact chains, which are assumed to be easier to control. On the evidence from this survey, however, it seems that the impact of the results agenda – in whatever form this manifests itself – should not be overstated. When asked in the survey which parts of their work had been changed most by the agenda, relatively few respondents prioritized changes in either how implementation occurs or what is implemented: only 7 per cent stated that changes in the implementation of programmes was the most important change resulting from the results agenda, with 13 per cent citing it as the second most important change. Perhaps predictably, respondents' main change related to liaising with donors through reporting (25 per cent stating that this was most important and 12 per cent second most important), followed by proposal writing (21 per cent most important, 8 per cent second most important).

Contrast 5: Burdening versus supporting relationships

The starting point of the survey was to map effects of the results agenda from the perspective of those being controlled by results requirements from higher up the 'aid chain'. Many of the experiences, however, were from staff members of intermediate organizations, often international NGOs, who both implement management-oriented controls and at the same time are themselves controlled by similar management practices. The fifth contrast concerns the way in which the results agenda affected how they could manage their partnerships and relationships. Several experiences from consortium heads described how they report to donors and, in turn, required others – national NGOs or other 'implementing partners' – to report to them. Of these, some felt that the focus on results was useful since it improves the planning discipline of their partners and their ability to coordinate their partners:

> By taking control of the reporting process ... and introducing a shared systematic process for identifying and describing outputs and results,

we have introduced much greater clarity and consistency into our engagement with partners funded.

Another positive aspect was the discipline people felt it introduced to thinking through more carefully the contribution of different organizations to development. One respondent described how the international NGO she worked with was rethinking its role and that of its partners. She said that a stronger results orientation had forced them 'to focus much more on the results we have in the realm of building the capacity of partner organisations to achieve their development results' – and to clarify the respective contributions of HQ and field-level staff.

Other experiences of reporting 'up' the chain were deeply problematic for respondents. Of the stories that dealt with reporting, several were concerned that the top-down definition of results targets led more often to inappropriate targets that were difficult to translate into useful management data. One experience said that the HQ definitions of indicators 'sometimes leave local staff and partners out – and so there is far less ownership of the results and little country level learning'. The hierarchical nature of reporting requirements caused some NGO workers to baulk and label the reforms as 'non-participatory'. Another critique focused on the damage done by the rigidity of year-on-year targets in a complex context:

> [This] doesn't lend itself to working relationally and facilitatively with partners in the global south...The result has been an increasing push in our internal organisational relations and systems towards inflexibility and 'upwards' accountability, increasing tendency towards the use of 'power over' in relationships both internally and externally, and has meant that we have had to invest more time and energy in trying to mitigate the negative effects of the results agenda on work going on in-country.

> Both partners and Programme Managers struggle to take large indicators and break them down into concrete measures of progress that [they] can practically use to support their own project management.

The stories indicate that the top-down and obligatory nature of the results targets often create tensions in the relationships between a consortium lead and their implementing partners. From the partners' perspective (those lower in the chain and subject to management controls), there was some talk of the frustration of adapting to the reporting requirements. Others accept the necessity with a tone of resigned acceptance:

> In one example that led/forced me to rewrite entirely a LogFrame which was the basis for regular reporting – this was somewhat time-consuming but made no difference in project monitoring. In my current work, we are slowly being moved to report more on results (including media outreach, which is a particular form of results), and I find the team with which I work almost without reluctance adopts new practices and gets on with the work it cares about.

As with earlier contrasts, the interpretation depends on the stance or position of the respondent. This factor, and the four others with some power to explain the contrasts, are addressed in the following section.

Four factors that may explain the contrasts

In the previous section, I identified five patterns of contrasting interpretations among the stories. What might explain these patterns? Here I turn back to the survey data to identify four factors that may partially explain the contrasting experiences.

Factor 1: Respondents' positionality and perspective

All five contrasts relate to a balancing act at management level: holding 'downstream' actors and ultimately fieldworkers to account, while delegating sufficient power to local experts to enable them to deal with the unique conditions of their context. The results agenda reinforces the accountability side of the equation and reduces delegated power. This tension resonates with what Power (1997) identifies as a growing audit culture, in which a generalist management class is empowered, while the 'professional class' is subjugated through a range of 'audit' processes. Accounts of similar reforms in other contexts suggest that professionals will resist management and audit processes in various ways (see Thomas and Davies, 2005; Bezes et al., 2012). Conversely, those in a management role and those empowered to undertake M&E (implementers of the 'audit culture') may be expected to benefit – and, therefore, to approve of the reforms.

Our survey responses give some support to the proposition that a person's role shapes his or her perspective of the results agenda. People with M&E responsibilities were more positive about how the results agenda had affected their ability to learn, compared with those with programme responsibilities (see Figure 3.1). Broken down by hierarchy rather than function, senior management were more positive than mid-level staff. Both these groups were more positive than technical advisers, who were ambivalent, while external experts and consultants, many of them academics, were the standout sceptics of all groups.

Similar trends and breakdowns were reflected in respondents' views of their organization's ability to achieve its mission as revealed by questions about

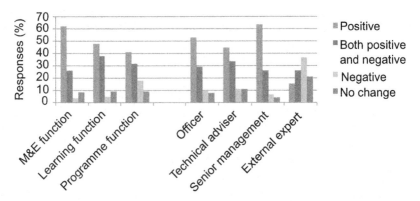

Figure 3.1 Response by seniority and function on how the results agenda has affected an organization's ability to learn

its ability to learn (see Figure 3.2), although, on average, the trends were more negative. The responses suggest that senior management and M&E people tend to perceive the agenda more positively than programme staff, lending support for a 'squeezed middle' group of programme or project officers who are producing information to be used by those higher up the management chain (see Chapter 2).

Perspectives on the effects of organizational daily practices or processes add further nuance to the proposition that position affects opinions about the results agenda (see Figure 3.3). Respondents with an M&E or learning function

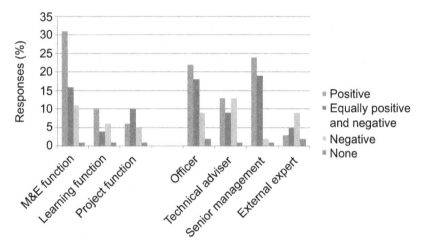

Figure 3.2 Response by seniority and function on how the results agenda has affected an organization's ability to achieve its mission

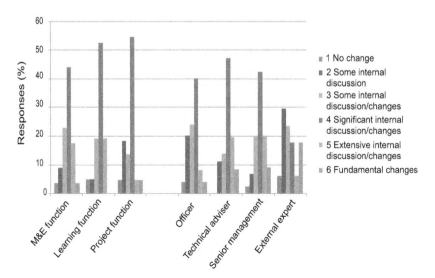

Figure 3.3 Extent of organizational changes affected by the results agenda

were slightly more likely to see extensive or fundamental changes than those who identified themselves as having project functions. Senior management and internal technical or policy advisers saw greater changes than mid-ranking staff members (41 per cent). External experts were deeply divided as to the extent of the agenda's impact. These survey results suggest that those closer to the 'results coalface' are less struck by any change in daily practice.

Factor 2: Reporting numbers obscures programming realities

The second factor builds on the importance of position and concerns respondents' relationships to the production and use of numbers. Sausages and laws are said to 'cease to inspire respect in proportion as we know how they are made'.[5] Numbers are similar. Reporting on results leads to a simplified and digested version of a project's or programme's effects, thereby losing the complexities of reality to a greater or lesser extent. Familiarity with the process of constructing numbers affects people's perceptions of their utility. Quarles van Ufford et al. observe that these management processes arise from the need to control the environment, a control that is comforting even if it is illusory (Quarles van Ufford et al., 2003; Hobart, 1993).

The stories provided some confirmation of this. The second contrast noted above suggested concerns about arbitrary decisions and choices forced by standard indicators that are unsuitable in a specific context. The complexity of development programming arose consistently in the stories as an insurmountable challenge that could not be overcome in results-reporting frameworks:

> The restrictive results-based reporting format did not allow for... collaborative impact attribution, was unduly linear, and encompassed unrealistic assumptions about the pace of change in gender relations.

Reporting requirements created restrictions on what could be claimed. One story noted that the 'reporting format did not allow for a more analytical and nuanced assessment of the overarching outcomes and impact of our program', which meant that attributable claims had to be made that the organization felt were unfair. Another described the consequences for the logframe of a relatively modest security reform programme:

> [It] means a small project like refurbishing police stations (which is needed) looks like it lead[s] to increased security for the whole country. This frustrates implementers, because they don't know how to fill out the log frame and feel we're making them jump through evaluation hoops without a real learning purpose.

Programme budgeting and reporting on costs and value for money are also simplified, leading to distortions:

> As part of a new institutional contract, we have been asked to divide our programme budget by the objectives included in our programme proposal, and by direct/indirect costs. However the division is quite arbitrary, as all our objectives relate to increasing civil society space and demand and respect for human rights, and are interlinked.

Such frustrations are compounded by the costs of implementing tightened reporting requirements: '[l]ots of time spent across the organisation ... of very little value to program improvement'; 'we and our partners have spent increasing amounts of time justifying our work...which has little perceivable benefit so far'; and the results focus 'has diverted staff and partner time away from other activities, and it's not clear what the added benefit of completing a "business plan" in addition to an application form should be'.The *use* of the numbers by management and processes of upstream aggregation were a source of worry in more than one story. This quote illustrates the concerns:

> I am involved in a large scale impact assessment of the aid sector funded by our government ... Synthesis will be done by economists with no understanding of assessing complex and dynamic issues like organisational capacity. We had to use standard indicators for all organisations, but how will the analysis by the synthesis team be done? Giving a mean score per indicator? These indicators are context specific and cannot be looked at separately.

Simplification and reporting against common formats, often for aggregation, turns a complex world into something easily understood and hence accessible to management,[6] giving managers grounds for decisions. Differing experiences on the quality of the numbers and their utility may drive the contrasting views.

Factor 3: How the results-oriented reforms have been implemented

A demand for reporting against performance or results frameworks is an exercise in control, and therefore of power. It makes sense, then, that a third factor that influences respondents' perceptions of the results agenda is *how* such exercises of power have been implemented and communicated. Have they been managed well or poorly? Were they introduced carefully or by diktat? Consider the reception of a new M&E system in this team:

> The M&E officer was responsible for developing the M&E system we would use based on our theory of change. We, the programmes' team, had to be proactive to be involved but it was clearly seen as 'his responsibility'. Our partners and country offices had no input. When the document arrived, I could hear the sighs around the desk as my team read it. It was hard to read for us, native English speakers, and when it was clear that, while it could be described as 'good' in M&E terms, it would not be possible to implement. It would take too long, was difficult to understand and, while it was not just about numbers, focused on collecting 'evidence' rather than listening to people's experience and learning from it. There was some good stuff in there – for the first time we would be able to have a more holistic view of what we were doing and what was happening as a result of it.

This quote encapsulates several factors about how the process is managed: the division of responsibility, the internal relationships between M&E and programming, and the manner of communication between divisions and involvement of key people in the process.

More negative perceptions about utility of information were linked to poorly communicated and extractive reporting requirements with limited obvious utility. Much depends on how the organization balances management versus operational needs for information. Respondents sharing experiences in which information is perceived as being purely for management also expressed more frustration. Their experiences suggest that results frameworks can be difficult to justify, especially as data collection for accountability purposes threatens to squeeze the space for learning at programme level (see Factor 1). But sometimes it can work well, for example in this experience where the reporting framework was linked to the principle of transparency and was accompanied by good change management:

> As a result of the contractual requirement in our PPA [programme partnership arrangement] to publish information on DFID-funded projects, we were able to use this requirement as a catalyst to focus our SMT's [senior management team's] minds on the value and practical implications of transparency, and secured a commitment and practical plan of action to publish information on all of our organisations projects, not just DFID-funded ones. We were able to plan to do this without causing too much angst among staff as the deadline for doing it was quite generous.

As with any internal change processes, communication and leadership are vital:

> I have learned that consistent, clear and simple messaging from leadership is key; that institutional change processes will take years to effect, and will require dedicated leaders to promote, facilitate and be responsive to the change process experiences.

Indeed, good management of an intermediate organization in the chain can even find benefits in inappropriate indicators:

> the indicator is of limited value to the programme and our partners as it does not measure what the impact of these media messages has been. Positive of indicator: having to adopt the indicator made us realise the sheer volume of messages that were being communicated through our partners ... It also made us think through the different types of message that our CSO Partners were using ... This has then led to a study to try and answer the questions of which types of messages [have] the most impact.

An inappropriate indicator can trigger an organization to think creatively about why the indicator is poor, if the relationships are in place to enable that process. Several experiences highlighted good change management practice: the need to generate buy-in among users of previous reporting frameworks; the need to clarify responsibilities between different departments (e.g. programming and M&E); and the need to coordinate closely between the coordinator and grantees. In each, organizational context matters, and this informs the fourth factor.

Factor 4: Organizational starting point: a typology of three

A fourth factor with explanatory value arises from the nature of the organiza-tion. The responses suggest a rough typology of three types of organization affected by the results agenda: 'sluggish bureaucracies', those with developed systems, and smaller organizations without developed internal systems.

Many positive experiences seem to emerge from managers or M&E champions within organizations that hitherto had not focused seriously on learning and for whom the results agenda has been an important wake-up call. The agenda has enabled them to leverage more resources for monitoring and learning and to become more disciplined. Several quotes stress the benefits of improved discipline in articulating and focusing on results, or in planning and identifying causal links, or in coordinating partners. For organizations doing little evaluation, the results agenda has galvanized their management into focusing on this, on pain of reduced funding. It has enabled internal champions to mobilize more resources for monitoring and learning and to shift internal knowledge management processes, sometimes quite substantially. For them, accountability does not have the same opportunity costs, since there was limited focus on M&E anyway.

The second type comprises organizations with existing systems and a capacity for learning already in place. The stories suggest that the agenda appears to bite hardest those organizations that already take learning seriously, with existing capacity and existing systems. They are unlikely to benefit from 'quick wins' generated by emphasizing results, since they already have systems for and commitments to learning, but are burdened by the more damaging aspects of the agenda, such as reductionism, risk-aversion, and standardizing bureaucracy. The following comment is illustrative:

> A very busy advocacy group in the 'Global South' that I evaluated had been subjected to several rounds of mutually contradictory training courses on 'results-based management', which took several full days of all senior managers' time. Attempting to classify their activities and outcomes according to a complex input–output–outcome–impact logic, the members of the advocacy group started to produce illegible progress reports...The system was incompatible with their own, quite sophisticated internal monitoring and learning system.

The impact of the results agenda in this context depends on how insistent the donor organization is on its particular version of the results agenda. One donor representative described an encounter with an organization whose systems were of such high quality that she eased the normal results demands, saying:

> Organisational capacity can cut through everything and 'win the day'. It also highlights, for me, the importance of organisations not being afraid to stand up for what they believe in and fight their corner – 'fund us like this or don't fund us at all'. Donors respond better to this than NGOs would [have us] believe.

A third set identified in the stories is the smaller, often national-level organization described as having limited administrative capacity – although not low capacity overall. These organizations struggle to translate their expertise and knowledge into the formal requirements of the results agenda, and risk funding cuts if they fail. The following responses are typical;

> Some partners do not respond – they have little or no resources or their IT infrastructure is not reliable enough.We are a multi-donor funded organisation and have an implementation approach of working (funding etc) with local organisations ... However, working with many and varied partner organisations (public sector, civil society, other non-government organisations) who on average have weak monitoring and evaluation practices presents constraints to what it is possible to deliver in terms of being results focused.

> partners have struggled with the lack of knowledge, capacity and resources to engage with them.

Several stories suggested that international NGO coordinators and funders considered local partners as having low administrative capacity – low in terms of translating nuanced contexts and programming in order to make them more comprehensible to standardized administrative formats, not necessarily low implementation capacity. Demanding one standard or one language of reporting often means cutting off funding to organizations that cannot make the translation – or increasing support to fill in results frameworks via intermediate brokers (Mosse and Lewis, 2006).

This typology of organizational context, albeit tentative and not exhaustive, can inform results agenda strategies, particularly those relating to effective ways of working with organizations with low administrative capacity. The tension is between supporting such organizations in the belief that they are vital to development, knowing that limited administrative capacity does not necessarily indicate poor work, and insisting on channelling funds only to those who can show that they are competitive and effective.

Concluding observations

In this chapter, I have sought to distil patterns from over 100 short experiences that can help those in the development sector be more nuanced about the diverse practical realities of the results agenda. Respondents viewed the results agenda as positive more often than not – but serious detractors remained. The agenda's impact is deeply ambiguous, with contrasting interpretations of many key facets: how it has helped understand the context, helped with learning, helped manage relationships – or not helped.

Parsing the qualitative and quantitative survey data suggests that the respondent's position in the sector seems to matter. Programme implementers burdened by its requirements are more likely to be detractors, while managers who benefit from report-based representations of reality, or M&E specialists whose functions have been bolstered, are more likely to be in favour. The chapter argues that the results agenda often entails translations of reality that obscure arbitrary choices and simplifications that go into formulating reports, and, as such, detract from learning and frustrate implementers. The analysis also gives some indication that a well-run, well-communicated, and participatory process can overcome these challenges and reduce negative impacts.

The survey on which this chapter is based was run on a shoestring, and it makes no claims to representativeness within the development sector. Nevertheless, it highlights the value of listening to the lived experiences of staff at different levels, more of which is needed. Listening can help the development sector consider whether the ways in which the results agenda is manifesting itself is what is needed and desirable.

References

Alvesson, M. and Willmott, H. (2002) 'Identity regulation as organizational control: producing the appropriate individual', *Journal of Management Studies* 39(5): 619–46.

Bezes, P., Demaziere, D., Le Bianic, T., Paradeise, C., Normand, R., Benamouzig, D., Pierruc, F. and Evetts, J. (2012) 'New public management and professionals in the public sector. What new patterns beyond opposition?', *Sociologie du travail* 54: e1–e55.

DFID (2011) *Annual Report and Accounts 2010–11*, London: Department for International Development (DFID).

Hobart, M. (1993) 'Introduction: the growth of ignorance?', in M. Hobart (ed.), *An Anthropological Critique of Development: The Growth of Ignorance*, pp. 1–31, London and New York NY: Routledge.

Lewis, D. and Mosse, D. (2006) 'Encountering order and disjuncture: contemporary anthropological perspectives on the organization of development', *Oxford Development Studies* 34(1): 1–13.

Mosse, D. and Lewis, D. (2006) 'Theoretical approaches to brokerage and translation in development', in D. Lewis and D. Mosse (eds), *Development Brokers and Translators: The Ethnography of Aid and Agencies*, Volume 1, pp. 1–26, Bloomfield CT: Kumarian Press.

Power, M. (1997) *The Audit Society: Rituals of Verification*, Oxford: Oxford University Press.

Quarles van Ufford, P. (1993) 'Knowledge and ignorance in the practices of development policy', in M. Hobart (ed.), *An Anthropological Critique of Development: The Growth of Ignorance*, pp. 135–60, London and New York NY: Routledge.

Quarles van Ufford, P., Giri, A.K. and Mosse, D. (2003) 'Interventions in development: towards a new moral understanding of our experiences and an agenda for the future', in P. Quarles van Ufford and A.K. Giri (eds), *A Moral Critique of Development: In Search of Global Responsibilities*, pp. 3–40, London: Routledge.

Shore, C. and Wright, S. (2000) 'Coercive accountability: the rise of audit culture in higher education', in M. Strathern (ed.), *Audit Cultures: Anthropological Studies in Accountability, Ethics and the Academy*, London and New York NY: Routledge.

Strathern, M. (ed.) (2000) *Audit Cultures: Anthropological Studies in Accountability, Ethics and the Academy*, London and New York NY: Routledge.

Thomas, R. and Davies, A. (2005) 'Theorizing the micro-politics of resistance: new public management and managerial identities in the UK public services', *Organization Studies* 26(5): 683–706.

Whitty, B. (2013) 'Experiences of the results agenda: draft experiences for discussion from the crowd-sourcing survey', Big Push Forward website <http://bigpushforward.net/wp-content/uploads/2011/01/Experiences-of-the-Results-Agenda-by-Brendan-Whitty.pdf> [accessed 27 June 2014].

Zoellick, R.B. (2010) 'Speech to the annual meetings plenary', 8 October 2010.

About the author

Brendan Whitty is interested in how institutions shape the translation of development policy into practice. Following research and evaluation work in Afghanistan, he worked for a UK think tank specializing in research on development accountability. Since 2010, he has concentrated on evidence- and results-focused controls in the development sector. He is presently researching for a PhD at the University of East Anglia relating to an ethnographic study on development discourses within a DFID country office. He was a Big Push Forward convener.

Notes

1. The author would like to thank Irene Guijt for the guidance and comments throughout the process of setting up the crowdsourcing survey and on early drafts of this chapter; and to Rosalind Eyben, Irene Guijt, Cathy Shutt and Chris Roche for comments on an earlier version of the paper, which was presented to the conference in Brighton on 24–25 April 2013. Errors remain the author's.
2. See, for example, DFID (2011: 2) and Zoellick (2010).
3. Rosalind Eyben, Irene Guijt, Chris Roche, Cathy Shutt and Brendan Whitty.
4. Personal pronouns have been chosen at random to anonymize respondents further.
5. This is often wrongly attributed to Otto von Bismarck, but the original quote is from US lawyer and poet John Godfrey Saxe (see <http://www.nytimes.com/2008/07/21/magazine/27wwwl-guestsafire-t.html?_r=0>).
6. For more on processes of translation from the field, see Mosse and Lewis (2006) and Latour (2005).

CHAPTER 4

The politics and practice of value for money

Cathy Shutt

Abstract

This chapter is for practitioners wanting to engage with value for money (VfM) politically, and in ways likely to encourage transformative social change. The author reflects on her own involvement in political debates and consultancy contracts to explore the evolution of VfM discourse and practice in the UK. She argues that, although VfM can appear hegemonic and sometimes contradict principles of transformational development, there is room to manoeuvre. Tactics that have been employed to mitigate unhelpful effects offer power-aware practitioners opportunities to increase accountability to citizens and each other. VfM also creates possibilities to debate what is valued in development.

Keywords: value for money, NGOs, DFID, transformational development, politics of accountability

This chapter is for practitioners wanting to engage with value for money (VfM) politically, and in ways likely to encourage transformative social change. Value for money is a relatively recent addition to buzz terms related to 'results' and 'evidence'. Arguably triggered by the British government's 2010 announcement of its commitment to secure maximum VfM for taxpayers, it has permeated the everyday language of British aid institutions and their partners – multilateral organizations, other bilateral agencies, international NGOs, and private contractors. The rapid spread of the concept has prompted enthusiasm, confusion, and concern. No one disagrees with its normative aim to use analysis of the relationships between the costs of inputs and values of outputs and outcomes to inform decisions to maximize impact. However, there has been intense debate about how to operationalize a somewhat ambiguous idea in ways that confront power relations that cause inequity, rather than reinforce them.

This chapter reflects on my participation in VfM debates. Who am I, and what qualifies me to undertake such an exercise? I have a disciplinary and professional background that straddles accounting, economics, and anthropology and has involved work in both the corporate and voluntary sector. My more recent VfM work is modest but diverse and includes consultancies with relatively small NGOs, larger ones that are household names, several Department for International Development (DFID) country programmes managed by private contractors, and some larger donor organizations – Comic Relief and the Nike

http://dx.doi.org/10.3362/9781780448855.004

Foundation. Given the small size of my sample, I do not present generalizable conclusions. Instead, the chapter raises issues and possible lessons for those who are interested in the politics of the agenda and want to make more informed choices about if or how to play, or influence, the 'rules of the game'.

My argument is simple: VfM discourse and its operationalization within a results paradigm can appear hegemonic and can sometimes contradict principles of transformational development. Nevertheless, there is room to manoeuvre. It can offer power-aware practitioners opportunities to increase accountability to citizens and each other; VfM also creates possibilities to influence discourse about links between value and money and to debate what kind of development is valued.

The argument is set out as follows. I begin by describing the evolution of VfM in the UK: the initial discursive ambiguity that prompted a confused and competitive response, and what followed next as practitioners collaborated to define meanings and shape practice. This leads into a discussion of tactics that have been employed to try to mitigate unhelpful effects while highlighting potential opportunities to make VfM more supportive of locally led transformational development.

The initial drive

> Our bargain with taxpayers is this. In return for contributing your money to help the world's poorest people, it is our duty to spend every penny of aid effectively. My top priority will be to secure maximum value for money. (Andrew Mitchell, 2010)[1]

Although the UK's National Audit Office directed public institutions to demonstrate VfM in 2006, its emergence in public discourse about UK aid is commonly associated with the 2010 election of the coalition government. In particular, it is associated with speeches made by the then Secretary of State for International Development, Andrew Mitchell. My first engagement with DFID's agenda was soon after, when considering tendering for the final evaluation of Christian Aid's civil society partnership programme agreement (PPA) with DFID. An annex accompanying the main scope of work gave an overview of what has since been reworked and become widely referred to as DFID's '3E VfM framework'. An adapted version is laid out for readers' convenience in Figure 4.1.[2]

PPAs, designed to provide strategic support for flexible organizational development needs, did not fit with this linear 3E VfM model. Thus, Christian Aid's suggestions of how to respond manifested pushback: evaluators were asked to 'adopt a broad understanding of value for money',[3] and comment on its relevance and usefulness as a performance criterion for assessing such funding.

Email exchanges with international NGO staff at the time indicated that they were not the only practitioners confused about how to proceed: DFID staff were also unsure about what to do. One wrote to me:

> It's quite frustrating because – as per DFID's TOR – we've only got 6 pages on results (from quite a complex, global programme) and yet 3/4 pages

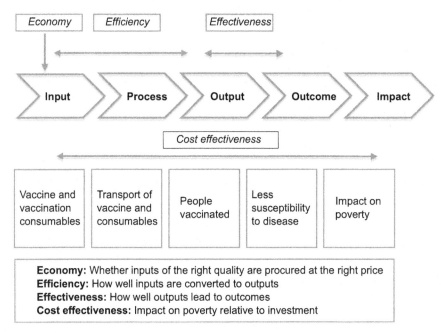

Figure 4.1 Adaptation of DFID's 3E value for money framework

on V4M with very limited guidance from DFID on what we should focus on (we were told they don't know yet and expect us to take the lead in defining).

By the time of the Big Pushback meeting in September 2010 (see Chapter 1), VfM had become a hot topic of conversation within the development sector. Issues discussed were typical of the sector's political preoccupations and practical worries. Academics, consultants, and NGO staff working on aid effectiveness policy were keen to highlight risks, such as a bias for simple programmes with results that were easy to achieve and measure. There was general agreement that we should categorically reject any attempt to put financial figures on work related to saving people from torture and human rights abuses. A proposal to resist the adoption of 'cost per beneficiary reached' as an efficiency metric was also popular.

Concerns raised at the conference reflected a broader set relevant to those keen to support locally led transformational development. Whose values or interests should be reflected in VfM questions, frameworks, analysis, and judgements at different levels of aid chains? How appropriate are economic tools that rely on the subjective modelling of linear relationships between costs, outputs, and predictable, observable, and measurable outcomes for transformative programmes with unknown outcomes that are hard to observe and measure? How can equity considerations be addressed? How should partnerships be valued? How can neoclassical concepts such as 'efficiency' be applied in aid relationships characterized by economic inequity in ways that reduce rather than increase it? How can non-financial costs like those of volunteers, particularly women – key actors in change processes and essential to sustainability – be valued appropriately? And, importantly, if the focus did have negative effects, what should be done?

The nature of the debate can be better understood when we appreciate its philosophical and ideological underpinnings, outlined in Table 4.1.

Table 4.1 Transactional and transformational development and VfM

Issue	Apolitical, managerial view of transactional development	Political, transformational development view
What is aid, who owns it and whose values count?	An investment by donors and taxpayers who set standards of what they consider good value using market prices as units of value	Part of a redistributive social justice project that incorporates valuation systems that recognize the importance of social relationships
What is aid/ development cooperation trying to achieve?	Short-term development results, often linked to donor government strategic, political, and commercial interests	Longer-term changes in power relations in support of social justice, e.g. between different groups of citizens; between governments and citizens; between donors and recipients
Who are the main learners and users of evidence and VfM analysis?	Donors and international policy-makers	Local governments and citizens
Nature of aid relationships	Contractual service delivery	Solidarity partnerships
Accountability priority	Taxpayers and donor governments	Local governments and citizens
What can we know about outcomes and contributions to them?	Everything is knowable providing we can find the right methodologies	Some things are unknowable
Ability to use VfM analysis objectively and neutrally	It is possible to overcome methodological problems and political interests and to make neutral decisions	Decisions are always political and shaped by subjective interests
Appropriate tools for VfM analysis	Cost efficiency, effectiveness, and benefit analyses	Social return on investment analysis or multiple criteria decision-making analysis that incorporates subjectivities of decision-makers and non-monetizable values
The appropriateness of using a neoclassical economic concept, such as efficiency	Efficiency is unproblematic and encourages healthy competition that produces benefits in terms of more people reached	Efforts to increase efficiency can increase inequity as less powerful suppliers/partners are likely to be squeezed more than more powerful ones

Discussions with practitioners indicated that, although fundraising, programme, finance, and monitoring and evaluation (M&E) staff appreciated some of the ideological issues, they needed methodological clarity about how best to respond pragmatically to new VfM requirements. Was VfM more about management or measurement, and was efficiency or effectiveness really DFID's main concern? Some seasoned financial managers argued that it was all about good management practices: risk management, procurement and planning, and M&E that enabled adaptation and continuous learning. But it was evident that NGO programme staff were already being asked to benchmark costs per units of outputs and outcomes; some had started to use economic tools to measure cost effectiveness or returns on investment. Examples of common assessment approaches assessed through a transformational development lens are included in Table 4.2, which draws on a VfM paper prepared by the New Economics Foundation (Vardakoulias, 2013).

Table 4.2 VfM approaches from a transformational development perspective

Elements of VfM assessment approaches	Description and possible weakness from a transformational development perspective
Economy analysis	Comparison of costs of key inputs, which can encourage the idea that cheaper is better. A superior approach is a procurement policy that allows agencies to justify decisions about price levels in line with their value propositions. Used in planning, implementation and evaluation.
Cost-efficiency analysis	Explores relationships between cost of inputs and outputs. Can be used during planning, implementation, or evaluation. Sometimes targeted using trend analysis of VfM indicators to improve over time. Also used to assess the relative efficiency of simple programme outputs, e.g. cost per person vaccinated or trained, but can be difficult to apply in complex programmes where linear relationships between inputs and outputs do not apply.
Cost–benefit analysis	Explores relationships between costs and the economic value of outcomes or impacts. Can be used during planning, implementation, or evaluation. Bases VfM judgements on comparison between similar programmes or with a subjectively chosen standard. Weaknesses include inappropriateness for non-linear programmes; using non-transparent or unrealistic assumptions and optimism bias to justify funding decisions; ignoring non-quantifiable or non-monetizable outcomes that are significant in transformational programmes.
Cost-effectiveness analysis	Explores relationships between costs and quantifiable outcomes or impacts. Can be used during planning, implementation, or evaluation. Characterized by weaknesses similar to cost–benefit analysis, although it avoids monetization challenges.

(Continued)

Table 4.2 VfM approaches from a transformational development perspective (*Continued*)

Elements of VfM assessment approaches	Description and possible weakness from a transformational development perspective
Social return on investment (SROI) analysis	Involves different stakeholders and partners in identifying costs and benefits that are then valued by assigning monetizable proxies. Includes social and environmental outcomes and values of different stakeholders in a cost–benefit analysis framework. Has been used by NGOs during planning and implementation, but can be used for evaluation. Challenges include the monetization process, ethical considerations, and the impossibility of comparison. Can be extractive if not used with empowerment objectives.
Basic efficiency resource (BER) analysis	Uses basic VfM concepts and qualitative approaches to assess the relative contribution of different units or projects/ organizations to complex multi-component programmes or activities given different levels of resources. BER analysis then offers a comparative perspective on performance, judged vis-á-vis other units within the organization or joint activity. Used for evaluation. A useful approach for encouraging participatory discussion and learning. It needs to incorporate other data to make full VfM assessments.
Multiple criteria decision analysis (MCDA)	Proceeds from the assumption that it is not appropriate to monetize social outcomes and that value is contested because of different interests/objectives. Thus, it includes a mix of quantitative and qualitative data and prioritizes debate and consensus-building among stakeholders rather than finding objective optimal solutions to problems. Variants of MCDA are widely used in aid agencies, e.g. DFID's business cases, although they are not explicitly recognized as such and include only a limited number of stakeholder perspectives. Potentially an important idea for practitioners promoting transformative development.

Emerging practice and effects

As a result of blogging on the Big Push Forward website, I was approached by individuals who were working on transformative programmes and struggling to respond to DFID's demands. This consultancy work, which included research into emerging practice and participation in VfM meetings, provided an opportunity to observe how collaboration among networks of individuals had begun to shape practice.

DFID Civil Society Department staff were honest about the challenges they experienced. Their guidelines seemed generally consistent with NGO efforts to respond in ways at least partly supportive of transformational development. DFID staff supported pilot tests of the social return on investment (SROI) methodology and advised NGOs against the application of narrow economic measurement approaches in discrete projects. More holistic approaches to integrating VfM consciousness in all stages of programme management cycles and organizational decision-making were recommended instead.

Despite ongoing debates among NGOs about the merits of VfM, in late 2011 the Bond Effectiveness Programme, which was leading efforts to improve transparency, evaluation, and learning by UK-based NGOs, produced a background paper. It included practical guidelines to help practitioners respond. Arguing that NGOs had a duty to help the government defend the case for aid and mitigate the risks of inappropriate approaches, the Bond paper suggested that NGO collective action could help shape the agenda:

> [i]n ways that will ensure inclusive and sustainable development. By proposing our own vision of value for money, NGOs can speak with a stronger collective voice and, in turn, will be positively placed to influence how donors and other development actors shape their approaches to these issues. (Bond, 2011: 3)

Tackling head-on the misunderstanding resulting from VfM's association with economic analysis, the paper provides an alternative framework for applying the 3E concepts. VfM is described in terms of the following approaches:

- Good management practice: building solid cases for funding allocations based on assumptions and evidence about costs and benefits that are consistent with social justice goals; using proper procurement and contracting procedures to achieve economy; robust planning, monitoring, and evaluation systems that include beneficiaries' perceptions of value; and so on.
- Comparison: for example, of salary benchmarks; different possible approaches to a project in a given context; a basic resource-efficiency approach to assess different stakeholder perceptions of the value of different approaches to development problems.
- Demonstration: for example, using multiple-criteria-type assessments in evaluations, or economic approaches such as SROI or cost–benefit analysis.

The Bond paper was a useful resource that partly addressed the thorny issue of 'whose values', but it failed to engage with the implications of applying VfM concepts in complex political contexts or get to grips with the issue of equity (Davis, 2012). The theoretical links between VfM, complexity, and equity are more fully teased out in a paper prepared by the Australian Council for International Development (ACFID) referred to in some of the discussion about practice below (Davis, 2012).

Diverse experiences

By the time of the Politics of Evidence conference in April 2013, most DFID grantees had some experience trying to apply VfM to their practice. There appeared to be nothing inherently empowering or disempowering about the agenda. Practitioner perceptions of its strengths and weaknesses were influenced by geographic and organizational contexts as well as individual values, positionality, and agency. Enthusiasts, like those involved in developing the Bond guidelines and some of my consultancy clients, were using VfM to encourage more transparency about financial decisions in their organizations. One used my involvement in helping a programme prepare for an external review to engage her senior management team in discussions she hoped would increase their accountability. Another was planning to use intuitive cost-driver analysis to make his colleagues aware of the hidden costs of strategic decisions to accept more institutional donor funding. (Analysis was highlighting the significant costs associated with servicing DFID's never-ending demands for evidence of results and procedural compliance!)

NGO attempts to use *ex post* VfM comparisons across programmes were generating useful discussions and learning. The HIV/Aids Alliance, one of the earliest adopters, found that comparisons across their portfolio raised sustainability issues that they could integrate in future planning. A similar exercise I undertook for a small grant-maker supporting women's organizations proved equally useful. Even in the absence of precisely quantified outputs and outcomes, it was fairly easy to undertake informal MCDA (multiple criteria decision analysis) that explored value in terms of efficiency; effectiveness; learning and adapting to improve during implementation; perceptions of project value by local partner organizations as well as by women involved; sustainability; and multiplier effects. This enabled identification of projects that showed outstanding value and some that were poor, which would have been impossible to predict *ex ante*. For example, one outstanding programme that began with a few women getting together to reflect on their lives led to a successful political and social movement, anticipated to provide economic empowerment for several thousands living in their community. The main reason was the extreme flexibility the grant-maker allowed the women in their use of funds (Blanch et al., n.d.: 6). Other useful lessons related to the risks of underfunding ambitious projects and the very different assumptions held by individual trustees about how VfM should best be conceived and measured.

Some smaller, but highly sophisticated organizations were finding VfM useful for helping them demonstrate their relative competitive cost efficiency advantage when compared with large multilateral agencies. For example, the Open Budget Initiative (OBI) – which has, in the views of some World Bank and International Monetary Fund (IMF) staff, been more effective at promoting budget transparency globally and nationally than either the World Bank or the IMF – uses a far more economic and efficient research methodology. The OBI research methodology costs about half as much as comparable World Bank and IMF studies and, by building the capacity of local organizations to undertake the research, it has the added value of increasing prospects for sustainable locally led advocacy (McGee and Shutt, 2013). By publishing a global dataset, it has also become a valued public good.

Regrettably not everyone experienced VfM in such useful and empowering ways. While the Bond guidelines may have resonated with me and won favour with champions of change within DFID, they unintentionally raised the bar for small NGOs lacking the resources or capacity necessary to use the advice. Some remained confused and concerned that they would be unable to measure or demonstrate adequate value and that their funding might dry up.[4] Everyone was cross about DFID's ubiquitous use of meaningless cost-per-beneficiary-reached metrics that most regarded as 'sausage numbers'. Jokes and confessions about making numbers up or not being sure about their validity were underpinned by much more serious ethical concerns, also voiced by teachers working under 'results-based management' regimes in the UK education sector.[5] And, even though there was no evidence to imply that long-term social change programmes were receiving less money, some working on such initiatives were frustrated that the focus on quantitative metrics denied adequate discussion of qualitative dimensions of value. One of my favourite 'pushbacks' was a comment on a business case for a programme to prevent female genital mutilation: the author 'refused to put a value on a clitoris'.

NGOs' efforts to resist narrow VfM interpretations were enabled by relationships with politically savvy DFID staff. Some of them had previously worked for NGOs and were equally frustrated with DFID's focus on economy and efficiency. They, too, were committed to ensuring that potentially transformational programmes continued to receive funding. Some initiated discussions within DFID about the need for special approaches to assessing the VfM of programmes with hard-to-measure benefits (HTMB), drawing on external expertise to shore up their cases. Lunchtime seminars – including one in November 2012 – bringing DFID staff and partners together to discuss issues relating to programmes with HTMB helped nurture a discourse about the inadequacy of linear results and VfM tools for transformational programmes.

Despite the well-intentioned efforts of DFID staff, Bond, and others, evidence in the public domain indicates that value for money remains a very donor-centric discourse. Whereas NGOs hardly mentioned it in their 2013 annual reports, DFID's (2013) report includes some 72 references. And the explanation used to satisfy taxpayers and the Public Accounts Committee promotes a very technical view of VfM. Boasts of 'saving' over £110 million by driving down suppliers' tender bids (DFID, 2013: 43) perpetuate the idea that international aid agencies can control the costs of development in a machine-like fashion. As noted by Eyben (Chapter 2), DFID's bold claims about achievement of results and cost savings suggest that development processes are apolitical and predictable. Ironically, then, rather than increasing political accountability to taxpayers, VfM threatens to mislead them (Leroy, 2012).

It is impossible to assess the impact of savings quoted in DFID's report on support to transformational development. In instances where they represent a cut in high administrative costs charged by private sector actors, the effects could be positive. However, if – as has sometimes been my experience – they have been achieved by excessive efforts to economize, they can have detrimental effects. For example, one of my clients reported being advised to accept the lowest bid for M&E services, even though she knew that the lowest-cost bidder lacked the necessary competencies to undertake the work. She felt furious and disempowered. Not only had her technical expertise been undermined, she was left having to manage a company that she knew could not deliver the value she required. Ironically, the selected provider eventually had to increase costs to build in the capacity to deliver the quality, making them *more* expensive than the original estimate submitted by her preferred bidder. Developing a nuanced understanding of how politics and power influence interpretations of VfM is key to more confident and informed practitioner engagement, so that such situations can be avoided or resisted.

Understanding our role in shaping politics and practice

It is easy to pinpoint the visible decision-making power of the government as initiating a focus on VfM. The disastrous effects of the international financial crisis and past UK economic policy, coupled with a rising aid budget, drove the need for new ideas to support the case for the 0.7 per cent aid targets. VfM was an obvious political solution for a right-wing government committed to neoliberal ideology. An ambiguous idea that tends to be invoked by governments to demonstrate accountability to taxpayers during periods of austerity (Power, 1997), it could be used to promote continued support for the aid programme, or to abandon it.

Although pushed by the government, VfM gained traction through diffuse power... driven by varied interests. Like other new public management ideas, it was powerful because it persuaded many of us practitioners that if we reformed the ways we managed and learned, we could enhance aid's impact on poor people's lives (Gulrajani, 2009) *and* achieve greater economies of scale. Such powerful ideas needed more than advocates to translate them into practice; they required a brokering of meanings and the reconciliation of diverse interests (Mosse and Lewis, 2006) in the development of approaches and tools. In the process, opportunities arose to shape politics and practice.

DFID staff created discursive ambiguity during the initial push, partly because different understandings of VfM within DFID meant that they did not know precisely how to respond. Arguably, it was also a deliberate tactic to create space for partners or suppliers to develop their own policies. Not everyone appreciated such vagueness. Research with Comic Relief partners in 2012 suggested that less confident practitioners would have preferred clear top-down instruction about how to comply. More confident individuals, such as those who developed the Bond paper, were keen to respond. Motivated by the desire to keep funds flowing *and* their belief that more responsible financial decision-making would increase impact, their strategic actions generated learning about the pros and cons of different approaches. It also helped prevent narrow interpretations that had begun to lead some NGOs to embark on inappropriate and ineffective cost-effectiveness analysis. But as some of the experiences above indicate, this did not always result in practice to effectively support transformational change.

Finding and creating room to manoeuvre

Earlier in the chapter, I identified questions raised by practitioners concerned that a rigid, hegemonic donor-driven VfM agenda would compromise the values and aims of those committed to locally led transformational development. In this next section, I introduce examples of specific tactics employed by practitioners trying to create room to manoeuvre and influence the rules of the game.

Defining context-specific VfM shaped by transformative values

> What appears to an economist to constitute good VfM, for example in reaching the extreme rural poor in a pilot district-level programme, may not do so for a government concerned with nationwide coverage and/or seeking approval from influential non-poor or vociferous urban constituencies. VfM assessments should always be contextualised. (White et al., 2013)

VfM is an inherently relative concept. Occasionally, judgements are based on cost–benefit or cost-effectiveness appraisals of various ways to achieve the same goal. However, many assessments are made within parameters that rely on more subtle and contextual decision-making criteria. A good example is the framework used by DFID to assess the VfM offered by its multilateral partners (DFID, 2011b). Each partner was given a score that reflected expert analysts' assessment of: 1) the extent to which it contributed to UK development objectives; and 2) its organizational strengths.

Thus, a position paper that defines and contextualizes the criteria that under-pin an organization's understanding of, and approach to, operationalizing VfM within its broader planning and M&E processes is an important negotiation and communication tool. It implicitly draws on MCDA approaches cited earlier and helps to make explicit assumptions about how resource allocations are expected to contribute to transformative change. Additionally, it can explain how different stakeholders' perceptions of value can be included in the scoring process.

Such frameworks are always going to be open to challenge and critique. But engaging colleagues and partners in defining what VfM means to them, why they think programme approaches and funding decisions will achieve it, and what can be done to manage, demonstrate, or compare it enables useful learning.

I often use Christian Aid's briefing paper (Christian Aid, 2012) in con-sultancy and teaching. It describes how Christian Aid defines VfM and seeks to apply it in ways consistent with its organizational values. The paper starts by explaining how an organization concerned with shifting power relations in ways that benefit the most vulnerable needs to balance economy, efficiency, effectiveness, sustainability, scale, and equity concerns.

As well as developing a definition shaped by key organizational principles, the paper also explains how Christian Aid intends to ensure that the operationalization is consistent with a social justice mission. Although Christian Aid does not underestimate the challenges involved, it outlines ethical approaches to giving poor people a voice in defining and assessing some VfM parameters. Awkward issues such as unequal power relations in 'partnerships' with local organizations and the risks of exploitative attempts by international agencies to drive costs down are confronted head-on. What I particularly like is the emphasis on context and complexity. The briefing makes clear that VfM judgements require deep understandings of context that go way beyond simplistic comparisons of unit costs. The implication is that VfM should not result in micro-management by donors or international NGOs. It needs to be managed 'locally' within trusting relationships with strong monitoring, evaluation, and learning frameworks that are flexible and allow space for adaptation due to unpredictable events and/or changes in context.

Despite the risks of VfM being used to squeeze small organizations' costs, some local organizations see the discourse as providing them a useful means to challenge international agencies for their seemingly valueless use of funds, such as holding meetings in expensive hotels.[6] A position paper like the one developed by Christian Aid could thus become a tool for these organizations to hold international agencies to account.

Identifying 'whose values'

A key concern underpinning the question 'whose values' is that a donor-driven VfM agenda would reflect individualistic, market-based values that do not resonate with the social value systems of many of those engaging with aid programmes. The British offices of Voluntary Services Overseas, WaterAid and the HIV/Aids Alliance piloted the SROI approach, which is widely viewed as the most promising tool for including local people's perceptions of values in analysis of cost-effectiveness. These organizations, as well as one of my VfM clients, found that SROI enhanced learning. In one instance it deepened a finance manager's understanding of the benefits of participatory M&E. Moreover, SROI tests supported by the New Economics Foundation linked practitioners to work on measuring well-being that gets beyond individualistic notions of value, paying more attention to the value placed on social relationships.

Reflections by those who have engaged in SROI suggest that, although it may be ideologically attractive, it is expensive and the monetization aspect quite difficult. Whereas it can produce figures to suggest that an investment is good enough for those making the assessment – a comparison against expectations – the value is so context-specific that it will not satisfy those keen to make comparisons across contexts. Furthermore, asking questions such as how a woman values her child's life poses ethical problems, but these can be overcome. ActionAid avoided suchdilemmas by using a 'SROI light' version, essentially a participatory cost-effectiveness analysis. Several of the NGOs that had piloted the approach and consultants (see, for example, McDonald, 2011) have concluded that SROI is only worth pursuing if totally integrated in a programme approach. If it does not provide 'aha moments' and utility for citizens or other 'local' participating stakeholders, there is a distinct risk that it could become yet another extractive process. This highlights the importance of including ethical considerations in VfM frameworks.

Appropriating complexity science for hard-to-measure outcomes

In order to avoid an overly reductionist approach, I encourage clients working on transformational programmes to appropriate the complexity science-informed frameworks increasingly used by DFID in its HTMB discourse. Justification can be included in position papers using thinking from the VfM piece developed in Australia by ACFID (Davis, 2012) and Ben Ramalingam's (2011) arguments. They both stress that focusing on unit costs and things that can be measured misses the importance of politics, relationships, and networks in creating exponential value through difficult-to-measure change that can result from relatively small investments. Ramalingam's framework (Figure 4.2) shows that linear, results-based management thinking and associated VfM assessment techniques may have limited use for complex transformational initiatives.

Ramalingam shows that programmes sitting in different quadrants lend them-selves to different management, evaluation, and VfM approaches. His argument is that agencies should manage risk by adopting portfolios that include mixes of programmes, some allowing more opportunity to manage results and measure VfM than others. 'Plan and control' measurement approaches using cost–benefit analyses are only suited to simple service delivery programmes with easily quanti-fiable outcomes – vaccination programmes, for example – implemented in stable contexts (top left-hand corner). At the opposite end of the spectrum – bottom right – are complex interventions in diverse and dynamic settings. Here, the goal is 'Managing turbulence'. Everything is so unpredictable that planning, action,

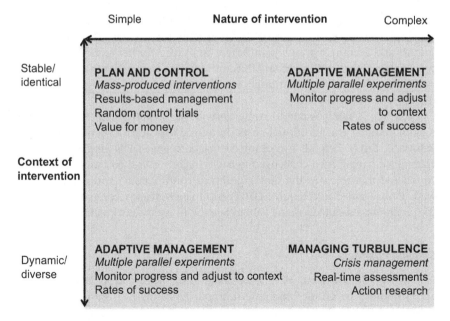

Figure 4.2 Ramalingam's portfolio-based approach to managing results and VfM

and assessment are fused together. In-between are innovative programmes being implemented in complex, dynamic, or diverse contexts that require 'Adaptive management': experimentation, M&E of progress, and learning from success and failure to enable adaptation in order to scale up and enhance VfM.

Alternatives for those not well versed in complexity science or who merely seek simpler solutions are: 1) to refuse to comply with donor demands to provide what they feel are meaningless VfM metrics; or 2) to accompany figures with a narrative that explains why they are relatively meaningless given the nature of the change being supported.

Incorporating equity

Equity is a central concern for those supporting transformational development. Although equity did not originally feature prominently in DFID VfM resources, support for it came from an unexpected ally – the Independent Commission for Aid Impact (ICAI), whose 4E framework (ICAI, 2011) adds equity to DFID's 3Es. Equity is relatively challenging to operationalize through quantitative analysis of the distribution of benefits, but plays an important discursive role in qualitative analysis that can prevent the adoption or misinterpretation of simplistic measures such as cost-per-beneficiary benchmarks.

Organizations wanting to ensure that a VfM emphasis does not favour projects with easy-to-measure results could develop multiple criteria decision-making approaches for deciding funding allocations that include and give additional weight to equity criteria. Alternatively, if a programme anticipates that it will appear relatively more expensive to a donor because it intends to work with vulnerable groups, it can highlight this in narrative discussions that should accompany any quantitative analysis. Another tactic is to include specific learning questions in an M&E and learning framework that encourages detailed analysis of the additional costs and benefits of focusing on enabling the most vulnerable people.

Even if it is not possible to come up with easy, off-the-shelf solutions, just making explicit the additional costs driven by decisions to benefit the most vulnerable can be helpful. Two of my clients, both large DFID programmes, were grateful for having been challenged to try to include it in their frameworks. Both considered that this was the most significant contribution I had made to their work. One regarded a subsequent DFID performance review recommendation that the programme should examine VfM in relation to equity as something of a coup.

Shielding partners

Pressure to demonstrate VfM risks demanding information that increases accountability to donors and international NGOs rather than to recipient governments and their citizens. Managerial demands can negatively impact on recipient organizations that spend so much time trying to learn to respond that they have little time for listening to the people they aspire to enable to transform their lives (Shutt, 2006; Wallace et al., 2006). Over the last few years

I have learned much from politically astute individuals working for donor agencies. They have influenced organizational decisions to avoid passing on ambiguous reporting requirements to small partner NGOs still struggling to develop effective M&E systems. Instead, they have chosen to absorb the costs of VfM analysis in their own appraisal processes while investing in the capacity of local partners to develop better evaluation and learning approaches driven by their contextualized learning agendas.[7]

Of course, trying to shield partners from having to assess VfM has a flip side. It could undermine the potential of local people to drive questions in ways that challenge donor power and contribute to locally led transformational development. Many talk about citizen monitoring or locally led transparency initiatives playing key roles in enabling local citizens to assess VfM. Yet this idea barely features in donor-centric political articulations.

Valuing relationships

In my own evaluation experience, the single most important determinant of whether VfM is achieved has nothing to do with tendering, beating down costs, or calculating cost-per-output figures. More seems to ride on the ability of management teams to support and respond to local power analysis and enable high-quality relationships between different actors involved in programmes. The OBI is a remarkable example, as illustrated by a quote from the mid-term review:

> Partners' preparedness to commit to the cost efficiency ethos of the OBI was demonstrated at a ... workshop in Pretoria. Partners arrived to find that they had been allocated shared rooms ... In evaluative comments collected in at the end of the first day, five expressed concerns ... in the workshop's final evaluation session several who had initially complained explicitly recanted, valuing the arrangement as having enabled them to develop useful relationships with roommates.

> Money saved on sharing accommodation may seem a trivial example of IBP's efforts to be economical with financial costs, but the partners' reactions are illustrative of the quality of relationships within the programme that have enhanced its cost efficiency and effectiveness ... IBP's trusting relationships with partners around the world – mainly OBI partners – enabled it to organize the Ask Your Government campaign within a three-month period across 84 countries. (McGee and Shutt, 2011: 23)

All VfM rationales and assessments need to comment on how and why particular approaches are expected to or have contributed to VfM. Including mention of the influence of individuals and relationships is an important way to counter a narrow technical understanding.

Using concepts such as efficiency to reduce inequity

Valuing partnerships has a double meaning. As well as communicating the importance of relationships, it also has an ethical dimension that requires finding respectful ways to operationalize approaches to managing for and assessing value. Driving small organizations at the end of aid chains to accept low administrative rates or refusing stipends can cause disharmony and inequity, generating opportunity and relational costs that outweigh the financial benefits of savings. This is a particular problem when financial cost-efficiency analysis ignores transaction and opportunity costs experienced by partner organizations and supposed 'beneficiaries'. I have been involved in several VfM exercises where underfunding, especially for the work of local partners and facilitators, has undermined the programmes' potential achievements.

Setting arbitrary ceilings on administrative costs as an efficiency indicator without understanding the nature of an organization or the structure of its accounts is a risky tactic. A meeting with UK grant-makers during VfM research for Comic Relief revealed considerable difference in accounting practices and definitions of administrative costs, which invalidated them as a comparable indicator of relative grant-making efficiency. At least two DFID-funded programmes I have worked with have similarly noted that unit cost benchmarking exercises are meaningless because of differing costing methodologies used by different organizations. This risk is highlighted in DFID's VfM guidance for cash transfer programmes (White et al., 2013), thus providing a useful tool for practitioners wanting to draw attention to the limitations of cost-efficiency analysis.

Valuing non-monetized costs

International donors and aid agencies have long struggled to acknowledge the contributions local actors make to the programmes they fund. Contributions from local people or governments are certainly an important indicator of the value they place on a programme and the potential sustainability of outputs and/or outcomes. Moreover, in some instances volunteer work can also be empowering for marginalized individuals who, by being associated with activities that benefit groups or communities, earn their respect. However, documented evidence about the sustainability of volunteer contributions to social change work is somewhat thin. Moreover, many community programmes that rely on women's time can significantly add to their existing unpaid care burdens.

SROI analysis can incorporate such costs and benefits. For example, an SROI of a Christian Aid HIV/Aids project explores the inputs of community volunteers and the benefits they experienced in terms of community esteem, among other things.[8] However, in the UK third sector, it has proved difficult to value volunteer time and estimate appropriate opportunity costs (Arvidson et al., 2010). Similarly, cost–benefit analysis should be designed to incorporate all of the costs of achieving outcomes. White et al. (2013) provide excellent advice about 'other' social and political non-project costs. The authors emphasize the importance of discussing these qualitatively in narrative text if it is not possible to quantify them.

As debates about valuing unpaid care gather pace, any VfM quantitative or qualitative analysis should draw attention to possible opportunity costs and benefits associated with women's contributions to programmes.[9]

Documenting negative experiences

As earlier examples suggest, inappropriate application of VfM approaches can have negative effects on the outcomes, as well as on practitioner confidence. Some people are more confident resisting or pushing back against inappropriate applications than others.

Documenting negative experiences can empower practitioners to publicize and debate the issue. Evidence of negative effects is essential for organized collective action to lobby against the overenthusiastic application of VfM concepts by technocrats who may not understand the relational and opportunity cost consequences of their actions. A good example is a case study written by Amy Pollard (2011) of CAFOD following a DFID country office decision to terminate a DFID programme before its sustainability and completion phase. Pollard notes that the action seemed to contradict Mitchell's commitment that a focus on VfM would not lead to a focus on short-term, low-risk, easy-to-measure solutions.

Conclusion

VfM is an attractive notion for all who believe that official and voluntary aid have roles to play in supporting 'development', poverty reduction, and social change. Despite being ambiguous and confusing, the normative ideals it conveys enable VfM discourse to win support and be reproduced. Yet, as the UK experience reveals, it can pose risks and dilemmas for practitioners wanting to support progressive social change. The transmission of management ideas that privilege certain conceptions of development and technologies of control can exacerbate inequitable relationships. It can create incentives for partners to engage in regressive learning of how to comply that ultimately incorporates them into the inequitable neoliberal capitalist system, rather than enabling learning for social transformation (Shutt, 2006). Fortunately, accounts of practitioner experience indicate that, for those sufficiently confident that they understand the strengths and weaknesses of different applications of VfM, it is possible to create or take advantage of room to manoeuvre. Narrow interpretations can be resisted, particularly by those empowered by relationships with other practitioners that enable collective action.

Collective action between individuals working in DFID, international NGOs, foundations, and private sector organizations appears relatively successful in mitigating the risk of funding for transformational programmes drying up. However, operationalization has not been problem-free. Incentivizing cost-cutting and efficiency savings appears in some instances to be undermining cost effectiveness. Furthermore, demands for relevant data can be burdensome and disempowering for those lower down the aid chain. Most concerning is the way in which VfM is communicated to the public, which reinforces the idea that development is transactional, technocratic, and within aid agencies' control. Since several studies have established that the UK public has an appetite for more complex stories about how development and change happens (for example, Glennie et al., 2012), a long-term goal for power-aware practitioners must surely be to influence more sophisticated public messaging. Whether implementing one's own VfM vision or responding to donor demands, there are a number of discrete actions that can be taken to mitigate the risk of unintentionally reproducing the idea that development is all about aid agencies 'delivering' results. These include developing positions that make clear whose values are being used to define VfM, explaining why linear approaches do not fit transformational programmes, refusing to make efficiency comparisons without considering effectiveness or equity issues, and always providing qualitative notes to explain the strengths and weaknesses of quantitative data and the extent to which it is likely to be transferable across contexts. It is vital to assess and articulate the possible impacts of approaches on partners, particularly if such impacts threaten to undermine transformational development approaches. Thinking carefully about how to frame citizen participation so that it captures real costs and benefits and documenting negative experiences or drawing attention to case studies written by others can be empowering and provide tools for collective action.

Love it or hate it, engaging with VfM is encouraging healthy and long-overdue debates that force practitioners to make explicit the reasons why we think we offer value and the values we use to assess that. By doing so transparently, the VfM discourse can offer power-aware practitioners opportunities to increase accountability to citizens and to each other. Furthermore, by developing approaches such as MCDA, practitioners also enjoy opportunities to contribute to debates being taken forward by organizations such as the New Economics Foundation, which challenge the idea that value can always be monetized.[10]

Examples of development practitioners' use of VfM tools and artefacts illustrate that it is possible to use 'political' consciousness to interpret VfM in creative ways, and that there are possibilities for collective action. However, it cannot be assumed that such efforts are always consistent with Eyben's normative ideas of 'expanding the politico-bureaucratic space for flexible and creative support of locally generated and transformative change' (Chapter 2). Practitioners who want to adapt, resist, or innovate in the field of VfM need to be equally conscious of our own politics. We need to continually interrogate assumptions that our actions necessarily provide better development alternatives. In order not to appear self-serving, we need to get better at demonstrating how and why the approaches we use, or propose that others adopt, will make a difference to locally led systemic change that is truly valued by those in whose interests we purportedly act. This requires those at the receiving end to be more engaged in conversations about what is valued. And that poses a fundamental challenge to the unequal power relations that constitute and sustain the aid system.

References

Arvidson, M., Lyon, F., McKay, S. and Moro, D. (2010) 'The ambitions and challenges of SROI', Third Sector Research Centre Working Paper 49, Birmingham: Third Sector Research Centre.

Blanch, A., Herzog, E. and Mahameed, I. (n.d.) 'Women reborn: a case study of the intersection of women, religion and peace building in a Palestinian village in Israel', in S. Hayward and K. Marshall (eds), *Women, Religion, and Peace: Exploring the Invisible*, Washington, DC: United States Institute of Peace.

Bond (2011) 'Value for money: what does it mean for NGOs?', London: Bond <http://www.bond.org.uk/data/files/Value_for_money_-_what_it_means_for_NGOs_Jan_2012.pdf> [accessed May 2014].

Christian Aid (2012) 'Christian Aid's value for money brief', London: Christian Aid <http://www.christianaid.org.uk/images/value-for-money.pdf> [accessed May 2014].

Davis, T. (2012) 'ACFID and value for money', Discussion paper, Deakin, Australia: Australian Council for International Development (ACFID) <http://www.acfid.asn.au/resources-publications/files/acfid-and-value-for-money> [accessed May 2014].

DFID (2011a) 'DFID's approach to value for money', London: Department for International Development (DFID) <https://www.gov.uk/government/uploads/system/uploads/attachment_data/file/67479/DFID-approach-value-money.pdf> [accessed May 2014].

DFID (2011b) *Multilateral Aid Review: Ensuring Maximum Value for Money for UKAID through Multilateral Organisations*, London: Department for International Development (DFID) <https://www.gov.uk/government/uploads/system/uploads/attachment_data/file/67583/multilateral_aid_review.pdf> [accessed May 2014].

DFID (2013) *Department for International Development Annual Report and Accounts 2012–2013*, London: Department for International Development (DFID) <https://www.gov.uk/government/publications/dfid-annual-report-and-accounts-2012-13> [accessed May 2014].

Emmi, A., Eskiocak, O., Kjennerud, M., Rozenkopf, I. and Schatz, F. (2011) *'Value for Money: Current Approaches and Evolving Debates'*, London: London School of Economics.

Glennie, A., Straw, W. and Wild, L. (2012) *Understanding Public Attitudes to Aid and Development*, London: Institute for Public Policy and Research and the Overseas Development Institute <http://www.odi.org/sites/odi.org.uk/files/odi-assets/publications-opinion-files/7708.pdf> [accessed May 2014].

Gulrajani, N. (2009) 'The future of development management: examining possibilities and potential', DESTIN Working Paper 9, London: Development Studies Institute, London School of Economics and Political Science.

ICAI (2011) *ICAI's Approach to Effectiveness and Value for Money*, London: Independent Commission for Aid Impact (ICAI) <http://icai.independent.gov.uk/wp-content/uploads/2010/11/ICAIs-Approach-to-Effectiveness-and-VFM.pdf> [accessed May 2014].

Leroy, M. (2012) 'The aid industry is threatening partner countries with its results obsession disorder', in *Value for Money in International Education: A New World of Results, Impacts and Outcomes*, NORRAG News 47, pp. 55–6 <http://www.norrag.org/en/publications/norrag-news/online-version/value-for-money-in-international-education-a-new-world-of-results-impacts-and-outcomes/detail/the-aid-industry-is-threatening-partner-countries-with-its-rod-results-obsession-disorder.html> [accessed May 2014].

McDonald, N. (2011) 'INGO experiments in impact monitoring – DFID programmes', conference presentation <http://www.intrac.org/data/files/ME_conference_papers_2011/Presentations/Plenary_presentations/Views_and_approaches_of_official_donors/INGO_experiments_in_impact_monitoring__DFID_programmes_-_Neil_MacDonald.pdf> [accessed May 2014].

McGee, R. and Shutt, C. (2011) 'Open Budget Initiative: mid-term review report', London: Open Budget Initiative <http://internationalbudget.org/wp-content/uploads/OBI-Mid-Term-Review-Report-for-DFID.pdf> [accessed May 2014].

McGee, R. and Shutt, C. (2013) 'Open Budget Initiative: final evaluation report', London: Open Budget Initiative <http://internationalbudget.org/wp-content/uploads/Final-Evaluation-Report.pdf> [accessed May 2014].

Mosse, D. and Lewis, D. (2006) 'Theoretical approaches to brokerage and translation in development', in D. Lewis and D. Mosse (eds), *Development Brokers and Translators: The Ethnography of Aid and Agencies*, Bloomfield CT; Kumarian Press.

NEF (2013) *Filling the Gaps: A Social Return on Investment Analysis*, London: New Economics Foundation <http://www.christianaid.org.uk/images/Filling-the-gaps-social-ROI-analysis-May-2013.pdf> [accessed May 2014].

Pollard, A. (2011) 'CAFOD's experience in Zimbabwe', London: Bond <http://bigpushforward.net/wp-content/uploads/2011/09/bondfeaturevalue_for_money_article-cafod-experience.pdf> [accessed May 2014].

Pollitt, C. (1990) *Managerialism and the Public Services*, Oxford: Blackwell.

Power, M. (1997) *The Audit Society: Rituals of Verification*, New York NY: Oxford University Press.

Ramalingam, B. (2011) 'Results 2.0: towards a portfolio based approach', in Aid on the Edge of Chaos [blog] <http://aidontheedge.info/2011/06/30/results-2-0-towards-a-portfolio-based-approach> [accessed May 2014].

Shutt, C. (2006) 'Money matters in aid relationships', in R. Eyben (ed.), *Relationships for Aid*, Oxford: Earthscan.

Shutt, C. (2012) 'A moral economy? Social interpretations of money in Aidland', *Third World Quarterly* 33(8): 1527–43.

Vardakoulias, O. (2013) *New Economics for: Value for Money in International Development*, London: New Economics Foundation <http://www.bond.org.uk/data/files/NEF_New_Economics_Jan_2013.pdf> [accessed May 2014].

Wallace, T., Bornstein, L., and Chapman, J. (2006) *The Aid Chain: Coercion and Commitment in Development NGOs*, Rugby: Practical Action Publishing.

White, P., Hodges, A. and Greenslade, M. (2013) 'Guidance on measuring and maximising value for money in social transfer programmes – second edition', London: Department for International Development (DFID) <https://www.gov.uk/government/uploads/system/uploads/attachment_data/file/204382/Guidance-value-for-money-social-transfers-25Mar2013.pdf> [accessed May 2014].

About the author

Cathy Shutt is an academic with over 20 years' experience within the international development sector. She is particularly interested in how different operations of power help or hinder social change. Cathy combines teaching on politics and power in aid institutions with consultancy work focused on learning for transformation and value for money. She was a Big Push Forward convener.

Notes

1. <https://www.gov.uk/government/news/andrew-mitchell-appointed-secretary-of-state> [accessed 24 August 2014].
2. This has since been adapted and a more recent approach can be found in DFID's 2011 paper on its approach to VfM (DFID 2011a).
3. Christian Aid Partnership Programme Agreement evaluation terms of reference, 2010.
4. <http://philvernon.net/page/4/> [accessed 20 April 2014].
5. A teacher's account of cheating in the target-driven UK education sector can be found at: <http://www.theguardian.com/teacher-network/teacher-blog/2014/jan/18/secret-teacher-cheating-schools-targets-results> [accessed 1 May 2014].
6. This sentiment was shared by feminists who have long been working on gender issues.
7. This was an argument made by managers in Comic Relief.
8. See NEF (2013).
9. Unpaid care was a major theme discussed at meetings to celebrate international women's day in March 2014. See, for example, <http://www.ohchr.org/EN/NewsEvents/Pages/DisplayNews.aspx?NewsID=14333&LangID=E> [accessed 24 August 2014].
10. <http://www.nef-consulting.co.uk/about-us/our-publications/perspectives/issue-2-december-2013/> [accessed 24 August 2014].

CHAPTER 5

The politics of juggling multiple accountability disorder[1]

Chris Roche

Abstract

This chapter describes and analyses the context and internal politics of Oxfam Australia's attempts to initiate a power-sensitive approach to accountability. The central proposition is that, despite some significant efforts by the organization to become more accountable to those it sought to benefit, this agenda never became 'mission critical'. I conclude that a greater focus on describing, analysing, and communicating the practice of transformational development (see Chapter 1) and associated forms of accountability may have been helpful.

Keywords: multiple accountabilities, Oxfam Australia, NGOs, politics of accountability

In 2014, I was 'admitted' to my local hospital having sat in the accident and emergency department for four hours. I had returned to the hospital due to a bout of severe pain following a surgical procedure that had been undertaken earlier in the week. When I asked why I was being admitted I was told that the doctors would let me know soon. Some four hours later, following the analysis of blood tests and a CT scan, I was sent home with stronger painkillers and the promise of an outpatient appointment the following week.

As I was leaving I had a chat with the slightly frazzled doctor who was overseeing the A&E department that day. He revealed that I had been admitted to the hospital despite the fact that the medical staff had not decided what to do with me, despite the fact that I was clearly still in the emergency department and under their care, and despite the fact that there were no beds available. Why? Sheepishly he admitted that this was to meet one of the key performance indicators (KPIs) for emergency care that are part of the performance-monitoring framework of the Victorian Department of Health, namely that '81% of patients [are] to physically leave the ED for admission to hospital, be referred to another hospital for treatment, or be discharged within four hours' (Victorian Department of Health, 2013: 9).

Eyben discusses (in Chapter 2) how the theory of the principal–agent problem underlies such a performance management framework. The assumption is that staff or the hospital service (agents) cannot be trusted to make decisions in support

http://dx.doi.org/10.3362/9781780448855.005

of their organization's or patients' (the 'principal') objectives if these should clash with their own interests. Hence management systems – such as those of the Victorian Department of Health – are established to assure staff accountability. Principal–agent notions of accountability are pervasive in the international development sector. This chapter describes and analyses the context and internal politics of Oxfam Australia's attempts to initiate an alternative, power-sensitive approach to accountability, avoiding the kind of performance monitoring that can lead to the perverse incentives I encountered as a hospital patient. This approach sought to move beyond a narrow contractual focus to also include accountability to one's peers, partners, and allies on the assumption that this was key to greater reflexivity consistent with transformational development, as described below. The chapter focuses on the findings of an external assessment of this process and looks at how this informed a broader review of the agency's strategic plan.

At that time (2007–12), I was Oxfam Australia's Director of Development Effectiveness and a key protagonist with the brief of driving this agenda, both within the organization and in the sector more broadly. This was in part a result of my past engagement on these matters, particularly in the domain of participatory impact assessments, and the fact that I had strongly pushed for this agenda to be a central part of how we could 'reimagine accountability' within the organization's strategic plan. The present chapter thus takes a critically reflective stance to an analysis of the strengths, weaknesses, and challenges of introducing such an alternative approach to accountability. I draw attention to the organizational and wider context that was driving the politics and shaping what kinds of evidence were considered appropriate measures of performance and accountability. I identify some tentative lessons that I have learned about what I may have done differently, which are possibly useful for others seeking to shift such organizational dynamics.

My central proposition is that, despite some significant efforts by the organization to become more accountable to those it sought to benefit, this agenda never became 'mission critical'. In part this was because of other organizational priorities becoming more pressing – particularly as growth in funding stagnated – and in part because we failed to recognize and align the many different perspectives on accountability that existed in the agency. Arguably, we underestimated the foundational reasons that underpinned these differences, and therefore did not address some of the ideological and political obstacles associated with them. I conclude that I should have placed a greater focus on describing, analysing, and communicating the practice of transformational development and associated forms of accountability.

The chapter is structured as follows. Firstly, I outline the organizational context and the revised approach to accountability that was adopted. This is followed by a summary of an external review of this strategy and the recommendations that were made as a result. Finally, I reflect upon what I believe can be learned from this experience, and what I or we might have done differently.

Reimagining accountability

In its 2007–13 strategic plan, Oxfam Australia outlined a 'central commitment' to 'active citizenship' and 'accountability' (Oxfam Australia, 2007). This was intended to capture a key aspect of how the organization saw progressive social change, or transformational development, occurring – understood as the engagement of citizens in holding governments, private sector agencies, and aid organizations to account. We also wanted to indicate the importance of Oxfam itself being held to account by those people and organizations that it sought to benefit. This was a view echoed in much of the literature at the time (Malena et al., 2004; Sirker and Cosic, 2007) and also based on Oxfam's own experience (Roche, 2009).

Oxfam used the One World Trust definition of accountability to guide its work during this period:

> Accountability is the process through which an organization balances the needs of stakeholders in its decision-making and activities, and delivers against this commitment. (Blagescu et al., 2005: 26)

The definition was based on the view that a developmental approach to accountability had to move beyond a narrow accounting and contractual mindset to also include accountability to one's peers, partners, and allies, as well as more robust ways of empowering those living in poverty to hold the more powerful (including international NGOs and aid agencies) to account. As such, Oxfam recognized the need to move beyond principal–agent definitions of accountability[2] to what have been described as more 'social'[3] and mutual models of accountability that are better suited to 'open systems' and multiple actors. This included more explicitly 'political' or power-sensitive approaches that recognized that transformational development processes are importantly about 'creating the checks and balances that ensure that the less privileged and powerful can challenge and re-shape the dynamic of social power' (Bonbright, 2007: 2).

The definition recognized that accountability could be described as being composed of a number of different elements, notably participation, transparency, learning and evaluation, and grievance and redress (see Box 5.1).

This definition was therefore much broader than those more closely associated with predetermined and narrowly defined notions of 'performance' in that it also sought to define the processes by which less powerful actors might hold more powerful actors (including Oxfam) to account.

As part of this emphasis on accountability, a number of processes were put in place. These included: a greater emphasis on engaging the board in *sense-making* about the international development programme, based on specific cases or thematic studies as opposed to simply receiving aggregated quarterly reports; attempts to link country-level, organizational, and board annual reporting and reflection processes; the establishment of clearer mechanisms for communities and partners to have access to more transparent complaint and redress procedures; and the introduction of 'What's Cooking' and 'Management

---

Box 5.1 The Global Accountability Project framework on accountability

The Global Accountability Project framework on accountability, developed by the One World Trust, categorizes accountability into four areas:

- *Transparency:* The provision of accessible and timely information to stakeholders and the opening up of organizational procedures, structures, and processes to their assessments.
- *Participation:* The process through which an organization enables key stakeholders to play an active role in the decision-making processes and activities that affect them.
- *Evaluation:* The processes through which an organization, with involvement from key stakeholders, monitors and reviews its progress and results against goals and objectives; feeds learning from this back into the organization on an ongoing basis; and reports on the results of this process.
- *Complaint and response mechanism:* The mechanism through which an organization enables stakeholders to address complaints against its decisions and actions, and through which it ensures that these complaints are properly reviewed and acted upon.

See Blagescu, M. et al (2005).

Team Question Time' sessions on a regular basis, as well as an annual country directors meeting, to provide opportunities for staff to engage in discussion of strategic issues, as well as provide feedback to, and ask questions of, senior management.

As a further element of the accountability and learning process, a mid-term review of this plan was conducted in 2010 which I led for the organization (despite the fact that I was responsible for a number of areas that were to be investigated).[4] As part of this, we commissioned researchers from Melbourne University to undertake an assessment of how well we had done in upholding the part of the commitment that related to becoming more accountable to those people and organizations we sought to benefit and support.

This assessment involved: a literature review of social accountability processes and, in particular, how this related to the practice of international NGOs; a survey of 76 Australian staff working in the Oxfam Australia head office and 86 locally engaged field staff; four country case studies undertaken in Zimbabwe, Sri Lanka, Cambodia, and the Solomon Islands; and follow-up workshops with staff.

Staff views on accountability

The review revealed some intriguing differences between head office and field staff's perceptions, meanings, and understandings of accountability.[5] In general, field office staff held more favourable perceptions than head office staff of Oxfam Australia's actual practice of accountability. The differences in response to the question 'To what degree *should* Oxfam Australia be held accountable for its overall performance to each stakeholder?' were relatively minor. However, when it came to *existing* accountability, field staff perceived the organization to be more accountable than home office staff in relation to almost all stakeholders.

Furthermore, the gap between field and home office staff perceptions was even greater when it came to the extent to which staff felt *personally* accountable to different stakeholders. What was also surprising was the relatively consistent picture that field offices presented, despite the difference in their context. Importantly, head office staff were more likely to have divergent views on the degree of accountability Oxfam Australia owed – which in part stemmed from different understandings and conceptions – and the level of personal accountability staff members felt towards different actors. In particular, the divergence of opinion between management, international programmes, and marketing staff was noticeable. This will be discussed in more detail below.

Interestingly, field staff also rated Oxfam's involvement of partners – and partners' participation – in planning, decision-making, and monitoring and evaluation (M&E) processes, as well as the organization's responsiveness to feedback from them, higher than Australia-based staff. In general, transparency to stakeholders on project-level matters was seen to be relatively high, but it was much lower in relation to broader strategy, policy, and organizational mission and values. Furthermore, in most cases, while Oxfam's partners were generally well informed, communities were less so.

Much of the transparency and accountability at field level relied on personal and relatively informal individual communication between staff, partners, and communities, which was built upon, and helped maintain, trust and strong relationships. These relationships were often forged in times of crisis, such as the political upheaval in Zimbabwe around the 2009 election, the conflict in eastern and northern Sri Lanka, and the post-tsunami reconstruction in Sri Lanka. These informal processes, which some have described as being at the heart of 'relational' accountability (Eyben, 2006), complemented more formal reflection and planning meetings. However, there were some differences of opinion between field and head office staff on the utility of more formal reporting mechanisms (head office staff saw these as more important), and, in particular, on the degree to which communication with local government was seen to be important (field offices saw this as more critical).

Communities and Oxfam's partners generally felt that Oxfam was open to receiving and addressing complaints and grievances, although it was clear that community leaders were generally better informed than the broader community. At the same time, there were some communities who, though aware of avenues for providing feedback, did not feel confident in doing so and were not always clear on what they had the right to complain about.

In line with the above findings, Oxfam was generally seen to be responsive to changing circumstances and feedback, particularly in responding to emergencies in Sri Lanka and Zimbabwe. However, field staff also expressed the view that the head office did not always achieve the right balance between managing risk and allowing field offices to respond to the specific factors they faced in their own countries.

In its report to Oxfam Australia, the research team conducting the assessment suggested three main reasons they felt might explain the findings – these are consistent with findings from other similar studies (cf. O'Dwyer and Unerman, 2008):

1. The different perspectives within Oxfam about the effectiveness of its accountability processes are explained by the different backgrounds, roles, responsibilities, and lived experience of the respondents. The variations in these roles and responsibilities result in differential attention to various dimensions of accountability, with greater implicit weighting being given to those relationships and practices most salient to people's own role. 'That is, their assessments may disproportionately reflect assessments of those dimensions of accountability systems with which they have most direct involvement or interaction in the day to day performance of their jobs' (Davis et al., 2012: 954).

2. There were quite different understandings of what was thought to be feasible or desirable in terms of social accountability, and indeed social change more generally, in specific contexts. Field staff in particular noted that the political realities of working in Cambodia, Sri Lanka, the Solomon Islands, and Zimbabwe meant that there were limitations to the degree of 'transformational change' that could be achieved, particularly in the short term (Davis et al., 2012: 955–7).

3. A more straightforward explanation of why field staff tended to suggest that the organization in general, and their field office in particular, was performing well would be that they wanted to look good. Given the power the head office has over field offices in terms of programme approval, funding, and employment, this would seem to be rational behaviour. This might also explain why head office staff responded in the way that they did:

The generally more critical relatively negative evaluations expressed by head office staff may have reflected a desire to signal self-awareness of their own power and position within transnational relationships, thereby communicating commitment to principles and practices of social accountability. Such an attitude would accord with the findings of internal surveys conducted among Oxfam Australia staff, indicating that such staff perceive Oxfam to be committed to forms of accountability that contribute to redressing power asymmetries between itself, partners and 'beneficiary' communities, but also perceive the organization as falling short in many cases of meeting those challenges. (Davis et al., 2012: 957–8)

Organizational debates

The report of the above study was one of several that had been commissioned for the mid-term review of Oxfam's strategic plan. As the lead author of the overall report, it was my responsibility – along with my co-author Annabel Brown – to take the findings of this and the other reviews and produce a summary report with recommendations for the senior management team.

As part of this process, we held a series of meetings with staff to discuss the findings and possible recommendations, before finalizing our report. These meetings were helpful in discovering where there was general consensus about the review's findings and where there were differences of opinion – and in creating some spaces to promote dialogue. We hoped that this would also help build on a recommendation from the Melbourne University study which suggested that, if a more comprehensive shift in agency accountability was to be achieved, this would require a more strategic conversation and negotiation across the agency as well as a more subtle understanding and accommodation of the power relations that exist within the agency, and between the agency and those with whom it interacts.

One meeting in Melbourne of country and head office staff was of particular note as it helped confirm and debate some of the divergent understandings that existed. For example, when presented with the findings of the Melbourne University research, field staff drew out the fact that they seemed to be much more concerned with accountability to local government in the countries they worked in than were head office staff, some of whom, they felt, seemed to feel more accountable to the Australian government.

As far as the organization's central commitments were concerned we noted in our report that the concepts of active citizenship and accountability – notwithstanding the different understandings that existed – remained central to many people's thinking about change and were also critical in creating the kinds of 'feedback loops' that many observers of the international development scene were arguing were 'broken or non-existent' (cf. Barder, 2009). However, field staff did note the challenges of translating notions of accountability into local languages and political contexts, particularly given the fact that direct translations may have different levels of meaning in various cultures. For example, in some places accountability may have more of a legal connotation that can be unwelcome, particularly in countries with repressive regimes. Furthermore, they noted that accountability was sometimes reduced to discussions about reporting, rather than encompassing the broader notion emphasized in the strategic plan.

Therefore, while we noted in our report the positive examples that the Melbourne University study had revealed of field offices attempting to develop social accountability processes, the meetings confirmed that staff were getting mixed messages regarding overall organizational accountability. We therefore argued that, while differences in understanding and experience of *personal* accountability and involvement were understandable, major differences in understanding and expectation of *organizational* accountability were a problem – not least because 'it can mean there is no common understanding and expectations that can guide staff when making decisions and dealing with clashes between the demands of stakeholders and sectional work programs' (Roche and Brown, 2011: 32). However, at the same time we also wanted to avoid what Dorothea Hilhorst described in other circumstances as singular, rational modes of accountability and a unified set of ethics that might diminish the importance of context, culture, and local politics in shaping the reality confronting NGOs and their staff (Hilhorst, 2003).

Furthermore, we suggested that the organization should do more to amplify the 'voices from the field' in order to shape its processes in ways that were likely to be more conducive to supporting work on the 'front line'. This built on concerns expressed at the meeting by field staff that they needed to be more engaged in strategic decision-making about systems and procedures, in addition to programming discussions.

As a result, we made a number of recommendations to the organization in order to address these issues. These included developing greater links between what were considered 'internal' processes and the change we wanted to see in the world, as well as developing more 'transformational' leadership skills across the agency that could embody more reflexive and collaborative practice. In particular, we argued for a better debate on the necessarily different ways of assessing performance across the agency and how different *accountability regimes* might best be understood and accommodated. This, we argued, would require a clearer hierarchy of accountabilities, which recognized the different contexts within which the work of differing parts of the organization are located, as well as Oxfam's organizational commitment to be more accountable to those we sought to benefit, which was often trumped by other considerations. We noted that this would also provide clearer decision-making processes for dealing with clashes between different stakeholder needs and expectations.

While these recommendations were largely accepted by the management team, and endorsed by the board, funding challenges and ongoing 'disruption' of the sector,[6] which led to subsequent restructuring at Oxfam, meant that other more pressing issues were prioritized. In essence, I am not sure that we were able to adequately indicate how the changes we proposed would address some of these more urgent agendas, or indeed concerns about their practicality.

The reflection

I have a privileged perspective as one of the key architects of both the Oxfam Australia strategic plan and its mid-term review (which, some would argue, would suggest a clear conflict of interest!), and indeed with responsibility in the agency for the accountability agenda until I left Oxfam in 2012. In this section I attempt to describe the experience, what I have learned, and what I think I would do differently if I had my time again.

Firstly, I became more convinced over time that the attempt to embed a broader definition and process of accountability into Oxfam's thinking was worth doing. In part this was because of the evolving political and organizational backdrop within which the plan was executed. There are perhaps three levels of this worth noting. At the level of the aid and development sector, the growing pressure for 'results', value for money, and an overly narrow definition of accountability meant that it was important that other ways of looking at this were being tested and discussed. At the level of the Oxfam family, the move to greater 'harmonization' between Oxfam affiliates ran the risk of high levels of homogenization, with a particular risk being that the 'highest' common denominator in terms of major donors' demands would be imposed across the confederation (i.e. the standards demanded by the most exigent and powerful back donor and affiliates would prevail). Developing practical and feasible social accountability processes that could be shared and debated across the confederation was therefore important. Finally, as Oxfam Australia itself grew rapidly following the Indian Ocean tsunami (2004), it became increasingly important to balance demands from more powerful stakeholders and donors with those of the partners and communities with which the agency worked. This demonstrated that becoming more accountable to those less powerful actors was not only a key means of meeting other stakeholder needs, but also consistent with the development philosophy of the agency, and therefore – in my mind – critical.[7]

Secondly, I felt that engaging more broadly with the sector on these matters was also important. I focused on two main processes: a piece of research for the Australian peak body for international NGOs, the Australian Council for International Development (ACFID); and my participation in the Big Push Forward initiative (see Chapter 1). The research for ACFID explored what other agencies were doing to become more accountable to those groups and people they sought to benefit, and, in particular, looked at innovations in this area. This involved developing a number of case studies of innovative practice, and a series of workshops with Australian-based programme, campaigns, marketing, and senior management staff. The final 'Voice and Choice' report (Roche, 2010) attempted to capture some of the generic obstacles that agencies seem to be facing and suggested how these might be overcome in a more holistic manner. Essentially, the report concluded that if alternative approaches to accountability were genuinely to be developed and tested, then this required a much more fundamental shift in organizational dynamics and processes.

In many ways the ACFID study and my engagement in the Big Push Forward provided me with access to a broader range of experiences and better understanding of some of the deep-rooted challenges faced by organizations such as Oxfam. Furthermore, it enabled me to engage and share thoughts with staff from other agencies, and with researchers who had a shared perspective on these issues. My thinking at the time was that there needed to be a degree of 'collective action' across the NGO sector as the power of individual agencies was insufficient to change the rules of the game.

However, this broader engagement also had a cost. In particular, it meant that I did not spend enough time engaging with programme staff in the field to understand their reality and their perceptions of what was feasible and desirable; as the Melbourne University research summarized above suggests, this was something that was important to do. I also probably did not spend enough time engaging with either those staff who were part of the 'squeezed middle' (see Chapter 1) or with those whose different roles and responsibilities in the agency produced some of the 'mixed messages' that undermined some of the alternative accountability processes we sought to build. As a result, I do not believe we managed to build the critical mass (or 'reform coalition', using other language) in the agency that was probably necessary to address the changes that were required at multiple levels across Oxfam Australia. I can now see that the challenge we faced in Oxfam, or indeed across the sector more broadly, was much more significant than I believed at that time. It has become much clearer to me that the pervasive nature of 'accepted' ways of doing things – project management, reporting, objective-setting, M&E, etc. (see Chapter 2) – meant that alternatives to these were completely and literally 'unthinkable' for many staff, particularly, but not exclusively, in head office.

So, while it was possible to achieve some important shifts in practice in some domains of accountability – such as becoming much more transparent in public reporting, which had the result of the agency winning the PwC Transparency Award in 2008 and being runner-up in 2010 and 2011 – in others this was much harder. Arguably where progress was made was in those areas where a CEO, who was personally committed to much of this agenda, could insist that certain actions were taken, where those actions were relatively straightforward to implement and monitor, and where the chain of command was relatively short. Furthermore, although some interests in the agency may have been uncomfortable with these changes (i.e. the more transparent reporting of the CEO's salary), the organizational risks were perceived by senior managers as being relatively low.

However, change proved much harder to initiate when it came to more fundamental issues that challenged orthodox ways of doing things, where a deeper transformation of behaviours and attitudes was required, and where organizational imperatives were sharper. In particular, the management team never really resolved some pretty major differences of opinion (arguably grounded in different world views) about the role of planning, performance management, and accountability. Some – especially those responsible for marketing and fundraising, as well as human resources and finances – consistently articulated the need for uniform, standardized approaches across the agency, with tightly defined objectives and SMART KPIs aligned from the organizational level to the individual level. Indeed, for those managers it was hard if not impossible to see why others, and in particular programme staff, could not and should not all be held to account in the same way.[8] For others – mainly those responsible for development programming, advocacy, and campaigns – it was important to recognize the different nature of the work carried out by different parts of the organization, and particularly that much of it was unpredictable, context-specific, non-linear, and long term and therefore not amenable to the kinds of planning and performance management that might have been appropriate in other areas.

Although attempts were made to develop a hybrid performance framework that sought to accommodate these different approaches in one overarching system, such a framework proved difficult to operationalize and was arguably overly conceptual in approach. This was in part because the more fundamental differences in perspective across the agency were difficult to reconcile, and in part because external funding and associated reporting demands produced additional incentives – particularly for programme staff and those charged with M&E systems – to privilege processes that delivered on those contractual accountabilities. As suggested by Brendan Whitty (Chapter 3), this alignment of external demands and internal interests of parts of the organization proved to be a powerful combination.

With hindsight, I think that while we were right to try to work internally and with others at the same time, we should have focused more on describing, analysing, and communicating the alternative practice that was already occurring – both within Oxfam and in other agencies. While some effort went into this in the Oxfam mid-term review and the ACFID 'Voice and Choice' report, the recommendations of both those studies focused on trying to address the cultural, organizational, and leadership challenges that had to be overcome for this alternative practice to become more common. This arguably had two effects. Firstly, it asked some senior managers, including those who were resistant to this agenda, to lead organizational change in a direction that did not align with their world view. Secondly, it did not provide those who wanted to pursue this agenda with enough practical information about how they might do it, given the external pressures they were under, and it did not include sufficient detail on how they might resist and 'bend the rules'. As others have noted, changing deeply held beliefs and assumptions requires more than admonishments to change; it requires deeper challenges to the status quo – and engagement in front-line practice, experiential learning, and 'immersions' can be a useful way of doing this (Chambers, 2014).

At the same time, the external public funding environment was becoming tougher – and this compounded things. Several agencies in Australia, including Oxfam, had grown very fast following the Indian Ocean tsunami. As a consequence, they had taken on more staff and more functions. Oxfam Australia, for example, created my post as Director of Development Effectiveness and started a research unit in 2007. In part, this growth was fuelled by funding from the Australian government for the larger NGOs (Pryke and Davies, 2014), which increased substantially between 2005 and 2013: the AusAID-NGO Cooperation Program increased from Aus$26 million to Aus$141 million over that period (Betteridge, 2013). Despite this, because of relatively stagnant public fundraising, by 2010 the annual growth in recurrent costs for a number of agencies, including Oxfam, started to be greater than their growth in annual income. The inevitable happened and agencies started to restructure, consolidate, and, in some cases, make staff redundant.

This increased dependency on government funding and threats to organizational survival also meant that the climate was distinctly unfavourable for more radical reforms to accountability processes. It is perhaps not surprising, therefore, that sector-wide proposals to take forward a research and learning agenda to test and share innovations in this area, funded through a pooling of NGO resources, came to nothing. In an even tougher climate, with a new set of government performance 'benchmarks' being developed and in a policy environment 'where standards are not met and improvements are not achieved within a year, investments will be cancelled' (DFAT, 2014: 10) it remains to be seen whether this will promote a greater sense of collaboration

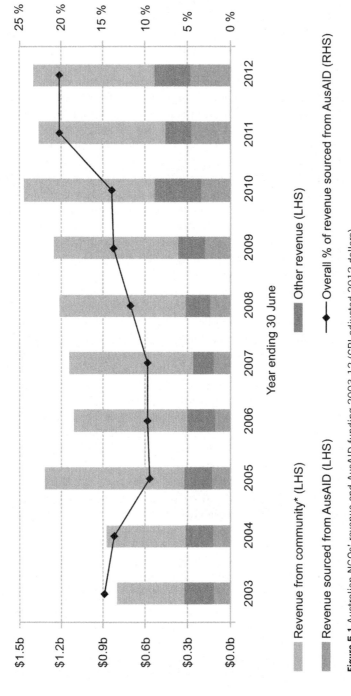

Figure 5.1 Australian NGOs' revenue and AusAID funding 2003-12 (CPI adjusted 2012 dollars)
Source: Wulfsohn and Howes (2014); ACFID data and annual reports; individual NGOs' financial statements; and authors' calculations.

Note: Values given in CPI-adjusted, 2012 Australian dollars.

* Donations, gifts, legacies, and bequests.

and collective action in the pursuit of a 'safe space' in which to operate, or whether it will drive further competition between agencies.

> We will strengthen the way we assess the performance of contractors, NGOs and multilateral organizations delivering Australian aid. We will build on what works so that funding will increasingly flow to the best performing organizations. When projects don't deliver the results we expect, they will be put on a rigorous path to improvement or be terminated. If a programme has failed we will call it for what it is and come up with a better way to meet the challenge. I am increasing significantly the rigour around performance management to ensure we achieve better value-for-money. (Bishop, 2014)

Conclusion

This chapter has described an attempt by an international NGO, and in particular by some of its staff, to resist the effects of power relations that drive standard performance monitoring by enhancing the agency's accountability to those people and organizations it seeks to benefit. It includes a summary of a study by staff at Melbourne University of this process. The researchers concluded that, while there were some positive findings, interestingly there were some significant differences in how field staff and head office staff assessed the agency's performance in this area, as well as significant differences of opinion within head office. They suggested that there were perhaps three possible explanations for these variances. The first was that these differences were due to the different roles and responsibilities – or 'positionality' – of staff, and in their understanding of accountability. The second was that there were actual differences of opinion about what was feasible and desirable in specific contexts and cultures. The third was that respondents were responding strategically to the questions they were asked and responses were therefore more a function of straightforward power relations than anything else.

In reflecting on these findings and on the process, as well as on my role as a key actor, I have tried to locate what was emerging in the broader context within which Oxfam Australia operated, and to explore how external and internal pressures and incentives interacted. I conclude that, although there were a number of attempts within agencies and across the sector to broaden approaches to accountability, and in particular to support the capacity of communities and counterpart organizations to hold others – including Australian NGOs – to account, a combination of factors has meant that this agenda has not produced much in the way of systemic change. These factors include: an increasingly unfavourable political and funding environment; a lack of appetite across the leadership of the NGO sector in Australia to build the kind of collective action across agencies that is required; and a poor understanding of how the messy reality of work on the front line of transformational development processes can best be supported, monitored, and communicated. Underpinning much of this are principal–agent notions of accountability and associated assumptions of neoliberal economics and managerialism (cf. Verhaeghe, 2014: Chapter 5). At the same time, it is clear that personal and organizational interests can act as a barrier to collective action, and thus help to reproduce the structures and constraints faced by the development sector. In other words, too many in the sector have accepted that they simply play the game, rather than playing the game with a view to changing the rules.

I now wonder whether a greater focus on exposure to – as well as analysis and communication of – the practice of transformative development and associated forms of accountability might be a more strategic way of both supporting those who are attempting to promote this agenda and possibly providing some encouragement and guidance to senior managers in NGOs to offer the right kind of organizational culture and support. Really understanding how successful practitioners and coalitions have brought about – and resisted – change, usually despite the organizational or policy straightjackets in which they find themselves, might uncover some original clues. For example, in the Big Push Forward we have noted the use of humour and 'rude' accountability[9] in putting informal pressure on decision-makers in contexts where effective formal systems for accountability are absent; others have analysed the role of gossip in enabling agency among NGO staff (Hilhorst, 2003). Are NGO leaders brave enough to constructively learn from their front-line staff and partners about how they currently bend the rules? The difficulty in shifting internal organizational culture, behaviour, and accountability processes, because of the politics, power relations, and interests involved, arguably provides an important basis for reflective learning about the complexity of the transformational development challenge itself.

In the same way that the staff of the accident and emergency department of the hospital I attended seemed to be able to tick the right box in meeting their four-hour KPI *and* maintain my ongoing treatment, so the development NGOs in Australia seem to behave as if they can meet more onerous results reporting and value for money demands placed upon them *and* promote transformational development. In both cases, one wonders whether the accountability demands are simply an unwelcome – but perhaps necessary – distraction, or whether they are in fact insidiously undermining effective practice.

References

Barder, O. (2009) 'Beyond planning: markets and networks for better aid', Working Paper 185, Washington DC: Centre for Global Development <http://www.oecd.org/dev/devcom/44251710.pdf>.

Betteridge, A. (2013) 'NGOs call for more aid...for NGOs' in Devpolicy [blog] <http://devpolicy.org/in-brief/ngos-call-for-more-aid-for-ngos-20130821-1/> (posted 21 August 2013).

Bishop, J. (2014) 'The new aid paradigm', speech at the National Press Club, Department of Foreign Affairs and Trade, Canberra, 18 June <http://www.foreignminister.gov.au/speeches/Pages/2014/jb_sp_140618.aspx?ministerid=4>.

Blagescu, M., de Las Casas, L. and Lloyd, R. (2005) *Pathways to Accountability: The GAP Framework*, London: One World Trust <http://www.oneworldtrust.org/

publications/doc_view/210-pathways-to-accountability-the-gap-framework? tmpl=component&format=raw>.

Bonbright, D. (2007) 'The changing face of accountability', talk at the International Seminar on Civil Society and Accountability, Montevideo, 16 April <http://www. keystoneaccountability.org/sites/default/files/The%20Changing%20Face%20 of%20NGO%20Accountability%20-%20David%20Bonbright_0.pdf>.

Brown, D. and Jagadananda (2007) *Civil Society Legitimacy and Accountability: Issues and Challenges*, Cambridge MA: CIVICUS and The Hauser Centre, Harvard University <http://www.civicus.org/new/media/LTA_ScopingPaper.pdf>.

Chambers, R. (2014) *Into the Unknown: Explorations in Development Practice*, Rugby: Practical Action Publishing.

David, R., Mancini, A. and Guijt, I. (2006) 'Bringing systems in line with values: the practice of ALPS (ActionAid's Accountability, Learning and Planning system)', in R. Eyben (ed.), *Relationships for Aid*, London: Earthscan.

Davis, T.W.D., Macdonald, K. and Brenton, S. (2012) 'Reforming accountability in international NGOs: making sense of conflicting feedback', *Development in Practice* 22(7): 946–61.

DFAT (2014) *Making Performance Count: Enhancing the Accountability and Effectiveness of the Australian Aid Program*, Canberra: Department of Foreign Affairs and Trade (DFAT).

Edwards, M. (2005) 'Have NGOs "made a difference"? From Manchester to Birmingham with an elephant in the room', keynote speech at 'Reclaiming Development? Assessing the Contribution of Non-Governmental Organizations' conference, University of Manchester, 27–29 June <http://www.gprg.org/pubs/ workingpapers/pdfs/gprg-wps-028.pdf>.

Eyben, R. (2006) *Relationships for Aid*, London: Earthscan.

Hilhorst, D. (2003) *The Real World of NGOs: Discourses, Diversity, and Development*, London: Zed Books.

Koppell, J. (2005) 'Pathologies of accountability: ICANN and the challenge of "Multiple Accountabilities Disorder"', *Public Administration Review* 65: 94–108.

Malena, C., Forster, R. and Singh, J. (2004) *Social Accountability: An Introduction to the Concept and Emerging Practice*, Washington DC: World Bank.

O'Dwyer, B. and Unerman, J. (2008) 'The paradox of greater NGO accountability: a case study of Amnesty Ireland', *Accounting, Organizations and Society* 33(7-8): 801–24.

Ossewaarde, R., Nijhof, A. and Heyse, L. (2008) 'Dynamics of NGO legitimacy: how organising betrays the core mission of NGOs', *Public Administration and Development* 28(1): 42–53.

Oxfam Australia (2007) *For a Just World Without Poverty: Strategic Plan for Oxfam Australia 2007–2013*, Melbourne: Oxfam Australia <https://www.oxfam.org. au/wp-content/uploads/2011/09/oaus-strategicplan2007-2013-0107.pdf>.

Pryke, J. and Davies, R. (2014) 'AusAID's favourite group of Australian NGOs gets a little bigger' in Devpolicy [blog] <http://devpolicy.org/ausaids-favourite-group-of-australian-ngos-gets-a-little-bigger-20130802/> (posted 2 August 2014).

Roche, C. (2009) 'Oxfam Australia's experience of "bottom-up" accountability', *Development in Practice* 19(8): 1009–22.

Roche, C. (2010) *Promoting Voice and Choice: Exploring Innovations in Australian NGO Accountability for Development Effectiveness*, Canberra: Australian Council for International Development.

Roche, C. and Brown, A. (2011) *For a Just World Without Poverty: Strategic Plan for Oxfam Australia 2007–2013. Mid-term Review Report Summary*, Melbourne: Oxfam Australia <http://resources.oxfam.org.au/pages/view.php?ref=594>.

Sirker, K. and Cosic, S. (2007) 'Empowering the marginalized: case studies of social accountability initiatives in Asia', WBI Working Paper, Washington DC: World Bank Institute (WBI).

Verhaeghe, P. (2014) *What about Me?: The Struggle for Identity in a Market-based Society*, Brunswick, Australia: Scribe Publications.

Victorian Department of Health (2013) *Health Service Performance Monitoring Framework 2013–14 Business Rules*, Melbourne: Victorian Department of Health <http://docs.health.vic.gov.au/docs/doc/The-Victorian-Health-Services-Performance-Monitoring-Framework-2013-14-Business-Rules>.

Wulfsohn, M. and Howes, S. (2014) 'How reliant are Australian development NGOs on government funding' in Devpolicy [blog] <http://devpolicy.org/how-reliant-are-australian-development-ngos-on-government-funding-20140327/> (posted 27 March 2014).

About the author

Chris Roche was one of the conveners of the Big Push Forward. He is Associate Professor of International Development and Director of the Institute for Human Security and Social Change at La Trobe University. He was previously Director of Development Effectiveness at Oxfam Australia.

Notes

1. The term 'multiple accountability disorder' was originally used in Koppell (2005).
2. Much of this thinking was inspired by the work by David L. Brown, captured, for example, in Brown and Jagadananda (2007).
3. However, I recognize that some forms of 'social accountability' adopt highly technocratic approaches that are arguably antithetical to more transformative processes that challenge power relations.
4. See Roche and Brown (2011) for a summary of this mid-term review.
5. For a fuller discussion of the findings, see Davis et al. (2012).
6. See, for example, the International Civil Society Centre report *Riding the Wave: A Proposal for Boards and CEOs About How to Prepare for Disruptive Change* <http://icscentre.org/downloads/RidingTheWave_web_spreads.pdf>.
7. This is notwithstanding the reality that the legitimacy and accountability of NGOs does seem to require a continual trade-off between 'developmental' and 'organizational' imperatives (see Edwards, 2005; Ossewaarde et al., 2008).
8. This is similar to experiences described in other international NGO processes of this kind (for example, see David et al., 2006).
9. See <http://bigpushforward.net/archives/1773>.

CHAPTER 6

Theory of change as best practice or next trick to perform? Hivos' journey with strategic reflection

Marjan van Es and Irene Guijt

Abstract

This chapter discusses the journey of Hivos, a Netherlands-based international NGO committed to transformational development, that since 2000 has sought a socially critical way to use the quest for evidence of results for strategic accountability. It describes how internal and external pressures have influenced efforts to improve programme quality, reflective practice, and learning, culminating in today's home-grown version of a 'theory of change' approach. The authors conclude that multiple factors work against its intended use, including an aid system that induces certain behaviours and limited incentives for staff. They raise the question whether an enabling environment for reflective practice is more decisive than the choice of any particular approach.

Keywords: theory of change, organizational learning, Hivos, Dutch development policy, strategic accountability

Introduction

'Theory of change' (ToC) has reached the status of development fad. It is the focus of books, planning protocols, guidelines, and resources, and the topic of many blogs. Much used by think tanks, NGOs, foundations, governments, and multi- and bilateral aid agencies, the term covers a wide diversity of practices and definitions (see, for example, Valters, 2014; Vogel, 2012). Most notable – and echoing the fate of the logical framework – is its almost contradictory use to describe on the one hand planning and review templates that fail to stimulate reflection, and on the other a process of critical thinking about assumptions and validity of chosen strategies. Advocates of both forms laud its contribution to better evidence-informed planning, implementation, and monitoring. Its use either as a technocratic management tool or for strategic accountability is shaped by capacities, attitudes, behaviours, power, and relationships – many of which arise from the politics of funding, results, and evidence.

We use the term 'strategic accountability' as an anchoring concept to reflect on the potential of ToC practice to foster the critical thinking essential

http://dx.doi.org/10.3362/9781780448855.006

for transformational development. The term focuses on learning about what seems to work – or not – in relation to one's mission (Cavill and Sohail, 2007; Ebrahim, 2010). While accountability is often equated with upward financial and output reporting to back donors, strategic accountability seeks to answer the question: 'Did we act as effectively as possible?' (Guijt, 2010). This requires knowing what an organization has undertaken, understanding the basis of strategic decisions and the underlying ToC, and, of course, knowing how effort and money was invested. Such accountability is intrinsically about identity – feeling committed to one's ideas and strategies (Fry, 1995).

Hivos' journey is described from the perspectives of Marjan van Es (monitoring and evaluation, or M&E, policy officer in Hivos) and her supervisor, who jointly initiated and steered the process, and that of a consultant (Irene Guijt) who supported the ToC learning process from 2010 onwards. Marjan's M&E position and her personal involvement strongly shaped our perception and analysis of the process. The Hivos M&E function, as in all organizations, is nested within a force field of internal and external pressures. Hence, this chapter also serves as a reflection on the manoeuvring space of M&E staff to influence the results agenda.

Our chapter reflects on three questions:

1. Is it possible to realize strategic accountability in a context where accountability is perceived as mainly for donors, predefined and performance oriented, and how does the politics of the results agenda influence this?
2. Is it possible to realize the potential of ToC or will it become an artefact for compliance?
3. Does the search for the right approach matter or are conditions more decisive for the level of uptake?

We describe three phases of influencing organizational reflective practice. The first focuses on capacity development for a more 'results-oriented practice' of Hivos' partner organizations (2004 to 2007), followed by two phases of advocating the use of a particular ToC approach[1] in partner and Hivos practice: one pre-ToC hype and one in the current ToC era. We reflect on why, in each phase, success in terms of extent and quality of uptake appeared to be limited and what seems to explain the similarities in the different phases. We close with considerations about the politics of and strategies for using ToC to institutionalize strategic accountability. In this chapter, we often use ToC in short, yet we are always referring to ToC as a practice, a thought process that can take different forms.

The transformational agenda of Hivos

Hivos started in 1968 as a relatively small international NGO; today, it raises €135 million per year for 700 initiatives in Africa, Asia, and Latin America, with five regional offices and one Netherlands-based head office. Since

1978, Hivos has been part of the Dutch Co-financing Programme (CFP) of the Dutch Ministry of Development Cooperation (DGIS).[2] Initially by far the main funding source, today DGIS accounts for 40 per cent of Hivos funding. Irrespective of its source, all income is accompanied by specific planning and monitoring protocols, the implications of which we discuss later.

Partnership with civil society organizations (CSOs) in the global South was and is seen as a reciprocal relationship, based on common interests and aims, trust, and clarity about respective roles. In Hivos, transparency regarding the rights and obligations of both parties is considered important in order to minimize the negative effects of inequality inherent in donor–recipient relationships and that shaped some of the dynamics discussed below. More recently, in addition to funding CSOs, Hivos also (co)implements programmes, collaborates in multi-actor initiatives, and initiates or participates in knowledge generation and social innovation. Its network has broadened to include private sector actors, think tanks, academia, social entrepreneurs, and social innovators.

Hivos explicitly supports initiatives working to shift power relations in favour of 'an open society...characterised by freedom, diversity and equal opportunities' (Hivos, 2013). It funds and co-implements efforts through active citizenship to 'challenge and check power' – for example, relating to freedom of expression, sustainable and equitable food systems, anti-corruption efforts, and taboo topics including LGBT rights. Such work, often in less democratic contexts, involves many unknowns, unpredictable twists, and long time periods from engagement to results. It entails collaboration in dynamic and diverse partnerships with organizations with limited management capacities. Furthermore, partners, engaged citizens, and Hivos itself often face strong forces that work to maintain the status quo and protect vested interests and privileged positions. At times, preventing deterioration of the situation of excluded groups or simply holding the line is a good result. Hence, in Hivos, the M&E challenge is truly one of dealing with complexity.

The monitoring and evaluation unit

Hivos' M&E unit is based in the Netherlands and in 2000 consisted of Marjan, as M&E policy officer, and her supervisor, the manager of the Audit, Evaluation and Quality Control Department. In 2003, a second policy officer joined the unit to guide programme evaluations. This small unit was responsible for developing planning, monitoring, and evaluation (PM&E) policies, guidelines, and instruments, and for supporting their use by programme officers and partner organizations. Capacity development for PM&E was one of Marjan's tasks and explains the strong focus on capacity development in this chapter.

Hivos had no other M&E staff in regional offices or in specific programmes. The original logic was that, with PM&E being part and parcel of everyone's work, creating specific M&E functions might be counterproductive. In later years, despite the need for more PM&E expertise, PM&E capacity did not grow because other investments were considered more urgent or strategic.

Until around 2000, Hivos was relatively free to define its own M&E systems and practice. Hivos worked solely through partner organizations, depending on their reports for results information. Programme officers monitored progress with each partner in a flexible way that recognized their diverse needs and approaches, allowing them to respond to changes and opportunities within their context. Hivos encouraged partners to write one annual report for all their donors and did not request specific reports. Although the logical framework approach (LFA) was widely used in international development, Hivos was critical and chose not to make this mandatory, shying away from donor-driven obligatory protocols. Particularly small, new, and activist organizations working on social justice issues, which formed a large part of Hivos' partner network, found the LFA ill-suited to the complexity and dynamics of their realities, difficult to use, and thus not helpful for improving practice.

Although the effectiveness of the CFP had long been discussed,[3] DGIS accountability requirements were limited to annual retrospective reporting, plus thematic programme evaluations by Hivos itself and jointly with DGIS and the other co-financing organizations (CFOs). Public accountability was based on information and case-based evidence from partners' annual reports, from Hivos staff, and from programme evaluations. Results information was recorded at the level of individual partners. However, Hivos had an internal learning need for more systematization and better M&E quality.

Hivos started to invest in what, with hindsight, we discern as three phases of strengthening strategic accountability, although initially the focus was on improving M&E practices. In what follows we introduce each phase by discussing the Dutch political context regarding development cooperation as the backdrop against which the M&E unit pursued its ambition of more strategic accountability, helping explain partner and in-house responses to these efforts.

Phase 1: Results-oriented practice, 2002–07

The early 2000s signalled a slow but steady shift in Dutch international development funding towards tighter results systems. The external pressure to demonstrate results grew as part of a general trend for tighter control in public management and a focus on short-term and simple results (see Chapter 2). A government-wide research framework (from Interdepartmental Policy Research or IBO) was one of the explicit manifestations of this trend.[4] In 1999, IBO research was initiated on the effectiveness and coherence of development cooperation, which included a study of the CFP (IBO, 2000). Pertinent to this chapter was the conclusion that CFP effectiveness could not be verified due to the lack of a clear policy framework from DGIS. This led to the DGIS 2001 policy framework, which formed the basis for grant applications for the period 2003–06. For the first time, the CFOs had to submit grant proposals, with objectives and anticipated results with measurable indicators. Yet the CFOs rarely knew long in advance which partners or proposals they would fund, working as they did in response to proposals from their Southern partners within the broad parameters of their policies and goals. Hivos, for example, strived for a 15 per cent annual renewal of its partner network. DGIS requirements were a push towards more top-down shaping and steering of programmes and relationships. Hivos faced the challenge of how to respect and deal with the considerable differences between partners against the backdrop of increasing standardization.

The approach to evaluating the CFP also changed, fuelling discussions about CFO effectiveness and the quality of their PM&E systems. Initially overseen by an independent steering committee, it was now up to the CFOs collectively, whose subcontracted efforts were assessed by DGIS's Independent Evaluation Unit. These assessments were sent to parliament and viewed by all political players and organizations as a means of formal accountability. During this period, politicians of right-wing parties and the media increasingly questioned the relevance and effectiveness of development cooperation. In the Netherlands, public trust in the merits of development cooperation started to decline.

Initiating results-oriented practice

From the early 2000s onwards, Hivos senior management, policy officers, and the M&E unit increasingly felt the inadequacy of existing instruments to effectively monitor results beyond the level of individual partners. Annual partner reports were mainly descriptive, with little analysis of change processes or results (see also Chapter 10). Programme officers generally felt that they had sufficient information through their personal relationships with partners. But senior management and policy staff wanted more insights on the relevance and effectiveness of intervention strategies for policy development and management. Furthermore, existing M&E practice failed to foster organizational learning about social change or for building new theory and practice. In Hivos' view, a more systematic results analysis would require a certain level of standardization, which it sought to avoid for fear of clipping the wings of partners. In effect, Hivos management and the M&E unit were seeking ways to strengthen strategic accountability and deal with the results agenda.

The M&E unit responded by investing in an organization-wide approach it called 'results-oriented practice'. The M&E unit aimed to improve strategic and public accountability by strengthening the capacity of Hivos and its partners to assess and use results for learning and accountability, enabling them to produce justifiable statements about effectiveness, while giving partners as much freedom as possible. Under the new approach, partner organizations still drafted programme proposals on their terms, but formulated objectives and intended results for the contract period as part of longer-term changes. Partners were free to choose PM&E methods and protocols that aligned with their vision, objectives, and activities, and that suited their needs. A new element was that partners were asked to propose a limited number of indicators that were relevant and meaningful to them and that would focus monitoring, reporting, and evaluation during the contract period. These indicators could be changed en route if necessary. Hivos assumed that selecting key indicators could aid partners in thinking through what changes they were expecting from their efforts, in focusing their M&E practice accordingly, and in facilitating interactions with Hivos on what really mattered to them and to Hivos.

In 2004, partner consultations involved around 200 partner organizations, plus Hivos regional staff and external consultants, to discuss the proposed results assessment approach and suggest how to make it work for everyone. Although partners appreciated Hivos' intention not to impose formats or standardize indicators, they worried that the approach might gradually lead to more rigidity and uniformity, making Hivos no different than other donors (see Box 6.1). Tough experiences with donors had made many partners distrust donor-initiated M&E. They also resisted 'from a political stance, which questions why social change investments and agencies are being so closely scrutinized for effectiveness and impact, when private sector actors are not similarly held to account for blatant violations of hard-won norms and standards' (Hivos, 2004a).

The approach changed results data collection and use in Hivos. A new administrative system linked each partner contract to specific Hivos objectives, in effect translating partner-specific results into contributions to those objectives for internal analysis and reporting to DGIS. Each year, programme officers qualitatively assessed partner progress towards objectives, using a scoring system that allowed for aggregation. Assessments were validated and results information generated by integrating quantitative and qualitative data

---

Box 6.1 Participants' quotes from India Partner Consultation, 2004

Positive voices

- Any organization committed to its vision will want to assess at every level any change it has brought about.
- It is a flexible approach and it offers an opportunity for self-reflection and capacity-building.
- This will enable us all to know where we are going, to learn, make mid-course corrections, and go forward.

Concerned voices

- I fear that result assessment will lead to a loss of plurality of organizational forms, and implicitly promote some models over others because they can better demonstrate results.
- What about contexts where we adopt different processes and stages to reach a target group; or multiple efforts are aimed at one target; or one target group needs multi-faceted indicators? In such contexts, we cannot use flat indicators which reflect one-to-one cause–effect relationships.
- In the context of result assessment, is Hivos acting as a donor or a partner?

from multiple sources. The new approach generated a demand for training, so, between 2004 and 2006, workshops were organized for programme staff and partners.

Experiences with results-oriented practice

Three years later, the M&E unit noticed that uptake was variable and not meeting expectations. Most annual reports remained descriptive, with little information on outcomes and often no reference to agreed indicators. Annual reports did not improve learning or strategic reflection between partners and Hivos due to the considerable time between implementation, reporting, and Hivos feedback. Proposals still had a gap between activities and goals and lacked realistic mid-term objectives and intended results.

Small, activist organizations struggled most. Larger, more professional partner organizations were familiar with PM&E requirements and language, although quality remained problematic. Most partners found it difficult to identify relevant indicators, so, contrary to their intention, many programme officers ended up suggesting indicators themselves. They played a central role in obtaining and using results information, balancing between insisting on justified requirements for accountability while maintaining a flexible attitude to enable responsive programming by partners. The programme officers were the Hivos version of the 'squeezed middle' (see Chapter 2).

The disappointing outcome may have been a problem of perception (see also Chapter 10). Hivos' administration system did not yet allow for systematic monitoring of capacity development efforts, so changes may simply not have been registered. But other reasons seem to substantiate limited uptake. The 15 per cent annual partner renewal policy meant phasing out partners after 10 years of cooperation or those able to attract other donors. As Hivos continually took on smaller, less developed organizations, overall quality did not improve. Furthermore, the new approach focused on improving the assessment of realized results. More attention to programme design and articulating ToCs could have facilitated indicator choice. Finally, many partners struggled with inconsistency in M&E practices and systems, due to resource-driven compromises for projects that did not align well with their programme (see Chapter 7).

Hivos' partners reacted to donors' stronger results orientation in three ways: 1) some saw the utility; 2) some complied out of fear of losing funding; and 3) some grew increasingly apprehensive and averse to donor demands for results measurement. Most partners fell in the last two groups – and a stronger results orientation negatively affected relationships. Hivos' position of allowing any format did not encourage partners to undertake results monitoring for learning because most other donors required logframes. Hivos accepted logframes too, but these were often of low quality and not used reflectively – a far cry from the strategic accountability intention driving the efforts.

Phase 2: Theory of change approach, 2007–10

While the M&E unit was pondering next steps, the external context had shifted the politics of results. DGIS announced its CFP framework for the 2007–10 period, accompanied by four critical changes. First, a logframe-like system became obligatory for CFO programmes, with articulation of objectives, results, activities, and inputs. Second, results had to be reported in quantitative terms 'where possible'. Third, 'tailor-made monitoring' was introduced, requiring CFOs to submit a monitoring protocol for their programmes with key indicators and targets for inputs, results, objectives, and sustainability. And, last but not least, co-funding eligibility required CFOs to raise at least 25 per cent of their income from other sources by 2009. This pushed all CFOs firmly into the fray of needing to please multiple back donors, each with specific requirements with regard to results. As Hivos was the most dependent of the CFOs on DGIS funding, much was set to change.

The shift towards logframes and tailor-made monitoring was intensely debated in the Dutch development sector. DGIS intended to push for more results orientation while respecting CFO autonomy, echoing Hivos' own intentions with Phase 1 and encountering similar problems. Focusing on a limited number of indicators jarred with the complexity of CFO programmes involving many partners, contexts, and monitoring practices. Compliance fuelled a tendency towards indicator-driven management at all levels. Several studies conducted in this period confirmed the dilemmas and tensions of accountability in the CFP, with the DGIS frameworks triggering mechanisms that proved counterproductive. These findings led to changes – not necessarily improvements – in the DGIS accountability framework for the next CFP phase.

Early days with theory of change

Consequences of more standardization and target-setting were that partners needed to provide specific results information related to Hivos' monitoring protocol. Hivos' own PM&E practice became a compromise between complying with these demands and with the approach introduced three years earlier, including an administrative system based on different principles.[5] Nevertheless, partners and staff continued to request capacity development in PM&E and the M&E unit searched for a more effective means of stimulating critical, strategic practice. Two triggers led the unit to propose a pilot with ToC approaches.

First, the M&E unit and programme officers concluded that problems with M&E often originated in weak programme design. Although the concept of ToC had featured in the 2004 policy for improved result orientation (Hivos, 2004b), the M&E entry point for Phase 1 had focused attention on the end of the process: how to measure results. A ToC model shifts the entry point of reflection to strategic design questions, such as: What do you want to change? What is the underlying theory of change? What strategy options exist and are there good fits? What role can you best play? How does context affect design? How can M&E help learn about these change processes?

The second significant trigger was the complexity debate in development. Organizations increasingly recognized that development initiatives seeking to shift power relations involved unpredictable and non-linear change processes, requiring alternatives to linear planning and reporting frameworks. This resonated with the search of the M&E unit. A ToC approach seemed to offer scope for considering the complexity of change processes. It emphasizes the need to understand context, including politics and stakeholder relationships, as a basis for planning and acting strategically and flexibly. The M&E unit hoped that making explicit the thinking underpinning partners' strategies would support more coherent organizational development, sharper strategic choices, and more learning about change processes.

In 2007, Marjan[6] introduced ToC thinking in the capacity development for partner organizations. Initial efforts consisted of an introductory workshop for small, less professionally developed organizations and an offer for facilitated in-house follow-up. This first round of ToC work consolidated the intention for more in-depth reflection of causal pathways, shifting partners' attention from indicators towards rethinking their strategies.

Between 2007 and 2010, ToC training efforts were regularly reviewed and adjusted. Hivos developed a perspective on ToC as a comprehensive approach to analysis, programme design, adaptive planning and management, M&E, critical reflection, and learning, using a series of purpose-driven methods and tools. This phase ended with documentation of the emerging Hivos version of ToC thinking (Retolaza Eguren, 2010), which helped build understanding, visibility, and credibility of ToC as an approach in the organization.

Reflections on first steps with theory of change

Results of Phase 2 were comparable with those of Phase 1 – the quality of partners' proposals and annual reports did not improve significantly. ToC workshops were highly appreciated by most participants but resulted in few requests for follow-up support. Organizations undertaking a policy review or longer-term strategic planning process were most interested as they saw the immediate utility. In 2009, analysis by Hivos M&E staff and consultants involved in the workshops identified several factors that limited uptake (Stolp and van Es, 2009).[7]

First, training efforts had limitations. Partner ownership was weak: limited pre-workshop preparation with partners and the results focus linked to the M&E unit made some partner organizations experience it as a donor-driven imposition. The choice to prioritize training for weak(er) partner organizations meant that ToC thinking was used in situations with additional challenges. Post-workshop support was complicated by a dearth of available (local) expertise on ToC thinking.

Second, the M&E unit did not sufficiently consider the (dis)incentives for uptake in partner organizations. Partners pointed to the planning and reporting requirements of other donors, reasonably fearing that ToC practice would imply an additional reporting burden beyond mainstream output reporting. Undertaking ToC thinking effectively demanded staff time and willingness, changes in organizational processes and habits, and, therefore, management commitment. A good ToC analysis entails self-critical reflection on organizational values, strategies, and practices. In some follow-up efforts this triggered resistance to change because sensitive issues were surfaced, such as existing power relations, gender dynamics, or the need to differentiate partnerships, pulling management and staff out of their comfort zone. Honest reflection thus sometimes led to outcomes that were undesirable for leaders in partner organizations, consciously or unconsciously inhibiting ongoing ToC efforts. The half-hearted response may also have been due to prevailing donor power relations, although many staff and partners valued how the case-based ToC process focused on substantive strategy questions and assumptions.

Third, partner organizations struggled with balancing complexity and emergence on the one hand, and the need to focus and take strategic decisions on the other. Managing this tension without slipping back into linear thinking and oversimplification was particularly difficult given the incentive mechanisms of the aid system and funding relationships, such as pressure for short-term results, blueprint thinking, upward accountability, and project- rather than programme-focused funding.

Finally, Hivos was not 'walking the talk'. There was a growing tension between Hivos' M&E intentions and its partnership values on the one hand, and, on the other, how results agenda pressures were dealt with in practice. The context of international cooperation was – and is – not conducive for approaches that acknowledge uncertainty and complexity or promote adaptive responses, pushing partner organizations and Hivos in opposite directions. Notwithstanding this wider systemic pressure, Hivos was legitimately asked by partner organizations how it was itself using ToC in its planning and M&E processes.

Phase 3: Theory of change approach, 2011 to date

In 2009, the Dutch government announced the next phase of the co-financing system (2011 to December 2015). Indications were strong that this funding mechanism would cease thereafter, leading Hivos to stipulate a goal of at least 50 per cent of non-DGIS income by 2015 and accelerating donor diversification. This further aggravated Hivos' own juggling of an increasing variety of donor requirements for accountability.

The co-financing funding framework again strongly shaped the PM&E systems of the Dutch CFOs. The logframe consolidated its position as a reporting format. Monitoring was now required across four result categories: DGIS priority results areas (including the millennium development goals); civil society strengthening; capacity development of Southern organizations; and international lobby and advocacy. The prescribed monitoring frameworks were partly based on existing instruments, such as the CIVICUS Civil

Society Index, but were simplified beyond recognition for accountability purposes. The Dutch CFOs and their M&E staff contested the purported utility of these frameworks, arguing that they would serve neither upward accountability nor strategic learning. All protests fell on deaf ears. Politics prevailed again, cascading down the chain. Political and public distrust of subsidized development cooperation pushed DGIS to develop narrower and more control-driven reporting frameworks with every new funding phase. Like Hivos, it juggled the political interests of different stakeholders and tried to marry accountability, learning, and autonomy, with little success. Hivos and DGIS were and remain part of the same system.

A simultaneous narrowing of what constituted valid evidence in formal aid circles and the quest for impact insights fuelled the ambition of the Independent Evaluation Unit of DGIS to advocate for quasi-experimental approaches to evaluation. The DGIS requirements for an extensive CFP-wide impact evaluation resulted in a quasi-experimental evaluation design dominated by econometric thinking, with problematic consequences (Chambille et al., 2012). This major effort diverted considerable energy from limited NGO M&E capacity, fuelling intense debates on what constituted rigour, whose values of 'evidence' dominated, and the likely limited utility of non-agile approaches for improving implementation.

A second attempt at theory of change practice

The CFP monitoring protocol further widened the gap between formal accountability requirements and field realities, requiring adjustment of the monitoring system again. In this period, Hivos was also taking on new roles and developing programmes itself. The CFP-based protocols were increasingly in conflict with the demands of the growing number of donors. Although compliance drained time and energy from staff and further reduced the M&E unit's space to shape processes for Hivos' own results information and learning needs, the unit continued to promote programme quality and critical thinking. But it changed course: based on the analysis of Phase 2, it stopped ToC capacity-building of partner organizations, continuing only on a request basis. Responding to the challenge to Hivos to use ToC actively itself and to programme officers' requests to develop their own ToC capacity, the M&E unit decided to invest in learning about ToC use in Hivos' practice. To this end, it established a ToC Learning Group with external expertise.[8]

A more varied and analytical approach to embedding ToC practice was initiated based on action learning, resource development and sharing, and staff-focused capacity-building. In many ways, this mix resembles the notion of a 'benign virus' strategy (Chambers, 1995), in which multiple parallel efforts slowly instil an organizational appetite, understanding, and expectation around a way of working.

First, the focus was strongly on action learning. The ToC Learning Group held annual reviews of collective efforts to build a more robust understanding, generating guidance notes on ToC practice that aligned with Hivos' values (Retolaza Eguren, 2013; Guijt, 2013; Brouwers and van Vugt, 2013; Koopmanschap and Schaap, 2014). Frank discussions were held about power issues that arose between Hivos staff, between regions and headquarters, with partner organizations and with donors to understand how ToC could be shared and applied in ways that brought all parties closer to a critically reflective practice.

Second, Hivos opted for a public good approach through the creation of a ToC portal on the Hivos Knowledge Programme website (see Chapter 5 for another example of using a public good approach). Given the emerging celebrity status of ToC and a burgeoning diversity of interpretations, the Learning Group wanted to make explicit the politicized version of Hivos' ToC. Several online discussions were held and published, and key resources shared. For example, one gap in ToC writing was that of assumptions, considered by Hivos to be the backbone of its ToC approach (Guijt, 2013). Another topic was what constitutes high-quality ToC practice, given the plethora of existing versions (Stein and Valters, 2012). However, staff did not engage much with the e-dialogues and the portal is used more outside Hivos than internally: feedback suggests that, under pressure, most programme officers preferred straightforward guidance rather than conceptual reflections.

Third, the capacity development focused on Hivos staff, including senior management, to ensure commitment. Training workshops are not an optimal mechanism for organizational transformation but they were within the mandate of the M&E unit and in demand. Workshops helped the M&E unit convene the people it sought to influence. The workshops explicitly included discussions on personal preferences, biases, and blind spots – vital for a less technocratic and more (self-)critical approach to programme design and M&E. These were case-based to ground ToC concepts in daily realities and to generate immediate relevance. For example, at one event the regional director stressed the need to compare ToC thinking with the widely required logframe:

> Donors continue to require logframes, some donors (such as DFID) are also asking for ToCs (not necessarily meaning the same by it as Hivos does) and partners are struggling to marry all the different – and sometimes conflicting – requirements. In addition, most of them do not know enough of ToC to benefit from its (potential) added value.

In Latin America, personal exploration of firmly held beliefs had more prominence: for example, the (understandable) resistance of activists to consider dialogue with long-time political enemies as a strategic option. In Indonesia, the focus was on facilitating Hivos staff through a ToC quality audit of their existing programmes, to identify gaps and options for strengthening gender and power analysis, causal pathways, and critical assumptions.

Reflections on theory of change, 2011 to September 2014

In October 2013, the ToC Learning Group reflected in detail on what headway was being made in shifting people's mindsets and abilities towards more critical reflection, and strengthening organizational habits of strategic thinking and action.

First, the group recognized the increasing methodological clarity about the Hivos concept of ToC (see Box 6.2), supporting societal transformation in ways that deal explicitly with power inequities, counterbalancing the many mechanistic variations of ToC. These elements help Hivos staff and partner organizations implement the idea of strategic accountability. However, time pressure and logframe domination are a constant threat to its use for critical reflection.

Second, ToC as both discourse and practice had started taking root in the organization – triggered by our efforts and consolidated by the growing ToC discourse in the wider development sector. The M&E unit obtained board approval for the Hivos policy on ToC (2014), holding firm on practice and principles rather than rigid protocols. Several Hivos programmes are using aspects of ToC practice to sharpen their programme design and strategies, while Hivos has been able to respond to DGIS' requirement for ToC in a long-term strategic partnership proposal. Hivos staff members increasingly appreciate and see the benefits of ToC. One early adopter uses ToC thinking in workshops with local CSOs to develop the programme for which he is responsible. He wrote us: 'Some participants were disoriented by this approach and asked for formats and schemes, whereas ToC is about critical thinking and self-reflection!' Another programme officer commented: 'Finally we are paying attention to the real questions again...In your enthusiasm about a programme, you tend to forget to ask other stakeholders for their perspective...This is fun!'

Discussions during training events generated many examples of how the thought process has helped staff spot weaknesses and gaps in their programmes and formulate improvements (see Box 6.3).

Particularly in 2013 and 2014, ToC has become more visible within Hivos. However, quality remains a problem and requests for follow-up support remain low. Staff still lack sufficient confidence to own ToC enough to make it their own ongoing reflection process, or they simply feel that the programme does

---

Box 6.2 Key elements of Hivos' theory of change approach

- Comprehensiveness of analysis (context, values, strategy, actors)
- In-depth power and gender analysis about 'how change happens' and the forces that help and hinder
- Making explicit underlying assumptions and values, including about power and gender dynamics
- Participation of different groups of key people in ToC development
- Active and dynamic use in organizations to guide the work

Box 6.3 Revisiting assumptions – examples from regional offices

Staff of a regional initiative on ending child marriage noticed that interrogating their information about potential partners led them to conclude that each geographic area would need a distinct approach, as stakeholders and local laws vary from district to district – in some districts there will be a more positive reception, in others more resistance. They also realized more clearly the strategic importance and value of local CSOs and how they could contribute to the programme.

In another office, programme staff undertook a ToC audit of existing programmes, questioning assumptions about power and gender relations, strategic choices, and logic. They particularly valued working on underlying assumptions, identifying gaps and unravelling and challenging implementation strategies and assumed impacts. Staff working in Timor-Leste, for example, noted that an aquaculture programme that aimed to increase protein intake was based on the questionable assumption that people would eat the newly available fish. In a different example, programme staff working on an ICT for social change initiative had thought about power but had not considered that gender relations might shape who used technologies and how, requiring a rethink of the entire logic from a gendered perspective.

---

not need such reflection. Importantly, some shy away from using it because of its implications. For example, staff see its potential to strengthen social change processes by involving local groups in ToC-led design or reviews. But they are concerned about the time investment needed, resist challenging organizational change models with which they feel comfortable, or are uneasy about fragile relationships between local actors. Moreover, opening up in-depth reflection on objectives, strategies, assumptions, and roles may bring to the surface conflicting views of those involved, challenging valued relationships or normative ideas about locally led social change. This can delay implementation of plans to which staff feel committed and reduce their control of the process.

We perceive that ToC is still largely viewed as an organizational require-ment or option for planning and M&E, rather than a political strategy. Perhaps the Learning Group did not sufficiently offer ToC in that vein; perhaps the group members' identity as M&E people still dominated how ToC was perceived; or perhaps expectations were unrealistic. As a group, we have struggled to create sufficient appetite for its sustained use by staff and partners in contexts that inhibit its use for critical reflection. Even Hivos' own administrative PM&E systems focus on upward accountability, to enable compliance with DGIS and other donor requirements. Hence, the risk persists of Hivos staff and partners taking up the ToC label, not its reflective practice.

Conclusions

This chapter has discussed how the Hivos M&E unit sought to strengthen strategic accountability using a ToC approach. The journey has been one of navigating against the stream of external and internal pressures to give priority to upward accountability, too often resulting in reporting data to back donors in a way that has little meaning for any of the parties involved. This does not imply that Hivos has no insight into the effectiveness of its work or is not learning. But the contribution of formal M&E processes has been limited, and the transaction costs in terms of bureaucracy, time and frustration of staff, and loss of valuable learning opportunities are high. While not naïve about the ramifications of ToC thinking as an alternative, those involved in the three phases *were* naïve about the effects of system pressures on people and organizations, affecting people's motivation, capacity, and opportunity to use ToC as intended. We were also over-optimistic about combining a comprehensive reflective approach with formal accountability, assuming a win–win result despite time pressures and logframe domination.

We end this chapter by returning to our three questions. On balance, is *strategic* accountability through ToC possible despite the politics of upward performance pressures? Or will ToC become an artefact for compliance? Is the search for the right approach relevant at all, or are the conditions for the application of any approach for critical reflection in practice more decisive?

Despite the bumpy journey and its ambiguous outcomes, we are still convinced of the potential of ToC for strategic accountability and critical reflection to underpin and guide Hivos' support of transformational development. The good news is that both in Hivos and in the development sector more broadly this potential is increasingly acknowledged. But advocates are urged to ponder three challenges: 1) the pressures and politics of upward accountability; 2) the investment in time and process it requires; and 3) the deep questioning that touches on power and challenges the status quo, thus triggering resistance. Regardless of its value and potential, these factors may cause a ToC approach to follow the logframe fate: appropriation of language, uptake of the label, simplification, loss of meaning, and just a new trick.

In particular, the dilemma posed by the push for standardization and obligation needs to be navigated with great sensitivity. In Phase 1, a donor–recipient relationship between Hivos and its partners was inadvertently reinforced, although the M&E unit had sought so hard to avoid this. The message that results-oriented practice and, later, ToC thinking would benefit partner organizations' own practice was infused with the energy of a donor obligation, for partners and Hivos staff alike. In the same vein, tailor-made monitoring as introduced by DGIS in 2007 sought to accommodate the diversity of Dutch CFOs and their partners, but resulted in reductionist and mechanistic monitoring practices and indicator-driven management, a tendency that was exacerbated over time.

Bearing these experiences in mind, the M&E unit refrained from enforcing ToC as a PM&E protocol. After shunning standardization, staff now want to be told how to 'do ToC'. Practice to date indicates the need for guidelines to ensure high-quality ToC that includes political analysis. Hence our dilemma, as we do not think that critical reflection of and for social change can be imposed, and 'tools' can easily lead to instrumental use. 'The Politics of Evidence' conference (see Chapter 1) saw much fulmination against making artefacts obligatory due to the disastrous effects of this approach on encouraging critical reflection. Yet, the converse of keeping ToC entirely voluntary is deeply problematic in a sector driven by the mechanistic conveying of results data.

Given the focus on upward accountability protocols, we have seen that, without strong and explicit investment in reflective practice, strategic accountability as a parallel track simply will not happen. The past 15 years have seen DGIS shift from a trust-based system to a largely protocol-driven approach. Over time, Hivos felt forced to move from prioritizing partners' objectives and indicators to concentrating on those of Hivos and of DGIS. Hivos' practice became a compromise of parallel tracks, with the as yet unfulfilled hope of merging the results track with reflection. Nevertheless, the ongoing commitment from the M&E unit to invest in ToC capacity development and the Learning Group's process and products provided a critical basis for generating a credible, deliberated approach in a context that does not reward such processes.

In the ToC process, supply and demand/uptake have not been aligned. Disincentives included the effects of the results agenda, the at times limited priority Hivos management gave to M&E, and the tension between ToC practice and administrative systems. Workload and staff resistance to changing habits also played a role. Organizations and individuals will invest time and energy in what they are appreciated and valued for. A necessary though insufficient prerequisite is for back donors and management to create conditions for critical reflection and learning, and to demand and reward such processes. As M&E staff and experts, we need to think more strategically and realistically about influencing those factors, and about our role and effectiveness in this ambition. The Hivos M&E unit tried, along with other Dutch NGOs, to resist the mandatory, problematic PM&E protocols – but they failed. The M&E unit could influence but not control the organizational reaction to external PM&E pressures. The organizational position of M&E staff – who juggle increasing results and accountability bureaucracy and wish to encourage organizational learning while limiting the workload of programme staff – limits their effectiveness in suggesting and rolling out an approach such as ToC. M&E functions' association with, and focus on, methods and content rather than strategy may well strengthen this effect.

A benign virus strategy requires multiple efforts and can help build the capacity for and legitimacy of an approach. An organization interested in ToC for reflective practice must learn what is needed for it to take root and must undertake complementary initiatives to embed it in organizational practice. Hivos developed its ToC approach within a learning process, building on existing insights and expertise, testing different methods and components in workshops with partners and staff, through ongoing reflection and adaptation. With hindsight, the public good approach helped obtain broader legitimacy for ToC as a practice. The involvement of external expertise and the public recognition of the well-received and referenced ToC resource portal and ToC guide (Retolaza Eguren, 2010; 2012) considerably increased the internal credibility and interest in training. But despite progress made, especially over the past year, more is needed to transform organizational practice.

The key question is not *which* approach, method, or protocol for strategic reflection is best. The potential value and quality of the tool or approach chosen, including ToC, do not determine whether it takes root in organizational practice. Even the most intrinsically motivated staff will not use it as intended if the conditions and incentives to do so are not in place. We anticipate that problems of uptake will continue as long as organizational and external pressures reward an M&E practice that focuses on checking performance. The challenge remains one of how to institutionalize critical thinking – independent of the form that the 'artefact' might take.

Epilogue: December 2014

We first started writing this chapter in March 2014, the beginning of a period of radical change for Dutch NGOs. Some signs give us hope for the potential of ToC practice to take root and contribute to strategic accountability; other signs make us despondent.

After 2015, the long-standing Dutch co-financing system will end. With 40 per cent of Hivos' income still from this source, senior management announced a radical shift in strategy and structure, which is taking shape as we finalize this chapter. Budgets and staff positions are being downsized by almost half. In the new set-up, PM&E positions are being transferred to the programmes and regions, with little M&E capacity maintained at the centre. Decentralizing responsibility and capacity offers opportunities for more integrated, hands-on, and context-specific support to programme teams, and programme-specific learning processes. However, the even greater pressure on Hivos to mobilize resources will continue to be a very strong incentive for upward accountability following donor formats. The ideal of an integrated process in which learning and accountability exist in a beneficial symbiosis (Guijt, 2010) is unlikely in a sector in which one version of accountability, the upward and financial kind, dominates.

On the other hand, in both Hivos and international development, we see a genuine growing interest in ToC. At the global level, many actors are actively pursuing ToC for strategic reorientation. In the Dutch context, ToC is now well and truly part of the dominant discourse. In September 2014, the Dutch Minister of International Trade and Development announced an internal event on ToC approaches to take place in 2015, and to which members of the Learning Group have been asked to contribute. The challenge will be to preserve its critical and political qualities, and prevent politics from turning it into a mechanical obligation. Organizations will need to deeply understand the merits of strategic reflection and be willing to invest in it.

Thus, the Hivos journey with ToC for strategic accountability and critical reflection has an open ending. We will continue to engage with opportunities such as the 2015 meeting to create spaces in which the risks of mechanistic approaches are discussed and challenged, sharing positive examples of how critically reflecting on the validity of assumptions can lead to more effective support for locally led social change. We see no other way than through critical, strategic reflection to continually revisit interventions that seek deep transformational change – and make them work better.

References

Brouwers, J. and van Vugt, S. (2013) *How to Facilitate a ToC Process and Help to Develop ToC Capacities?* The Hague: Hivos.

Cavill, S. and Sohail, M. (2007) 'Increasing strategic accountability: a framework for international NGOs', *Development in Practice* 17(2): 231–48.

Chambers, R. (1995) 'Making the best of going to scale', Participatory Learning and Action Notes 24, London: International Institute for Environment and Development (IIED) <http://pubs.iied.org/pdfs/6093IIED.pdf> [accessed 23 December 2014].

Chambille, K., Das, P., Es Y., de Groot, D., Guijt, I., Huyse, H., Locadia, M., Rutten, R., Rijneveld, W. and van Zorge, R. (2012) 'Joint evaluation of Dutch development NGOs', joint presentation at the European Evaluation Society Conference, Helsinki, 3 October.

Ebrahim, A. (2010) 'The many faces of nonprofit accountability', Working Paper 10-069, Boston MA: Harvard Business School.

Fry, R.E. (1995) 'Accountability in organizational life: problem or opportunity for non-profits?', *Non-profit Management and Leadership* 6: 181–95.

Guijt, I. (2010) 'Exploding the myth of incompatibility between accountability and learning', in J. Ubels, N. Acquaye-Baddoo and A. Fowler (eds), *Capacity Development Practice*, pp. 277–91, The Hague: SNV.

Guijt, I. (2013) *ToC Reflection Notes 3: Working with Assumptions in a Theory of Change Process*, The Hague: Hivos.

Hivos (2004a) *Report: Hivos India Partner Consultation on Results Assessment*, The Hague: Hivos.

Hivos (2004b) *Hivos Policy Framework for Improved Result Orientation and Result Assessment*, The Hague: Hivos.

Hivos (2013) *Hivos Annual Overview 2013*, The Hague: Hivos <https://hivos.org/sites/default/files/annual_review_2013.pdf>.

Hivos (2014) *Policy Brief: Hivos and Theory of Change*, The Hague: Hivos.

IBO (2000) *Interdepartmental Policy Research. Round 1999 nr. 2: Co-Financing Programme*, The Hague: Ministry of Foreign Affairs, IBO Working Group on Effectiveness and Coherence of International Development.

Koopmanschap, E. and Schaap, M. (2013) *ToC Reflection Notes 4: Visualising your Theory of Change: A Must?*, The Hague: Hivos.

Retolaza Eguren, I. (2010) *Teoría de Cambio: Un enfoque de pensamiento-acción para navegar en la complejidad de los procesos de cambio social*, The Hague: Hivos and UNDP.

Retolaza Eguren, I. (2011) *Theory of Change: A Thinking and Action Approach to Navigate in the Complexity of Social Change Processes*, The Hague: Hivos and UNDP.

Retolaza Eguren, I. (2013) *ToC Reflection Notes 1: What is the Purpose of a Theory of Change?*, The Hague: Hivos.

Stein, D. and Valters, C. (2012) *Understanding 'Theory of Change' in International Development: A Review of Existing Knowledge*, JSRP Paper 1, London: Justice and Security Research Programme (JSRP) and The Asia Foundation <http://www.lse.ac.uk/internationalDevelopment/research/JSRP/downloads/JSRP1.SteinValtersPN.pdf>.

Stolp, A. and van Es, M. (2009) 'Report of Hivos exchange workshop on the pilot programme "result-oriented practice for learning and accountability"', Internal document, The Hague: Hivos.

Valters, C. (2014) *Theories of Change in International Development: Communication, Learning, or Accountability?*, JSRP Paper 17, London: Justice and Security Research Programme (JSRP) and The Asia Foundation<http://www.lse.ac.uk/internationalDevelopment/research/JSRP/downloads/JSRP17.Valters.pdf>.

Vogel, I. (2012) *Review of the Use of 'Theory of Change' in International Development: Review Report*, London: Department for International Development (DFID) <http://www.dfid.gov.uk/r4d/pdf/outputs/mis_spc/DFID_ToC_Review_VogelV7.pdf>.

About the authors

Marjan van Es is senior policy officer for Monitoring, Evaluation and Learning in Hivos, a humanist organization for international cooperation based in the Netherlands. Marjan has worked in international cooperation for over 20 years, 15 of which have been in her current position. She introduced ToC thinking in Hivos.

Irene Guijt is a rural development specialist with 25 years' experience in participatory processes in planning and M&E. She is particularly curious about how to understand what we do not know we need to know that is critical for transformative change. She works as a research associate for the Overseas Development Institute on impact evaluation. She is active in global evaluation capacity-building through BetterEvaluation and on ToC with Hivos. She was a Big Push Forward convener.

Notes

1. <http://www.hivos.net/toc> [accessed 23 December 2014].
2. The Dutch CFP was adopted in 1968 to direct Dutch government support via key NGOs to thousands of NGOs in the global South. Hivos became the fourth co-financing organization in 1978. This privileged status, replete with power relations, was increasingly questioned and ended in 2007, when all Dutch NGOs or alliances became equally eligible for funding.
3. This discussion started around 1987, resulting in the CFOs commissioning the so-called impact study (1990–92).
4. In 1998, DGIS initiated a research framework 'Steering for results', triggering several interdepartmental policy research efforts.
5. Introducing a functional administrative PM&E system in a large, decentralized international NGO takes years and cannot be easily adapted to new requirements, a major problem for all Dutch CFOs.

6. With Hettie Walters.
7. Hivos recognized that organizational change capacity on these topics cannot be measured easily or attributed to specific efforts, as they take time to materialize. Limited requests for follow-up do not mean that partners were not using new tools for thought.
8. The Centre for Development Innovation (Wageningen University), Irene Guijt, Iñigo Retolaza, Sue Soal (CDRA until 2011) and Isabel Vogel (from 2012).

CHAPTER 7

Aid bureaucracy and support for disabled people's organizations: a fairy tale of self-determination and self-advocacy

Ola Abu Alghaib

Abstract

Donors' approaches to monitoring and evaluation can undermine disabled people's organizations. Most donors behave as if societies were predictable machines and that change occurs through cause-and-effect processes attributable to a given intervention. Relatedly, current monitoring and evaluation approaches are used to demonstrate accountability, rather than as an opportunity for learning. This can leave little space for organizations to learn about what is happening in ways that strengthen their work, as I demonstrate in a case study of how our organization became a stranger in our own project. The chapter concludes with three principles for supporting the promotion of real change in the lives of people with disabilities.

Keywords: aid bureaucracy, Middle East, disabled people's organizations, rights, monitoring and evaluation

This chapter is for practitioners wishing to effectively support people with disabilities and other marginalized groups to transform their worlds. It reveals how the power of results-based donor approaches to planning and monitoring and evaluation (M&E) can utterly undermine these aims and proposes collective action to address this issue. What follows is based on my personal experience and research on the role and dynamics of donors in supporting disabled people's organizations (DPOs).[1]

My identity is shaped by my experiences as a woman with a disability, a DPO founder and leader, who is a senior staff member in a disability INGO (international NGO) that supports DPOs, and a board member for an international fund for DPO support. As a DPO leader, I not only witnessed the excitement of the potential for change following the adoption of the UN Convention on the Rights of Persons with Disabilities (CRPD) but also became a key actor in negotiations with various donors. This led to first-hand experience of the struggle that DPOs face in complying with donor requirements. At the same time, being a staff and board member of an INGO that supports disability rights familiarized me with the internal politics and

http://dx.doi.org/10.3362/9781780448855.007

dynamics that influence donor decision-making on funding directions, grantee selection, and partnership approaches. This puts me in a privileged position as an intermediary between local partner DPOs and the INGOs, which has influenced my approach and work practice in multiple ways: it enabled me to promote a deeper understanding of the realities of DPOs and the need of additional INGO support for them. At the same time, it allowed me to widen the horizon of DPOs, for example by enabling their access to information about funding opportunities and related mechanisms or partnerships.

My varied experience of DPO relationships with INGOs inspired my choice of dissertation topic on which the present chapter is based. My decision to focus on donor planning and M&E approaches was guided by the potential they have for learning and to help DPOs develop the capacities needed to qualify for the funding opportunities that emerged with the CRPD. The findings in this chapter are based on key informant interviews, questionnaires, an analysis of calls for proposals for DPO support from across the global South, and personal experience through a DPO, the Beyond the Stars Society. Informants included donors with specific funding streams for supporting DPOs who work at national levels and address cross-cutting disability issues. The spectrum of DPOs was limited to grantees of the Open Society Foundations, Disability Rights Fund, and Handicap International.

My research confirmed the need for a greater understanding of donors' assumptions about the role of DPOs, and provided new insights into how such assumptions influence funding schemes and M&E approaches. It also confirmed that my experience with donors in the Beyond the Stars Society was not an isolated one, but rather systemic across the sector. I contend that, if we are to live up to the DPO motto 'Nothing about Us, Without Us', it is vital for DPOs to be able to influence donors' funding strategies, priorities, and the ways they work with us, particularly their willingness to support us to learn from *our* mistakes. This has implications for other marginalized groups and requires collective action.

My argument is laid out as follows. The next part of this chapter identifies the conceptual and legal frameworks that form the basis for current discussions around disability. It looks at the identity and evolution of DPOs in general, and some of the assumptions that underpin most donors' participatory M&E approaches. It argues for the need to respect DPOs' rights to develop their own theory of change, and the importance of DPO demand-driven, bottom-up, inclusive, and participatory approaches to M&E. Finally, it considers alternative M&E approaches that respond to DPO realities and bolster persons with disabilities' (PwDs') voices on the issues that affect them.

Disability and development

Until recently, PwDs have traditionally been viewed using either the medical or the charity (or welfare) models reflected in international development rhetoric and practice. PwDs were defined as 'people whose lives are defined by medical and rehabilitative needs (the medical model)' or as 'individuals who were considered to be appropriate recipients of social and economic support (the charity model)' (UN DESA, 2012). The medical model implies that PwDs are '"sick" and therefore in need of a "cure" or rehabilitation' (Coleridge et al., 2010: 29). The charity model defines them as 'unable to take care of themselves, live independently, or earn a living'. Put bluntly, PwDs were considered 'objects who only receive and who do not participate in the processes which shape their lives' (Coleridge, 1993:47).

It was not until the last 20 years or so that the human rights-based approach (HRBA) challenged these models. The HRBA 'provides a clearer understanding of the constraints faced by persons with disabilities that reflect social, cultural and economic barriers, and are not inherently part of living with a disability' (UN DESA, 2012). The adoption of the CRPD by the UN General Assembly in 2006 further strengthened this view. The CRPD came into force in May 2008 and currently has 158 signatories and 174 ratifications (UN, 2013).

The Convention on the Rights of Persons with Disabilities: a paradigm shift

The CRPD is the first legally binding international instrument that views PwDs as subjects with equal human rights. Its core message is that 'people with disabilities should not be considered "objects" to be managed, but "subjects" deserving of equal respect and enjoyment of human rights' (WHO, 2011: 34). The UN has also changed its description of PwDs from a 'handicapped' or 'disabled person' to 'a person with a disability', placing more focus on the person rather than their type of impairment.

The CRPD has created momentum for development stakeholders in two key ways: namely, the principle of 'full and effective participation and inclusion', and the explicit obligations of state parties to ensure that 'international cooperation, including international development programmes, is inclusive of and accessible to people with disabilities' and to 'closely consult and actively involve persons with disabilities' (UN, 2006).

States are now obligated to 'use international cooperation as a means to realize the human rights of PwDs', which includes a 'socio-economic development dimension that recognises the importance of development to the full realisation of the rights spelled out in the CRPD, and the role of international cooperation in support of national efforts to implement the CRPD' (UN, 2010: 5). Such obligations provide for 'consultation with persons with disabilities and their representative organisations, underlining the disability organisations' (Lansdown, 2009: 20). In short, 'development actors must now rethink their approach to disability' (Wapling and Downie, 2012: 12).

Many development practitioners are optimistic about the opportunities for change that stem from the paradigm shift toward the HRBA. Questions remain, however, about whether there has been any real change in DPO access to donor funds, and about the real impact of this approach on DPOs' capacity to act. The following sections look at the concept of capacity-building, the role of DPOs, and the effectiveness of new funding schemes in supporting DPOs.

Disabled people's organizations and the disability movement struggle

DPOs are representative organizations for PwDs. DPOs must be governed and/or led by PwDs, and their main purpose is to articulate their members' aspirations and goals (HI, 2011). DPOs advocate for PwDs' rights, empower PwDs to control their own development, and strive for social inclusion. They have general agreement regarding their priorities, roles, and action plans. These include self-representation; representation in government, service providers, and UN bodies; and grass-roots needs identification (Enns, 2010). DPOs are generally perceived as essential players in the full realization of equal opportunities for PwDs (Katsui, 2005).

A key mandate of DPOs is identifying PwDs' needs at the grass-roots level. DPOs argue that PwDs must identify their own needs and how to meet them. DPOs have developed various tools and systems to identify these needs and determine action priorities. These include establishing self-help groups and local branches to ensure that local PwDs' voices are represented at all levels (Enns, 2010). DPOs have adopted a twofold strategy to combat vulnerability: they begin by empowering individuals through self-awareness activities; this leads to collective empowerment, which enables PwDs to fight against structural discrimination that many face (Katsui, 2005).

DPOs became the authoritative voice for PwDs during CRPD negotiations. The success of the disability movement was epitomized by Articles 32 and 33 of the CRPD, which recognize the role of DPOs in implementing and monitoring development programmes. However, most representatives who participated in the negotiations came from the small elite of the disability movement that represented well-structured DPOs in wealthy countries. Furthermore, despite the paradigm shift embodied in the CRPD, DPOs worldwide remain locked in a state of limited capacity, mainly due to inadequate funding. This lessens their ability to effectively mainstream disability into development programmes and achieve their objectives (Coleridge et al., 2010).

Despite their important role in representing PwDs in development arenas, DPOs are usually much smaller and less well resourced than other key players in the disability field. There are many other disability-focused NGOs – most of which are not controlled by disabled people – with far greater financial resources than DPOs (Stone, 1999). Stone suggests that the impact of such organizations varies considerably: 'At best development professionals are forming real partnerships with DPOs, supporting them to undertake the work they have identified as important. At worst, development professionals continue to function in "charity mode" or "expert mode" or "rescuer mode", where full control on direction and resources is taking place' (2002: 1).

The allocation of funds for DPOs can also be an issue. Donors tend to allocate resources to well-established organizations, bypassing smaller groups – especially those in developing countries – that often need support (Bhanushali, 2007; Hurst, 1999). Moreover, many smaller DPOs have difficulty obtaining the funds needed to maintain daily operations. The educational level of DPO members is generally low due to discrimination against PwDs in accessing education. Consequently, their organizational skills and management capacities can be fragile, making it difficult to access funding. Despite the momentum created by the CRPD, many DPOs remain isolated and unable to fulfil their roles and aspirations (DCDD, 2004). A lack of funding becomes a barrier to effective leadership training and networking, both common advocacy strategies for DPOs. The centrality of the 'charity mode' has created a funding environment in which donors support what they think is appropriate.

Experience of the Beyond the Stars Society

Together with a group of women with disabilities (WwDs), I established a DPO called the Beyond the Stars Society (BSS) in 2007 to promote the rights of WwDs in Palestine. BSS is one of the few organizations that addresses disability regionally from a rights-based perspective. Its annual budget is around US$500,000, with diverse funding sources. While this level of funding may be considered a great success, the following case study reveals the struggle to protect BSS's identity and vision for building a self-empowered disability movement. In addition to key findings identified through questionnaires and interviews, it discusses evidence from BSS's experiences with donors regarding their impact on the organization's mandate and identity.

Strangers in our own project

In 2011, BSS submitted a concept note to a rights-oriented and large global donor organization (for which I will use the pseudonym LGDO) in response to a call for proposals to support women's political participation in the Middle East region. We proposed a three-year project covering Palestine, Jordan, Yemen, and Egypt with a budget of US$450,000, and with the aim of promoting the rights of WwDs. Following this application, BSS was excited to receive an acceptance letter from LGDO, since this was the first time BSS was able to access much-needed funds from a big donor agency.

Despite this initial optimism, however, it soon became clear that accepting the grant also meant much compromise and struggle on the part of BSS. For example, donor staff generally focused on capacitating BSS to perform administrative and bureaucratic tasks to 'fit' *their* systems, systems that suggested they had very simplistic assumptions of how social change happens in a WwDs project. LGDO also made a number of unilateral decisions and imposed a set of bureaucratic requirements that BSS had to meet. These included reducing BSS's budget by half without explanation and questioning country choices, showing a lack of interest in Yemen and more interest in Lebanon (BSS eventually dropped Yemen given its tight budget). BSS also had to reduce the project duration from three to two years to match the new funding limit.

A short time later, BSS was asked to use an advance instalment of funds to recruit technical support to develop the programme document and logframe, programme work plan, and programme budget. Access to the remaining funds was contingent upon approval of the submitted documents. LGDO sent a funding and technical assistance package with specific guidelines on results-based management, including templates for the full narrative proposal, results chain, annual work plan, and logframe. LGDO also requested that the programme or reporting officer have a good understanding of results-based management fundamentals and project cycle management key concepts, and that they, or at least one member of the team, be able to report in English (correspondence from LGDO to BSS, 12 February 2012). BSS hired an external consultant to complete the necessary documents, as requested by LGDO.

Further to these unanticipated additional requirements, issues arose during the negotiation phase. For example, correspondence from LGDO to BSS indicated:

> While BSS lists the importance of training sessions in international human rights frameworks (e.g. CEDAW), social networking opportunities amongst stakeholders, media engagement for intervening in representations of WwDs, and advocacy work for influencing governmental policy, the proposal does not present a strong plot that demonstrates how such interventions will be implemented ... WwDs consistently receive a lower priority within women's rights and political participation frameworks and BSS is working to shift these unequal frames. However, given the layers of discrimination and lack of resources BSS and the women within it face, the programme should be developed on clear grounds showcasing how ... the organisation [will] be overcoming the persisting challenges to shift these unequal frames, and what expertise ... the organisation [shall] be deploying in light of the relatively new organisation's life. (18 March 2012)

BSS staff were shocked by this feedback, and felt that it placed them in a defensive position regarding their strategy and capacities; that is, BSS felt that LGDO had questioned their competence and approach during the reporting phase. Nevertheless, BSS resubmitted the necessary documents in an attempt to address LGDO's concerns. Shortly afterwards, LGDO responded with additional concerns and directions:

> The results chain needs to be revisited ... to systematically understand the different interventions, this is how we recommend your key entry points [should look]: Outcome 1 – on building the WwDs' and DPOs' capacities and collective work competencies to lobby for their rights; Outcome 2 – to execute the advocacy and lobbying campaigns through a set of interventions (situation analysis, national committees formations, action plan) ... and then the third outcome which is initially about the exchange of the best practices is one form of advocacy tool ... I do not see why are we separating the two and confusing the whole results chain. It should be reflected under the same Outcome 2. The third outcome is then to reflect

forming the linkages at the national level with decision makers and sensitising duty bearers to push for women's political participation at the national and regional levels, which the programme is [failing] to relay through a clear set of interventions. The programme in its current design fails to establish the strong linkages at the policy level. (21 April 2012)

While BSS felt that these later comments did not relate to their original strategy, and included excessive 'guidance' and demands, they subsequently hired another consultant to develop a new theory of change in order to meet LGDO's requirements. While generally satisfied with the amended documents, LGDO requested further changes on the design of the project programme and logframe, project outputs, and grants scheme. LGDO suggested adding new activities despite budget limitations, and wanted BSS to gain access to political processes, despite their claimed understanding of the complexity of predicting the means to achieve this:

We are pleased to have reviewed your programme documents, which reflect excessive work in further solidifying your programme strategy and details. The drafting style, content and observed RBM principles are indeed of high quality. However, we still require some annotations and propose a few final tweaks on certain interventions. We thank you for reviewing and streamlining as appropriate. You are presented below with our general key observations for a final review:

1. Number of targeted Direct Beneficiaries is too low...You are kindly requested to reconsider the proposed beneficiaries number, as they are disproportional with the grant size and nature of interventions.
2. As Result 2 will seek to enhance the political participation of WwDs with key stakeholders, output 3 will need to link to [the] ultimate outcome of gaining access to political processes ... The programme fails to present a clear strategy in reaching out for policymakers and duty bearers. Our comments on both the log frame and narrative suggest going [a] few additional steps to strengthening this intervention.
3. More coherence is required between the different outputs (i.e. Outcome 3) and here comes a suggestion to add [a] few more activities that would fortify the consultative role this Outcome is promulgating as well [as] requesting to strengthen the traditional media role in advocating for WwDs' role in public and political spheres.
4. The grant scheme remains unclear although we found it an effective instrument. (27 July 2012)

BSS regarded these 'few final tweaks' as additional unrealistic demands. BSS continued to try to clarify and adapt their project to meet LGDO's requirements, despite being unclear about the purpose of many of the requested changes.

One year after initial approval, BSS received a message from LGDO giving them the green light to go ahead with the programme:

> We wish to congratulate you for the well-done job and the clearance of your programme documents that underwent several rounds of revision. We will proceed with the disbursement of the remaining first instalment and wish to request that you complete the highlighted in red cells on the attached... However, we are granting this clearance on the grounds that BSS review its programme design to observe the following below comments that mainly centre around clarifying tangible results beyond capacity building and creating more linkages to concrete legislation/policy in countries. We strongly recommend that you get a technical advisor that might support you streamlining your programme strategy. (9 October 2012)

By this stage, however, there was little motivation to continue with a project that was substantially different to the one that BSS had begun with. In effect, although the project was implemented, staff felt that it had become a project designed by 'consultants' based on a methodology prescribed by LGDO's staff. The budget was reduced by half and there was no match between activities and resources. BSS also found itself with a complicated logframe built on results-based management that required external experts to help it comply with the formal requirements. BSS's initial enthusiasm for the project was replaced by uncertainty about whether they would be able to report against the progress anticipated by the donor. The ultimate goal of promoting political participation by WwDs became less important than the need to impress the donor. The project was approved and started, accompanied by the team's discomfort and fear of what might be coming next.

Donors' monitoring and evaluation approaches

The experiences described above led me to conclude that donor planning and M&E approaches have created further obstacles for DPOs: donors tend to view DPOs as 'delivery agents' rather than 'drivers for change' (Reeler, 2005: 3). I believe that there are three main assumptions in donors' planning and M&E approaches that are problematic: 1) donors assume that they understand what actions will achieve social change within development contexts; 2) to assess progress, a one-size-fits-all strategy works best; and 3) existing M&E approaches are easily understood and stimulate learning for both donors and DPOs. Such assumptions prevent donors from responding effectively to an unpredictable and dynamic policy environment, and need to be re-evaluated to facilitate DPO objectives. Each of these assumptions is discussed in more detail below.

Donors' theories of social change

Donors often presume to know what actions lead to social change within developing country contexts. Moreover, donor support for DPOs is informed by their own assumptions about the role of DPOs. Almost all the DPOs interviewed said that their primary mandate concerned empowerment, mobilization, advocacy, and capacity-building. In contrast – and arguably somewhat ironically, given their empowerment mandate – donor responses showed that they expect DPOs to perform more 'advanced' functions (for example, influence policy reform, monitor policies, promote equal access to services, promote anti-discrimination, and enact inclusive policies). This discrepancy in understanding significantly limits the positive effects of newly created financial resources and opportunities, and illustrates what Eyben et al. (2008) identify as the consequences of donor-informed theories of change for the work of NGOs. The BSS experience highlighted the unrealistic expectations from donors around DPOs capacities, with the end result that BSS had to struggle to maintain its identity and goals.

When I did further research, donors and DPO representatives were asked for their opinions on the weaknesses of the disability movement and barriers to its progress. A donor staff member from Norway declared that:

> For 20 years we have been trying to support DPOs following the Norwegian model by working very closely with DPOs in Norway and a large part of our funding is received by them. We are very frustrated by DPOs in Palestine failing to follow the [foot]prints of their counterparts in Norway. (A donor's senior staff member, December 2012)

This comment illustrates donor assumptions that what works in a developed country such as Norway can work in a developing country such as Palestine.

The findings of the questionnaire survey administered to DPOs confirm the priority donors give to their own theories of change. Half of DPOs surveyed indicated that they had to realign their proposals to fit donor priorities. Donors themselves confirmed this as well. One donor board member commented:

> By providing the grants, the donor follows its own agenda, which, in some cases, is not on the agenda of the DPOs. It can certainly be because DPOs lack knowledge, and they do not even have the big 'objectives' in their minds, while the donor sees 'further' and knows better what to do. On the other hand, [the] donor's agenda can be politically motivated (by their country's foreign policy) – and in such cases, the 'real interest' of DPOs might be neglected/ignored, and donors would 'make' DPOs do what the donors want.

Bridging the gap between donor assumptions and the realities of working in a DPO should be made a priority consideration (James, 2011). Donors should try to respond more respectfully to the disability movement's understanding of what constitutes development and social change, rather than impose fixed prescriptions (Reeler, 2005). Limited experience of the disability movement in development frameworks leads to donors behaving in ways that seem to equate development with charity (Hurst, 1999). Hence their actions often seem to contradict their espoused empowerment goals.

Determining the best methodology to assess social change is difficult (Guijt, 2007). There are at least two main issues with measuring social change. The first is the failure of many externally driven M&E approaches to make the link between short-term interventions and long-term change. The second is donors' weak understanding of context and their inability to keep track of contextual changes, which can lead to misinterpretations (Guijt, 2007). Understanding cause and effect – and choosing the most effective means for change – can also be difficult when there are multiple actors (Reis, 2010).

The second issue is donor's limited understanding of the causal link between DPO activities and on-the-ground results. Donors increasingly pre-select grantees who have already demonstrated 'impact', so as to be able to demonstrate success. However, donor claims that their funding or support has been the main contribution to long-term development are often unsupported (Carden et al., 2009; Reeler, 2005; CDI, 2013). Finding the link between intervention A and outcome B can be almost impossible if the context and interactions that may affect a process are not considered (Burns, 2007; Batliwala and Pittman, 2010). At the same time, there is currently no single assessment framework that can adequately capture all dimensions of social change (Batliwala and Pittman, 2010).

The perception that many development projects do not produce the anticipated changes often stems from the parameters for success or failure established in a project's planning stages. For example, some donors' indicators might interpret the choice of WwDs trained in rights and advocacy *not* to join planned advocacy actions in a project as a failure. A more positive interpretation may be that such a decision indicates empowerment and the ability of WwDs to make independent choices. In fact, the training itself might have opened up new ways of thinking for them. The belief that people are 'predictable machines' is an implicit assumption that persists in most project proposals, in spite of the overwhelming experience that they are not.

Unrealistic expectations from donors

BSS struggled to reach an agreement with LGDO when lobbying for expected results framed by realistic indicators. LGDO followed the one-size-fits-all approach to M&E, using a results-based management framework. Results that fell outside this framework were not considered relevant, even if context and evidence suggested otherwise (CDI, 2013). The debate between BSS and LGDO regarding capacity-building plans for WwDs is a case in point. BSS sought to assess progress toward an increase in women's self-confidence and their ability to mobilize other groups and act together to achieve full engagement in policy processes. BSS's five years of experience working with WwDs gave them an understanding of how discrimination against WwDs hinders their ability to act and reduces their self-esteem, and that empowerment cannot be achieved until the problem of discrimination is properly addressed (itself a long-term process requiring time and resources). LGDO did not accept BSS's position on capacity-building since it did not coincide with their framework indicators designed for women's programmes worldwide. BSS eventually complied and reluctantly changed its indicator from 'the number of women interested in mobilizing other WwDs and engaging in planned actions to demand change' to 'the number of trainees that self-report that the acquired knowledge has positively impacted on their advocacy with civil society organizations (CSOs) and public authorities'. It remains unclear how this indicator could be measured and whether it could be achieved through the limited training provided by BSS to WwDs.

The following example also demonstrates unrealistic donor expectations about how change occurs through WwDs' engagement in policy-making processes. BSS was aware of the constant political instability and the marginalization of WwDs in Palestinian, Jordanian, and Egyptian societies, and within human rights and women's movements themselves. Project aims were therefore based on what BSS considered realistic, achievable results within the project's two-year time frame: for example, wider acknowledgement of WwDs issues to support the creation of a network of trained WwDs who generate long-term opportunities for greater participation of WwDs in decision-making and self-advocacy. This network could in turn pressure decision-makers to work towards changes in policies, laws, programmes, and budget allocations aimed at WwDs. Donor expectations were, however, that BSS would reach the following results within the same budget and time frame:

- greater visibility and recognition of WwDs' political rights at the policy-making level;
- increased knowledge and skills among WwDs and DPOs to communicate their political rights;
- greater coalition-building between DPOs and civil society to advocate for WwDs' political rights;
- increased regional and national–regional cross-fertilization of ideas, experiences, support, and development, and further replication of good practice;
- greater participation of WwDs in related dialogue and decision-making;
- increased opportunities for WwDs to exercise their political rights.

BSS's experience with LGDO shows how DPO teams see development projects as steps towards advancing PwDs rights, whereas donors view them as interventions leading to full accomplishment on the ground (Reeler, 2005; James, 2011). Agreeing on what to measure – particularly in relation to the ability of indicators to capture what is really happening on the ground and how that can guide us to further action – was (and is) BSS's main concern. Project results are seen as a means to achieve long-term changes over the life of the project. LGDO, however, viewed the project as an end goal rather than a means to an end (Batliwala and Pittman, 2010).

Two-thirds of DPOs interviewed for this study indicated that almost all donors focused on project-specific results with no consideration of the feasibility of achieving such results in short-term projects (often less than a year). Three of the respondents from donors' teams answered that the main objective of their M&E policies was 'to evaluate to what extent the projected activities are contributing to meet our own goals and logframe'. These results show that donors commonly behave to disability programmes in ways that suggest they respect DPOs' theory of change but actually end up pushing potential beneficiaries to promise exaggerated results to ensure compliance with their results chain.

Donors' assumptions that monitoring and evaluation approaches are easy to understand and encourage learning

M&E approaches need to be built upon equal ownership and utility, and adapted according to both parties' needs, in order to be a stimulating learning experience for both DPOs and donors. Both DPOs and donors need evidence to show what works, what does not, and how and why. When we talk about improving learning through M&E processes, do we refer mostly to a need on the part of donors? Does this include recognition of the local actors' right to learn from their mistakes? The quest for local actor participation often has an instrumental sense, geared more towards actor consultation than to effective local participation in decision-making.

Development agencies must place their M&E approaches in a broader context, and they must design them with the full participation of all stakeholders. This study suggests that there are very limited spaces for learning within existing M&E approaches. Less than a quarter of DPOs interviewed considered existing M&E approaches as enabling a holistic, participatory, and learning-oriented environment. Two-thirds, on the other hand, indicated that donors were mainly concerned with measuring the achievement of expected results, with no real interest in understanding links with other actions implemented by DPOs, or any attempt to explore or support DPOs' understanding of the reasons for failure or success.

Despite donor rhetoric regarding the importance of facilitating learning within organizational settings, the concept of 'learning' remains vague (Guijt, 2010). Learning is interpreted as not only the accumulation of knowledge but also the ability to improve the efficacy of action by reflecting on visions, strategies, and contexts. M&E approaches can be designed to create real learning spaces for DPOs. However, debate remains over how best to use M&E mechanisms as spaces for reflection and learning. M&E becomes 'a common site of a tug-of-war' between the need for 'accountability' and the desire to ensure 'learning'. Often neither term is clearly defined, yet many development practitioners are convinced that the two are methodologically and practically irreconcilable.

The map becomes the world

Documents produced during the project-planning phase are, naturally, only theories about what development practitioners think might happen. However, they often become reality – as Irene Guijt suggests, 'the map becomes the world' (2010: 279). Adaptive learning is a significant challenge for many donor agencies, given their 'disconnectedness' from the field. On the ground, this sometimes feels like top-down supervision carried out within rigid frameworks and requirements.

If the 'map' becomes the 'world', then how can DPOs have the capacity and time to ask the 'why' questions regarding project actions (Guijt, 2010; Batliwala and Pittman, 2010)? The literature suggests a constant tension between 'learning' and 'donor accountability' (CDI, 2013; Guijt, 2010). Donor reporting requirements are often automatically prioritized by small organizations (Woodhill, 2005) since they view satisfying donor requirements as their only mode of survival. In response to the question 'Why do we measure change?', two-thirds of DPOs in this study selected 'Donors require it' and 'To sustain or obtain more funding'. Only five of the 25 DPOs considered M&E approaches as ways to promote organizational learning and empowerment.

Changing identities

Such accountability demands not only take up time and energy; they start to make a difference to who is selected to work in an organization, ultimately changing an organization's identity. As one interviewee (a DPO leader in Iraq) noted:

> I am always accused by our members that our DPO is not hiring paid staff with disabilities. The complexity of donors' reporting requirements forces us to seek experienced staff to help us write what donors want to hear. Most of our members were not fortunate enough to access higher education and I am always torn between our principles as a DPO versus our obligation toward donors.

M&E frameworks are demanding in terms of deadlines, resources, and technical expertise. The compliance expected from DPOs often far exceeds their capacity. As a result, DPOs are constantly concerned about their ability to comply with donor reporting requirements. DPOs often have no option but to hire external consultants to help them make their case (as in the case of BSS), which drains their financial resources (Batliwala, 2011). However, it is still the grantee's responsibility to allocate resources appropriately and to make sure that contractual promises on indicators and results designed by external experts are met.

We are still far from replacing the external accountability approach with an actor-specific learning approach (Woodhill, 2005). LGDO spent one year in negotiations with BSS to ensure that their predetermined indicators were well integrated within BSS's project. The resources expended on this process could have been conserved if the donor had respected the BSS team's knowledge and experience.

Although there is no universal definition of accountability, it generally means holding actors responsible for their actions. DPOs have many levels of accountability – to their donors and to their beneficiaries. DPOs around the world face tremendous challenges in revising and strengthening their strategies and capacities within increasingly complex economic and political contexts. Balancing donor requirements and member expectations is very demanding (Batliwala, 2011). Donors are not aware that existing M&E approaches actually lower DPO accountability to their members.

The demand from donors that DPOs demonstrate value for money increases the risk of upward instead of downward accountability (Emmi et al., 2011; Guijt, 2010). DPOs are obliged to provide information about their activities, give clear justifications for their choice of interventions, and 'suffer sanctions from those dissatisfied' (Goetz and Jenkins, 2002). If the various voices are not prioritized, downward accountability mechanisms tend to fall on the weakest side of the power play (Emmi et al., 2011).

A DPO leader in Egypt stated:

> We get support from three international donors. Each organization has its own reporting requirement and deadlines; for the same activities, we have three sets of indicators matching each donor's requirement. We tried so hard with them to accept unifying the templates, but we failed. Therefore, half the time of our resources goes into working on their sheets and translating them. For the last three years, the only reports I bring to our general assembly meetings are the donor ones as we have no capacity to work beyond that.

It is unclear how long BSS will be able to withstand the pressure of directing its actions towards the wishes of donors instead of its commitments to its members. The organization's survival relies on project funding; refusing to adapt to donor requirements will mean tough decisions about BSS's operation and existence. BSS argues that 'doing something is better than nothing'. Putting members' expectations ahead of donors' requirements means that the organization runs the risk of being 'turned off like a tap' (Reeler, 2005); many organizations live under the same threat and end up becoming donor vehicles for projects.

Rethinking planning and monitoring and evaluation approaches in support of disabled people's organizations: the way forward

In this final part of the chapter, I consider the core principles necessary to support the impact of DPOs in promoting real change in the lives of PwDs.

Shared understanding of change and capacity development

There needs to be mutual understanding between donors and DPOs regarding who leads change and how best to measure this change. It is important that donors respect a DPO's right to define their own theory of change, and to ensure a demand-driven, bottom-up, inclusive, and participatory M&E approach in which the DPO 'owns the process'. The involvement of DPOs as development actors should be a valued process, not just an outcome. Progress towards social change is gradual and should be monitored and measured accordingly, and adapted if necessary.

The empowerment of DPOs through capacity-building requires that DPOs create spaces where they have control over their own behaviour. Donors need to provide long-term capacity-building, technical, and financial support for DPOs through a comprehensive, tailored, and harmonized approach, based on permanent dialogue to shape priorities and policies.

Participatory approach to monitoring and evaluation

Donors should undertake a participatory approach to planning, monitoring, and evaluation in partnership with community members and other stakeholders, using processes that are culturally and socially appropriate, creative, and based on mutual trust, openness, and transparency (Lennie and Tacchi, 2013: 27). Donors should enact transparent and consistent policies that define the role of DPOs according to DPOs' own ambitions and interpretations of reality; these should then be integrated into donors' strategic frameworks and plans.

M&E approaches should ensure downward accountability and promote a space that progressively builds a culture of organizational learning, results orientation, and internal advancement. Development programmes are generally 'messy and non-linear'; it is important to avoid one-size-fits-all approaches when assessing results, and to remain positive about the possibilities for learning and adaptation (CDI, 2013: 4). Adaptive approaches could include experimenting with hybrid designs (including elements of thinking from theory-based approaches, participatory and case study designs) to monitor progress and encourage learning (CDI, 2013: 4).

M&E should be undertaken in partnership with community members and other stakeholders, and, wherever possible, involve long-term engagement with these groups. The evaluation process should respect, legitimize, and draw on 'the knowledge and experience of community members and stakeholders, as well as relevant experts and outsiders' (Lennie and Tacchi, 2013: 31). M&E requirements need to be based on an appreciation of the long-term benefits of taking a participatory and inclusive approach that considers the experiences of DPOs and PwDs.

Equal access to funds

If donors are to contribute to real social change and empowerment, they should make their application processes more accessible to DPOs. They should target the DPOs most in need, rather than encourage DPOs who already have funding and capability. For this, donors need to keep their application processes as simple as possible, simplify their reporting requirements, and adapt communication methods to increase accessibility.

Conclusion

This chapter has explored how donors' attitudes and behaviours expressed through planning M&E artefacts can contribute to or hinder the process of social change for PwDs. Many of the capacity development tools and methodological processes commonly used by donors assume a change process that is predictable and linear. They also believe that they have a strong grasp on the kind of strategies or activities most likely to produce change. Such assumptions mean that many of the processes and approaches favoured by donors are unsuitable in many situations, or do not generate the expected significant changes.

Capacity challenges that DPOs face are complex and uncertain. It is unclear how far the funding opportunities that have emerged following the CRPD address DPO realities. Donor staff's understanding of reality is often not the same as a DPO's on-the-ground experience.

However, DPOs and other CSOs are often expected to act immediately to address power relations and inequality, and to articulate long-term impacts on policy change through linear short-term interventions using results-based management systems that fail to reflect a systemic understanding of development (Eyben et al., 2006; James, 2011). The findings from this case study indicate that most DPOs have limited capacity to oppose donor directives that are overwhelming or mismatched with their needs; they are afraid to refuse these 'opportunities' and they often consent to a donor's assumed knowledge, even though this may be contrary to their own beliefs.

As mentioned in the introduction, my views are shaped by my identity as a woman with a disability, with significant experience working at different levels in aid chains. While initially I expected that DPOs and donors would be on a par in negotiations on funding and partnerships, my experiences and research changed my understanding of the power relations and decision-making at the donor level. I became aware of a dangerous imbalance of power in the non-profit world and the dominance of donor agendas and policies, which severely limit the access of DPOs to grant-makers: DPO are frequently too small and immature to stand up for their needs and what they believe should be done. They therefore often fail to successfully challenge 'strategic' grant-making and the unwillingness of donors to allow them a greater role in driving the agenda. Based on these experiences, I feel the particular need for greater determination and unity of position among DPOs in their interactions with donors, particularly on the issue of genuine and equal participation in the design and implementation of projects and M&E processes.

The more knowledgeable I become about the politics of development agencies, the harder it is for me to accept the subordination and lack of control that seems to come with development support. I feel an increasing discomfort when I see how grass-roots partners struggle with daily expenses, while donors decide, according to their own beliefs, how resources should be spent and why. While it is understandable that donors grant funds to priorities they focus on, DPOs should not be considered merely as contractors for implementing the ideas of others.

As such, BSS has rejected in the past funding that did not match our beliefs or came with a strong sense of donor control. Yet other DPOs, especially smaller ones and those that find it difficult to access funding in general, may not be in a position to do so, or to effectively challenge donor processes that fail to promote answers to local problems. I therefore encourage DPOs to resist the 'strategic philanthropy' of donors and develop greater collective action in demanding equal participation in terms of partnership modalities and implementation. This more unified approach could, I believe, prove influential in making donors more accountable to PwDs and other minority groups, allowing them more space to prioritize *their* learning needs. This may mean advocating for space to learn from our own mistakes.

The motto 'Nothing about Us, Without Us' has been used by DPOs for many years as part of the global movement to achieve equalization of opportunities for PwDs. It is my belief that in order to apply this motto – which relies on the principle of meaningful participation – it is vital for DPOs to be able to influence donors' funding strategies and priorities in interventions that aim to help them develop the capacity for achieving social change for PwDs.

References

Abu Alghaib, Ola (2013) 'Aid bureaucracy and support for disabled peoples' organizations: a fairy tale of self-determination and self-advocacy', unpublished master's thesis, Sussex University, Institute of Development Studies.

Batliwala, S. (2011) *Strengthening Monitoring and Evaluation for Women's Rights: Twelve Insights for Donors*, Toronto: Association for Women's Rights in Development (AWID) <http://www.awid.org/Library/Strengthening-Monitoring-and-Evaluation-for-Women-s-Rights-Twelve-Insights-for-Donors>[accessed27 May 2013].

Batliwala, S. and Pittman, A. (2010) *Capturing Change in Women's Realities*, Toronto: Association for Women's Rights in Development (AWID) <http://www.awid.org/About-AWID/AWID-News/Capturing-Change-in-Women-s-Realities> [accessed 27 May 2013].

Bhanushali, K. (2007) 'Changing face of disability movement: from charity to empowerment' on Social Science Research Network (posted 8 March) <http://papers.ssrn.com/sol3/papers.cfm?abstract_id=965999> [accessed 27 May 2013].

Burns, D. (2007) *Systemic Action Research: A Strategy for Whole System Change*, Bristol: Policy Press.

Carden, F., Earl, S. and Smutylo, T. (2009) *Outcome Mapping: Building Learning and Reflection into Development Programs*, Ottawa: IDRC.

CDI (2013) 'Improving the evaluability of INGO empowerment and accountability programs', CDI Practice Paper 1, Brighton: Centre for Development Impact (CDI) <http://bigpushforward.net/wp-content/uploads/2011/01/CDIPractice-Paper01finalR.pdf> [accessed 27 May 2013].

Coleridge, P. (1993) *Disability, Liberation, and Development*, Oxford: Oxfam, pp. 45–62.

Coleridge, P., Simonnot, C. and Steverlynck, D. (2010) *Study of Disability in EC Development Cooperation*, Brussels: European Commission <http://eeas.

europa.eu/delegations/tanzania/documents/press_corner/20101201_01_ en.pdf> [accessed 27 May 2013].

DCDD (2004) *Disability, Self-Organizations and Aid: Finding an Empowering Mix. Symposium Report*, The Hague: Dutch Coalition on Disability and Development (DCDD).

Emmi, A., Ozlem, E., Kjennerud, M., Rozenkopf, I. and Schatz, F. (2011) 'Value for money: current approaches and evolving debates', London: London School of Economics and Political Science <http://bigpushforward.net/wp-content/uploads/2011/09/vfm-current-approaches-and-evolving-debates. pdf> [accessed 27 May 2013].

Enns, H. (2010) 'The role of organizations of disabled people: a disabled peoples' international discussion paper', Farsta, Sweden: Independent Living Institute <http://www.independentliving.org/docs5/RoleofOrgDisPeople. html> [accessed 27 May 2013].

Eyben, R., Harris, C. and Pettit, J. (2006) 'Introduction: exploring power for change', *IDS Bulletin* 37(6): 1–10.

Eyben, R., Kidder, T., Rowlands, J. and Bronstein, A. (2008) 'Thinking about change for development practice: a case study from Oxfam GB', *Development in Practice* 18(2): 201–12.

Goetz, A.M. and Jenkins, R. (2002) *Voice, Accountability and Human Development: The Emergence of a New Agenda*, New York NY: United Nations Development Programme <http://hdr.undp.org/en/content/voice-accountability-and-human-development> [accessed 27 May 2013].

Guijt, I. (2007) *Critical Readings on Assessing and Learning for Social Change*, Brighton: Institute of Development Studies (IDS).

Guijt, I. (2010) 'Accountability and learning', in J. Ubels (ed.), *Capacity Development in Practice*, London: Earthscan.

HI (2011) *Support to Organisations Representative of Persons with Disabilities*, Lyon: Handicap International (HI) <http://www.hiseminars.org/uploads/ media/Support_to_Organizations_Version_electronique__2__02.pdf> [accessed 27 May 2013].

Hurst, R. (1999) 'Disabled people's organisations and development: strategies for change', in E. Stone (ed.), *Disability and Development: Learning from Action and Research on Disability in the Majority World*, Leeds: The Disability Press, pp. 25–35.

James, C. (2011) *Theory of Change Review: A Report Commissioned by Comic Relief*, London: Comic Relief <http://dmeforpeace.org/sites/default/files/ James_ToC.pdf> [accessed 27 May 2013].

Katsui, H. (2005) *Towards Equality: Creation of the Disability Movement in Central Asia*, Ithaca NY: Cornell University, ILR School <http://digitalcommons. ilr.cornell.edu/cgi/viewcontent.cgi?article=1333&context=gladnetcollect> [accessed 27 May 2013].

Lansdown, G. (2009) *See Me, Hear Me: A Guide to Using the UN Convention on the Rights of Persons with Disabilities to Promote the Rights of Children*, London: Save the Children <http://www.crin.org/docs/See_me_hear_final.pdf> [accessed 27 May 2013].

Lennie, J. and Tacchi, J. (2013) *Evaluating Communication for Development: A Framework for Social Change*, London: Routledge.

Reeler, D. (2005) *A Theory of Social Change and Implications for Practice, Planning, Monitoring and Evaluation*, Cape Town: CDRA.

Reis, L. (2010) 'Evaluating social change: a funder–social movement dialogue', Santa Cruz CA: Forging Alliances South and North <http://www.for-al.org/english/documents/Evaluating_Social_Change_ForAL.pdf> [accessed 27 May 2013].

Stone, E. (1999) *Disability and Development: Learning from Action and Research on Disability in the Majority World*, Leeds: The Disability Press.

Stone, E. (2002) 'ADD programmes and partnerships' [online] <http://disability-studies.leeds.ac.uk/files/library/stone-chapter-4.pdf> [accessed 27 May 2013].

UN (2006) 'Convention on the Rights of Persons with Disabilities' on United Nations Enable [website] <http://www.un.org/disabilities/default.asp?navid=14&pid=150> [accessed 4 March 2013].

UN (2010) *Including the Rights of Persons with Disabilities in United Nations Programming at Country Level: A Guidance Note for United Nations Country Teams and Implementing Partners*, New York NY: United Nations Development Group <http://www.un.org/disabilities/documents/iasg/undg_guidance_note.pdf> [accessed 27 May 2013].

UN (2013) 'Convention on the Rights of Persons with Disabilities. Chapter IV: Human Rights' on United Nations Treaty Collection [website] <http://treaties.un.org/Pages/ViewDetails.aspx?src=TREATY&mtdsg_no=IV-15&chapter=4&lang=en> [accessed 9 March 2013].

UNDESA (2012) 'Examining disability issues and the MDGs' on United Nations Department of Economic and Social Affairs (UN DESA) [website] <http://www.un.org/en/development/desa/news/social/disability-and-the-mdgs.html> [accessed 27 May 2013].

Wapling, L. and Downie, B. (2012) *Beyond Charity: A Donor's Guide to Inclusion*, Boston MA: Disability Rights Fund <http://disabilityrightsfund.org/files/beyond_charity._a_donors_guide_to_inclusion.pdf> [accessed 13 March 2013].

WHO (2011) *World Report on Disability*, Geneva: World Health Organization (WHO) and World Bank <http://www.who.int/disabilities/world_report/2011/report.pdf> [accessed 4 March 2013].

Woodhill, J. (2005) 'M&E as learning: rethinking the dominant paradigm' <http://jimwoodhill.files.wordpress.com/2010/01/me-as-learning-chapter-woodhill1.doc> [accessed 27 May 2013].

About the author

Ola Abu Alghaib has over 15 years of experience working on issues of inclusive development, disability and poverty, and inclusive social services in low- and middle-income countries, including gender and disability research. She has an MA in Power, Participation and Social Change from the Institute of Development Studies and is currently a PhD researcher at the University of East Anglia. Her research interests encompass the association between disability and poverty in the Middle East and North Africa region.

Note

1. For further details on the methodology, see Abu Alghaib (2013).

CHAPTER 8

The results agenda in Swedish development cooperation: cycles of failure or reform success?

Janet Vähämäki

Abstract

Sida, the Swedish International Development Agency, has repeatedly, over decades, tried to introduce a stronger focus on 'results' and it has always resulted in a (re-)introduction of a management technology based on a derivate of the logical framework. Since 2006, the 'results agenda' has been a top political priority, with large organizational and cultural changes within Sida. The chapter concludes that, although there might be factors that support the success of the current effort, these changes may hamper the achievement of development results on the ground and be just another 'tide of reform'.

Keywords: donor practice, management technologies, Sida, reform cycles, results

Managing and demonstrating 'results' has always been a concern for Swedish development cooperation. As early as 1962, the first government bill for development cooperation defined the achievement of results in terms of 'downward accountability' that appeared supportive of transformational development: a 'major task, which also ought to lie in the interest of the recipient' and 'would require a mutual cooperation between the donor and the recipient' (Proposition 1962: 100). Ever since, the Swedish International Development Agency (Sida) has sought to operationalize this political ambition, although the agenda has gradually shifted in ways that privilege accountability to governments and taxpayers in donor countries.

While the quest for results is a permanent feature of the public sector, this agenda receives an extra push during a 'tides of reforms', when national governments shift from 'getting and spending' to 'achieving' (Ferlie et al., 2009). In Sida, results initiatives received such a push in 1971, 1981, 1998 and 2012. Each initiative included the introduction – or reintroduction – of certain 'new' and obligatory management technologies or artefacts (see Chapter 2), such as the logical framework, to help generate evidence of results. Yet each technology encountered severe difficulties, such as staff resistance and low usage, resulting

http://dx.doi.org/10.3362/9781780448855.008

in continual cycles of surge and decline. Since 2006, in particular, the results agenda has been a top political priority heavily pushed by the right-wing alliance government in Sweden. To meet political reform ambitions, Sida has been reorganized and re-staffed with new routines established in ways I will describe below.

The Sida case illustrates the difficulties a donor agency faces when it seeks to interpret and translate political demands from government to produce and communicate evidence of its results. It reveals how people in organizations respond to powerful drivers, sometimes resisting and at other times appearing to comply. I show how they sustain hope and optimism for reform and how they innovate within the set agenda. Tracing the history of cycles of results-oriented reform efforts illustrates how such reforms can – or cannot – induce change.

As an employee at Sida from 1998 until 2011 and at the Ministry for Foreign Affairs in 2012, I saw from the inside how a donor shifted from analysing and understanding the needs of intended beneficiaries to mainly focusing on controlling, reporting, and communicating the 'results' that aid projects and programmes achieved. As a consequence, very little time and space was left to try out different 'out of the box' approaches for actually achieving results. I became interested in discovering what was driving these changes. The documentation of these results initiatives now forms part of my PhD thesis within a Sida-funded research project on the 'results agenda'. My hope is that the Sida case can stimulate discussion and learning about results-oriented management reforms in general – and the extent to which they contribute to the transformational intentions of international development.

I start the chapter by discussing the relationship between reforms and results-oriented management technologies. Then I describe the rise and fall of earlier results-oriented management technologies. Much of the chapter details the current strong 'results agenda' and how it made its entry into Sida. In particular I examine how Sida staff members experienced the challenges and possibilities of the new agenda. Finally, I reflect on whether the current incarnation of the results agenda is yet another 'tide of reform' or has the potential to be more.

Management reforms and technology

Western political democracies are built on the idea that governments go to elections promising new reforms. Political ideas or programmes, such as more focus on 'results', are translated and formed into institutionalized practices or technologies which become concrete tasks, routines, or regulations. However, these always encounter difficulties and fail to live up to their promises. Miller and Rose (2008) argue that this failure allows the surge of new optimism for yet another round of reforms.

The logical framework approach (LFA) is a classic example within international development, used since the 1970s to strengthen results orientation.

The logframe consists of a matrix, which allows users to map out how resources and activities will contribute to achieving objectives and results using quantifiable indicators to measure progress (Coleman, 1987; Binnedjikt, 2001). The logframe, or subsequent derivatives, serve to encourage strategic, linear, rational thinking in change processes and to express, simplify, and reproduce complex processes by using numbers for comparison (Espeland and Stevens, 1998; Vollmer, 2007).

Some scholars discuss repeated reforms based on these logic models as a stable element in an endless pursuit of a more rational world (Brunsson, 2002). This type of logic model is reintroduced in policy fields and organizations, despite little proof of the model working even remotely as hoped (Brunsson, 2002; Sundström, 2007). Some argue that their downfall is due to their very basis in rationality, with failure inevitable since people and organizations are never fully rational, nor do they strive to be (Brunsson, 2006). Newly incumbent government officials responsible for designing new information and control systems ignore history (Sundström, 2007). In the end, change initiatives appear to lead to new initiatives rather than to changed practice (Sundström, 2007). Nevertheless, Brunsson (2006) argues that such optimism and hope is necessary for organizations; the opposite would imply despair and cause organizations to lose their legitimacy.

Other scholars argue for more understanding of how people make sense of and use technologies in organizational day-to-day practice. Political ideas and their subsequent technologies need to be studied *in situ* prior to reaching this understanding (Christiansen and Varnes, 2009). Also, this school of thought stresses how, since their inception in the 1960s, results reforms have emphasized changing staff mindsets away from the 'activity trap' towards results- and goal-oriented thinking (Drucker, 1964), a process requiring time (Sundström, 2007). However, since results management techniques most often imply an increased search for provable, quantitative evidence, in practice people 'become obsessed with measuring, weighing, and calculating' (Espeland and Stevens, 1998: 322). Thus organizations need to balance stronger goal-orientation for more robust policy-making with offsetting the risk of 'obsessive measurement disorder' (Natsios, 2010).

Understanding whether the current results agenda in Sida is simply another reform or is occurring under more positive circumstances requires an in-depth analysis of day-to-day-practice and staff reactions, specifically on the management technology implemented within the reform.

Early results initiatives in Sida

The Swedish International Development Authority (SIDA) was formed in 1965. In 1995, four development organizations, including SIDA, merged to form Sida, the Swedish International Development Agency. Sida is a government organization under the Swedish Foreign Ministry. It administers about half of Sweden's aid budget, which in 2014 amounted to 38.4 billion

Swedish kronor or US$5.7 billion. Sida's role is to manage aid projects and programmes and to make available Swedish resources (knowledge exchange, personnel, and money) for achieving agency objectives. Sida also monitors results produced and checks on the proper use of resources. Sida is governed mainly through two mechanisms: government guidelines and the Government Annual Letter of Appropriation. The guidelines describe how Sida should perform its work and the Letter of Appropriation sets out Sida's objectives, total budget, and allocations. Follow-up occurs through annual reports from Sida to government, which detail costs, revenues, and results. Swedish aid operations in specific countries, organizations, or thematic areas are decided upon through strategies that are guided by specific government guidelines.

I now turn to early attempts in Sida to implement results initiatives. I will explain the 1971 initiative in some detail and highlight similarities and differences with approaches in the 1980s and 1990s. I then focus on the current results initiative within Sida from 2012 onwards.

The 1971 'results valuation' initiative

The 1960s saw a strong drive for rationalization and effectiveness of public administration, alongside substantial increases in public aid for developing countries. Internationally, aid agencies were increasingly concerned about the need for evaluation and follow-up to ensure successful aid projects, as well as the need to demonstrate 'results' from public funding. When SIDA was formed in 1965, the main pressure to demonstrate 'results' and control aid funds came from parliament and a parliamentary audit report that claimed that 'despite several calls from the parliament there had so far been limited efforts to achieve such control of funds through results measurement and evaluation efforts' (Riksdagens Revisorer 1966). Hence, at its inception, SIDA was roundly reprimanded for failing to do enough on the results agenda.

In 1971, SIDA responded by establishing the 'results valuation' initiative to 'assist developing countries in their follow-up and evaluation of results of their development work' (SIDA, 1971: 7). The approach was oriented towards ensuring benefits from results valuation for recipient countries and organizations, and therefore it focused on the conduct of the valuation by recipient countries. The programme also stated, 'as a consequence, also SIDA will benefit from improved access to results information for its decisions' (ibid.).

The requirements for managing SIDA-funded aid projects and programmes were extensive. During planning, programme officers were expected to include quantitative indicators for the expected main goal, partial goals, production goals, activities, and costs. This data was assumed to be part of recipient organizations' proposals, and, if absent, the organization undertook a valuation to obtain the information. Data was intended to calculate planned effectiveness. It was simplistically assumed that regular monitoring would reveal 'actual effectiveness' by dividing the degree of goal-fulfilment by costs to date. The assumption was that improved results data would facilitate planning and administration, in contrast to the prior practice of guessing goals and hoping they were fulfilled. Thus results were considered fully predictable and their tracking feasible – provided staff transferred 'reality' into a calculation model.

Unsurprisingly, difficulties arose during the initiative's roll-out: goals were absent in recipient organization proposals and in SIDA agreements; reporting did not always follow agreements, nor align with programme goals; and if reports arrived, they were seldom read. Thus, in practice, SIDA staff could not do the requisite calculations:

> There was a constant discussion [about] this: 'How will you be able to measure? How will you see the results?' And the whole time the discussions were about the fact that the abstraction level for the targets was too high to be able to measure. (Head of SIDA's Result Valuation Function in 1971, interview in 2013)

> There were always difficulties to prove the relation between Swedish funding and its impacts. The role of aid was...different than today [For project implementers] ... the matter of aid was not to produce impact, but to get e.g. the water pumps to work, to get the local community to understand how water pumps should be maintained, etc. (Head of SIDA's Evaluation Unit in 1974, interview in 2013)

SIDA field offices noted that the approach had negative consequences for recipient countries. For example, the head of SIDA Kenya wrote to SIDA headquarters in 1974 after having observed how the valuations affected Kenyans:

> Observations on how results valuation affect the Kenyans [have] given me goosebumps over my whole body. I believe that we ought to master our curiosity, if we are not to participate in a massive 'perversion of intelligence' in this part of the world ... From Kenyan perspectives these laboratory experiments are rather uninteresting ... and ... the costs of these perversions are large, even though the donors always are more than happy to pay for the costs ... Also, large amounts of money flood to purposeless activities that are not operational ... since typically nothing operational can be done until the studies have been conducted. (Letter to the Evaluation Unit from Gösta Edgren, Head of SIDA office in Nairobi, 9 June 1974)

Despite much effort, a 1973 parliamentary audit found that only 10 per cent of SIDA's project portfolio had fully met planning and reporting requirements, and of that only 9 per cent of valuations had been undertaken by recipient countries. The audit noted the great difficulty of valuing social and economic effects of public sector programmes, and stated that it was not possible to attribute the effects of Swedish funding. It therefore recommended that SIDA should focus on demonstrating agency, not project results. In 1974, the National Audit Office also critiqued SIDA's recipient-oriented approach.

Subsequent discussions between SIDA, the government and the audit offices led to a new results valuation programme in 1974. One key difference was around purpose: results valuation now also had to 'contribute towards improved knowledge among the Swedish public and parliament of the long-term effects of aid as well as the results and effectiveness of Swedish aid' (SIDA, 1974). Another difference was replacing the requirements for the calculations with a narrative description of project intervention logic. It was decided not to use the logical framework, about which the then head of SIDA's Evaluation Unit commented:

> We sent one of the evaluators to the US to participate in the first 'logical framework' conference...and we deliberately chose *not* to [use it] because it was not WE who should do it. If someone were to use the method it was the aid recipients. It was completely crazy if we were to introduce some kind of 'logical framework' for someone else...it did not match up with the view that development takes place in the beneficiary countries and not in Sweden.

These changes sought to simplify results requirements. Between 1974 and 1981, efforts focused on demonstrating results through narrative studies and evaluations of SIDA-funded projects and programmes. In the meantime, the difficulties met in the 1971 programme and the difficulties of SIDA to disclose resutls had heightened interest from parliament, the public, and the audit offices in seeing SIDA demonstrate results. Notwithstanding this first resounding failure, the notion of using management technology to operationalize a results focus had taken root.

Results initiatives in SIDA/Sida in 1981 and 1998

In 1981, SIDA launched an initiative called Project before 'Programme Follow-Up', which aimed to store and systematize project-level results data for an annual 'catalogue'. A three-year pilot led to two catalogues in 1984 and 1987 that merely sought to meet parliamentary and public requests with regard to SIDA. The original focus on benefiting recipient countries was abandoned, instead shifting to piloting new reporting formats.

However, it was difficult to identify the best level of results information. Until 1984, SIDA headquarters requested information only on intended and actual disbursement, activities, and production targets. Later, information was also requested on goals and actual impacts. SIDA staff strongly criticized the different templates, for example because of how results were linked to goal achievement.

In 1984, a project performance rating 'fashioned after the World Bank' was included to ease some of the difficulties – characterizing projects along a scale from 'problem free' to 'major problems' and a trend from 'improving' to 'deteriorating' (SIDA 1984: 2). However, staff doubted its overall utility and said it was too time-consuming.

Eventually, the information collected through both reporting models was deemed to be of inadequate quality to qualify as official SIDA results for disclosure to parliament and the public. In 1987, the initiative was terminated because of limited utility and lack of enthusiasm for its implementation. It took another 11 years before the next attempt to systematize agency-wide results hit the agency. In the interim, different attempts were made to report on results through other means, such as evaluations and specific reports on themes, countries, and projects or programmes.

In 1998, the parliamentary audit and other bodies applied additional pressure on SIDA to demonstrate and attribute corporate results, and Sida's director general launched an initiative called 'Sida internal Rating System' (SiRS). SiRS sought again to systematize agency-wide results and improve management, this time through an IT-based system for the recurrent rating of projects and programmes. SiRS focused solely on results information with no link to any planning or other decision-making function. Sida staff had to write an *ex post* narrative on why results had or had not been realized. SiRS included an annual five-grade rating of risks and performance per project or programme.

Like earlier initiatives, SiRS was heavily criticized and questioned by staff and also by several senior managers in Sida's Board of Directors. Compared with the situation in 1981, criticism focused less on lack of internal competence and more on the consequences of rating. How was Sida going to validate what was a poor- or a well-performing project? And what would happen to projects rated 'bad'? Enduring technical difficulties, particularly for field offices, compounded the resistance. In the end, SiRS was used by only 25 per cent of those required to do so, and in 2008 it was made voluntary.

From 2006 onwards: 'results, transparency, and accountability'

Reforming Swedish aid

In 2006, the new government issued guiding principles for Swedish aid known as 'results, transparency, and accountability', making results central to the reform. In the government bill of 2007 (Gov, 2007) the reform was rationalized in terms of 'value for money' (see Chapter 4). 'There is a need, both for the populations in the recipient countries as well as for the Swedish public, to know that Swedish aid really is used in the best way' – the Minister of Development Cooperation, Gunilla Carlsson, sent a clear message: management reforms in the sector were essential and urgent. Amidst similar discussions in other countries, Sweden was to spearhead policy and methods in the field of 'results' (Carlsson, 2006), switching, said the minister, from 'passive disbursement politics to active development politics' (Carlsson, 2007). Results-focused management was considered critical for the success of these reforms. The government bill of 2007 stated that 'We must now realize a results thinking that permeates the whole aid administration', and this intention took shape in a new model for results management. A new Sida director general, known for reforming management in another aid organization, was appointed. A new independent Agency for Aid Evaluation (SADEV) was established.

External critique of Sida administrative routines increased, for example by the National Audit Office regarding budget support, support to civil society, and capacity development. Triggered by findings of corruption relating to

Swedish funds in Zambia, the minister criticized Sida in an article entitled: 'It is time that we start an honest discussion of aid' (Carlsson, 2009). The criticism and the new management reforms provoked pushback from civil society organizations, opposition parties, and notably Sida staff. In 2009, the minister received two headline-generating letters: one from five of Sida's department heads (Sida, 2009a) and a Christmas letter signed by 172 staff members at Sida (Sida, 2009b). Both letters expressed the difficulties and complexity of applying results management in development cooperation. The department heads' letter stated that:

> We will therefore probably never be able to prove the cause and effect relation and the role of Swedish aid in that way. It is subsequently not reasonable to require that from aid and it is also [not reasonable] to build up a hope among the public that this is possible.

> We are concerned about the image that you [the minister] give of Swedish development assistance in articles and interviews in the media. It is not based on the results that development cooperation actually achieves. It does not highlight the complex reality for managing results in development cooperation. The image you convey outwardly makes us and many of our staff wonder about how you look at the value of the aid profession in your work for change.

The staff members' letter broached the contradictions, complexity, and difficulties of the new requirements:

> According to government instructions, we try to work through partner countries' own systems and harmonize requirements with other donors, but at the same time we need to be able to show results just for the Swedish money. We try to make wise analyses and take into account a variety of problems, but are groaning under increasingly grotesque requirements that everything must be documented. However, the requirements are becoming so extensive that insufficient time remains for making wise assessments.

The results reforms disrupted relations between Sida staff and the minister, generating a harsh debate about the utility and feasibility of increased requirements to quantify precisely how Swedish funds had been spent and how to attribute results. In her response, the minister wrote:

> I will not give up. We must work in a more results-oriented manner in development aid. We must be able to tell the parliament and the voters of all [the] positive things that are done in a comprehensive way. We must also have a totally different documentation and systematization in how we think of results in aid. (Ekot, 2009)

> Of course it is possible to measure. One only has to develop measurement methods; internationally this is possible. (Härdmark, 2010)

> A challenge we have in this relation is how we look upon our respective roles. I am doing my work and I expect Sida to do theirs. (ibid.)

At the time, staff viewed the reforms with despair because of their probable counterproductivity. However, the minister maintained her optimism about the reforms by stressing that they would eventually lead to transformational development, with current difficulties being only temporary.

Reforms were introduced during a time of intensified public debate and media coverage about the raison d'être of development cooperation, adding to the pressure for transparent disclosure of results information. The 2010 'Guidelines for cooperation strategies' included increased focus on aid effectiveness, including more rigorous continuous reporting directly to the Ministry for Foreign Affairs on results at different levels. The government instructed that 'the agency's core task is to administer aid assistance or other financing that contributes to the fulfilment of development goals' (Gov, 2010), deprioritizing Sida's earlier core tasks on policy and knowledge. A new board replaced the advisory council, rounding off a set of ministerial decisions that provided 'solid ground for Sida's carrying through of...open and results-oriented aid' (ibid.).

The situation was aggravated by budget deficits caused by an overspend on Sida's administration and closer scrutiny with more frequent reporting. In May 2010, the government had showed its dissatisfaction by replacing the director general and by appointing a deputy director general. Tasked with balancing the budget, the new leadership cut staff by 25 per cent, inducing many voluntary departures. A total reorganization led to the redeployment of all Sida staff, who were now all personally affected by government reforms.

In 2011, the newly appointed Secretary of State for International Development (the minister's deputy) further intensified the results agenda. The Swedish Agency for Public Management evaluated the model for results management from 2007. One conclusion was that 'the control system is so difficult to understand that the government's priorities may fail to make an impact' (Statskontoret, 2011). The evaluation recommended: 1) reducing the number of steering documents; 2) developing an aid platform that would clarify government priorities and the link between different goals; and 3) balancing annual result reporting with more analysis of results. Sweden also wanted to make its mark internationally. For example, before the High Level Meeting (HLM) on Aid Effectiveness in Busan in 2011, the Swedish minister invited a new group of like-minded donors (United Kingdom, United States of America, Germany, Denmark, and Canada) to discuss how to work jointly towards an increased results focus, transparency, and accountability in aid.

More new reforms were introduced, bolstered perhaps by additional criticism of the aid sector. The minister went on record to state that the Busan HLM was an 'alarm clock for an aid industry that had fallen asleep' and that it signified 'a long-awaited farewell to oldie-aid which was more about form and theory than practice and results' (Carlsson, 2011). These reforms required replacing and revising all recent government aid guidelines. In addition, SADEV was closed down after five years as its evaluations had underemphasized the actual results of Swedish aid, thus not fulfilling original expectations (Statskontoret, 2012).

After 2011, Sida's plans of action reveal that it had visibly become focused on 'results', cost-efficiency, and transparency: for example, 'We report and communicate results and lessons learned in a simple and fair way' and 'We have built expertise through a systematic use of country, regional, and global analyses in assessment of results offers and implementation of results strategies'. By this stage, the huge organizational changes, cutbacks, and administrative reforms had greatly affected Sida's culture and mandate. One of the signatories to the directors' 2010 letter to the minister stated in an interview with the author:

> Sida is today a disabled organization. We have complained, we have not retreated, we ... have produced evidence, saying that this will not work, we've done it here and there. However, we don't any longer have the strength to stand up and say 'we do not think this works' ... It has become clear for us, since 2006/2007 ... that our job is not to fight poverty; they have narrowed the agency's mission ... our largest responsibility is to have a strong apparatus for managing grants and strategies.

Another staff member working with Sida's results-reporting instructions expressed deep resignation. 'Even though there is resistance towards it now as well, there is no alternative now. You just have to do it.' Both quotes show that Sida staff, one year after the huge organizational changes and public dissent with the minister, had started accepting that resistance towards the reforms was no longer a valid option.

Results management reforms in 2012

During 2012, the enhanced results ambitions led to two new agency-wide projects (Sida, 2012a). The 'results communication' project aimed to make 'results' from Swedish aid visible in response to demands, for example from the government in its budget bill of 2013, which requested that results be quantified and aggregated 'to the extent possible and reasonable' (Sida, 2012b). To support this project, coordinating staff analysed the required culture and attitude change within Sida. Figure 8.1 shows how they visualized the transition from staff currently in denial and angry about the 'results agenda' but changing as a result of the communication efforts and coming to accept and implement the agenda. The figure was used with Sida directors to discuss how organizational resistance could be counteracted, illustrating Sida management's belief that success with the results reform required working with staff attitudes and feelings.

The second project was on 'standard indicators', driven by Sida's internal need and external wish to increase the use of quantitative indicators. One of the project deliverables was an aggregation framework with indicators at different levels that would give an overview of results to which Sida had contributed (Sida, 2013a).

This renewed round of result reforms occurred in an organization that had, perhaps surprisingly, a new sense of hope and possibility for the reforms.

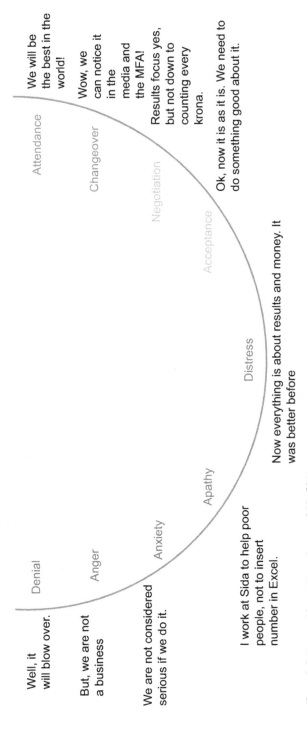

Figure 8.1 How to drive culture change within Sida

Note: Image taken from a presentation of the 'results communication' project by the Communication Department to Sida's board of directors, 2013. Translated by the author.

Different explanations for this turnaround existed. For example, the head of communication stated in an interview with the author:

I believe that we, as an agency, have probably come to the conclusion that it is better that we drive the results agenda and results communication, instead of someone else driving and pulling us, because then we have the momentum, we are the ones who know the field and can be clever in how we move forward.

Another Sida director responsible for corporate results reflected on how organizational changes had affected Sida's culture:

One can accomplish things today that could not be achieved before, but perhaps we should not shout out that we are through it yet ... The strong organizational culture that existed before, which was [mainly] where the resistance came from, has of course been removed. In combination, there has been a generational shift ... People just disappeared with the reorganization, and also, naturally, people from the old generation, which were used to do whatever they wanted, and who could say that 'I go down to Tanzania and start a project and then I have my darlings that I support', are now gone.

In 2012–13, senior management was keenly aware of the failure of previous results reforms, ensuring that new efforts were given high priority within the agency. A new sense of optimism for the reforms could thus be envisaged within Sida.

Operationalizing the results agenda through the 'results summary' initiative

In 2012, a new procedure was launched to operationalize the results agenda. This made obligatory a results summary for each project or programme, including a baseline, annual targets for outputs, interim outcomes, and final outcomes. The summary was to be updated annually with actual performance values. This same requirement had been tried during each reform era: in 1971, 1981 and 1998. However, this version differed in two respects: 1) it required annual targets as well as an annual update of results information; and 2) it identified which organizational function had to account for the correct fulfilment of specific aspects. Thus, standardization was sought through a form of 'responsibility audit'.

Despite the prevailing optimism about the success of the results agenda, there was pushback from within the agency to return to obligatory results data, which was understood by many as an obligation to quantify all data. For example, one sector specialist, tasked with suggesting indicators for her thematic area, critiqued the all-consuming task of calculations and indicators:

There is a huge speed in Sida right now, everyone is trying to interpret the various control signals and what the government wants. There is a lack of history, everything goes very fast. We do not understand what is meant by 'results' and the indicators that you want in order to measure results. Nobody wants analysis ... Our advisory role is completely reduced to only defining a measurable indicator; we no longer devote ourselves at all to any whole sector analysis or advice.

A staff member working with the methods and templates for corporate-level results reporting encountered implementation difficulties. 'It feels like what is methodologically reasonable does not matter...Thus it may well be that we are expected to report on it anyway, even though it is not possible.'

Programme officers commented on the recurring time conflicts between ensuring results and administering management technologies:

> Actually, one would just like to ignore the results matrices; they destroy so much and everyone knows that it is not leading to results. We do not have time to do anything else.

> Sida is only systems these days, and then you change everything all the time – it's very confusing.

However, another staff member from the Communication Department, while acknowledging the difficulties, saw them as an opportunity to be transparent about the complexity of quantifying development processes:

> We need to be transparent about 'this is the way we think', 'this is the way we attribute', 'this is the way we aggregate', 'this is the way we use the indicators', 'this is the way we use reporting'. We want to measure, and therefore we do it in this way....Then someone else, so to speak, can say 'It is very complex.' Then we can agree, but we should not avoid taking this step because we think it is complex.

Staff in the Communication Department viewed these difficulties as part of initial implementation that would be resolved over time:

> I am absolutely convinced that both the new grant management proce-dure and the standardized indicators and monitoring of results will give stability in the working processes. The working atmosphere for the indi-vidual programme officer will become much clearer … It will become very easy to relate to, and then I get space for my expertise instead of using time thinking about the procedure or the formats.

In January 2013, the new procedure underwent an internal quality review (Sida, 2013c) that found that results summaries were missing in 40 of 45 decisions taken between 7 March and 30 April 2012, and in 11 of 30 decisions between 1 May and 30 June 2012 (Sida, 2012c). Despite prioritization and reforms, only 12 per cent of the staff in the first case and 36 per cent in the second had respected the new requirements.

To improve one problem – the low quality of funding applications and related results matrices – Sida programme officers were encouraged to offer recipient organizations consultancy support. However, the consultancy firm soon realized that it had inadvertently become the translator of what 'results' meant in reality. In an interview with the author, one consultant commented:

> My impression is that there is often a linguistic confusion between the Sida programme officer and the recipient organization, that they simply

do not talk the same language and do not understand each other. And then we jump in as a translator.

The consultancy firm started to question Sida about unfeasible requirements: for example, questioning the requirement for annual targets. They also noticed the power these requirements had over programme officers and their ineffectiveness:

> The new requirement with the results summary is counterproductive. The only officer who can meet the demands is the one using 'copy and paste'. It has not enabled people to think more, but rather less. A programme officer must answer 30 different questions for the system to be satisfied.

In May 2013, the Evaluation Unit decided to revise the requirements. They presented three alternatives to Sida's decision-making board guiding the grant management process: 1) increase internal control to comply with the results summary; 2) remove the compulsory nature of reporting; and 3) shift requirements to only narrative reporting (Sida, 2013b). Following indecision by the board, the director general chose option 2.

Thus, Sida replaced the results summary requirement with a 'results register' (Sida, 2013c), removing the obligation to prove causality between outputs and outcomes, and allowing for voluntary decisions about which outputs and outcomes to report on. It introduced a rating function (red, amber, green) for project performance. Both tasks are the responsibility of Sida programme officers, thereby reducing the involvement of recipient organizations. The results register is currently being implemented.

Current status of the results agenda in Sida

In August 2013, a new government decision on 'Guidelines for results strategies' came into effect, requiring, for example, *ex ante* identification of anticipated in-country results. Project results are expected to contribute to overall strategy goals. Future financing of aid projects will increasingly be guided by whether results are achieved. Upward performance accountability has therefore won over *in situ* and policy learning. At their launch, the minister stated that the guidelines implied a 'system change to strengthen the focus on concrete results for poor people' (Gov, 2013).

The following month, a cabinet reshuffle led to the replacement of Gunilla Carlsson, who had been Minister for Development Cooperation for seven years. While ostensibly a requested departure, since 'a lot of our policies are now in place' (Rosén, 2013), it followed shortly after a heavily critical consultancy report on the minister's management of her portfolio. While the new minister, Hillevi Engström, reiterated the importance of results and transparency, she also stressed the need for openness about internal decisions.

Around this time, both the results communication project and the standard indicator project reported on the one-year pilots. The results communication project noted some success with simplified, quantitative results (Sida, 2013d). Interestingly, it was also open about the complexity of results communication, confirming that 'measuring effects of aid can take time; it is therefore easier to measure outputs/deliverables' (Sida, 2013e). However, the data used in communication has not been from the results summary process, but is rather a by-product from other processes. Thus, in an echo of earlier results initiatives, the information gathered through systematized efforts has not, until now, been used for official reporting. Moreover, critique from Sida's field offices highlighted that the requested standardized numerical information poorly conveys field realities, and a director commented to the author on the extremely low reliability of the data.

The second project has not delivered an agency-wide framework of standard indicators. 'Sida will not be able to present aggregated results for the agency, since this would have required similarity in the expected results decided upon in the results strategies' (Sida, 2013f). Delays in the government's decisions on the aid platform and 'Guidelines for results strategies' were contributing factors. In April 2014, the government approved an aid platform that provides a goal hierarchy and anticipated results of Swedish aid. The platform states that aid results can vary due to their nature and context, with implications for the ease of assessment. It also cautions:

> the difficulties in measuring results should not imply that the aid administration stops trying. The difficulties also do not imply that Sweden should focus its aid only on short-term results or results that are easy to measure. Sweden should also not refrain from [providing] support in unstable situations where it can take a longer time until aid achieves results or where results are more difficult to measure. (Gov, 2013: 42)

So, despite the aid platform emphasizing quantitative goals and results, it also opened up the possibility of seeing transformational development as context-specific.

Reflecting on the eras of results initiatives in Swedish bilateral aid

Swedish aid has long been driven by the simultaneous wish and need to demonstrate the results of aid. Repeated failures of previous reforms have underpinned hope and optimism for new rounds of reform (Miller and Rose, 2008). In Swedish aid, the efforts have intensified during certain periods, stimulated by results initiatives that have largely been driven by the wish to systematically show results achieved by Sida's aid investment to the Swedish public and parliament.

All initiatives have pinned hopes on (re)introducing a management technology based on some derivative of the logical framework. The technology designers have been spurred by the need for 'commensuration' (Espeland and Stevens, 1998): that is, to reduce disparate information from recipient organizations in diverse complex realities into numbers to be compiled by Sida programme officers for easy comparison and aggregation. However, implementation repeatedly encountered difficulties. These problems conform with what Espeland and Stevens (ibid.) refer to as the 'sociology of commensuration', where people and organizations search for the 'perfect tool' that can transform qualities into quantities and difference into magnitude, in order to manage – or at least appear to manage – uncertainty. Notwithstanding adjustments made in subsequent rounds, staff experienced difficulties in applying rules to the practical realities of aid initiatives and subsequently resisted, resulting in the inevitable decline of each initiative. Sida's cycles of management technologies have been ensnared in implementation problems, yet driven by the hope for a techno-logical solution.

Given Sida's history of implementing results-oriented reform, is the current reform just another round doomed to fade away? Or is Sida different today, in a way that might make the current version of the results agenda work? Evaluations of earlier organizational result-based management revealed insufficient political will and management support and a weak organizational results culture (Vähämäki et al., 2011). Today, several factors are different, possibly suggesting that the current reform may face a different destiny. The combination of strong political imperatives, new steering documents, and organizational changes have made 'results' a key priority for Sida. Formerly a low-status issue, this has become the agency's prime preoccupation along with transparency and accountability, prioritized above content themes such as gender and poverty reduction.

The Swedish government is more clearly the goal-setter today, with pub-lic agencies the implementers (Tarschys and Lemne, 2013). Results reforms occurred alongside intensive reforms to consolidate Sida's role as an admin-istrator and manager of funds, in the process reducing its role as a policy and knowledge organization. Spurring such organizational reforms is the primary aim of 'new public management', 'to give public sector organisations a new orientation and, in so doing the way they operate' (Diefenbach, 2007: 894). Several interviewees noted the consequent changes in Sida, where 'doing things right' now seems to be at the core, leading to a stronger culture of compliance with government policies. Another factor is the change in views on the intended primary user of results information. The 1970s reform, like others over the decades – for example, those resulting from the 2005 Paris Declaration – were strongly oriented towards assumed benefits for in-country recipient organizations, with effort (at least in theory) invested in designing more recipient-friendly management technology. Attention has now shifted towards domestic results management reforms, with the current primary user increasingly understood to be the Swedish parliament and citizens.

Nevertheless, as with previous initiatives, current data reliability and staff use of the results register continue to be difficult. But because Sida currently operates in a wider political system that considers policy and goal definition as the responsibility of government, not staff, the space for staff to resist what they experience as a counterproductive management technology is reduced. One danger with consolidating a culture of compliance is that 'doing things right' becomes more important than 'doing the right things', and the need for organizational legitimacy supersedes its actual task. One Sida director said: 'Sida is more anxious to appear transparent and communicate results than to actually work for results in practice.' And another commented:

> Our weakest link is where development is produced, i.e. the recipient countries. The government's new steer has probably not had any impact on the ground … but maybe it will come later.

Another danger of the current reform, with its narrow donor-centred approach and growing pressure to quantify, is that it could lead to 'obsessive measurement disorder' (Natsios, 2010), which in turn blocks the achievement of results on the ground.

However, despite reforms not meeting expectations, the current results reform – with its harsh debate between Sida staff and the minister, discussions about the agenda, and several pilots – seems to have led to other positive changes. Implementing the current results agenda has inadvertently increased staff knowledge and understanding of the pros and cons, possibilities and difficulties with results measurement and management. Recent comments by a Sida field director reflect this:

> My feeling is that the process of results strategies stimulated many conversations about results and thus increased the competence at Sida on the issues. I fought hard for us to distinguish between results and how to analyse development trends, and had a hard uphill battle to begin with. But retrospectively attitudes have changed. The same has applied to the struggle to formulate qualitative results. There was for some time a hard push to quantify what can be quantified but now the attitudes have changed.

A recent statement by Sida's director general echoes this optimism: 'Our new process for assessing, managing and following up aid interventions provides us with improved possibilities to base decisions on evidence and previous experience' (Petri Gornitzka, 2014). So far, yet another results reform is being implemented, spurred on by the hope and optimism of further improvements.

My own hope and wish, when pursuing these questions further through my PhD, is that the dynamic dialogue and attempts to implement the current reform will also lead us closer to the intended goal of the reforms –achieving actual results for transformative development.

Epilogue

This chapter was finalized in August 2014, shortly before a new minority government consisting of the Social Democratic Party and the Green Party took over and declared: 'Public sector professions need to be strengthened. New management models that create greater freedom for public sector workers will be developed' (Gov, 2014). As far as development cooperation was concerned, the proposed budget bill stated the preconditions for results management to be 'trust, dialogue and learning', emphasizing the importance of qualitative analysis and the need to rely on recipient country systems for results information. In the bill, 'results strategies' became 'strategies' – 'results' was removed.

These signals represent a 'softer' view of the management and results agenda, with more emphasis on human relations and analysis and less on administrative routines and indicators. The stress on quantitative results seems to be fading away. Discussions are focusing on what 'qualitative analysis' means and what type of management model can generate greater freedom. But these discussions have been halted, as the new government failed, in 2014, to get the budget bill passed by parliament.

The ever-changing story of the results agenda seems to continue, a story with no end.

References

Binnedjikt, A. (2001) *Results Based Management in the Developing Co-operation Agencies: A Review of Experience*, Paris: DAC Working Party on Evaluation, OECD.

Brunsson, N. (2002) *The Organisation of Hypocrisy: Talk, Decisions and Actions in Organisations*, Copenhagen: Copenhagen Business School Press, Abstrakt Forl.

Brunsson, N. (2006) *Mechanisms of Hope: Maintaining the Dream of the Rational Organisation*, Copenhagen: Copenhagen Business School Press.

Carlsson, G. (2006) 'Ny myndighet för bättre bistånd', speech at the inauguration of SADEV, Karlstad, 8 November <http://www.government.se/sb/d/7735/a/72195> [accessed 16 June 2014].

Carlsson, G. (2007) 'Den nya utvecklingspolitiken', *Dagens Nyheter*, 27 August.

Carlsson, G. (2009) 'Dags för en mer uppriktig debatt om biståndet', *Newsmill*, 28 August.

Carlsson, G. (2011) 'Tal av Gunilla Carlsson: Vad händer med svenskt bistånd efter Busan?', speech at Sida, 20 June <http://www.regeringen.se/sb/d/15823/a/184518> [accessed 16 June 2014].

Christiansen, J.K. and Varnes, C.J. (2009) 'Formal rules in product development: sensemaking of structured approaches', *Journal of Product Innovation Management* 26(5): 502–19.

Coleman, G. (1987) 'Logical framework approach to the monitoring and evaluation of agricultural and rural development projects', *Project Appraisal* 2(4): 251–59.

Diefenbach, T. (2007) 'New public management in public sector organisations: the dark sides of managerialistic "enlightenment"', *Public Administration* 87(4): 892–909.

Drucker, P.F. (1964) *Managing for Results*, Bombay: Allied Publishers.

Ekot (2009) 'Carlssons krav är groteska', Swedish Radio [website] <http://sverigesradio.se/sida/artikel.aspx?programid=83&artikel=3329520> [accessed 16 June 2014].

Espeland, W.N. and Stevens, M.L. (1998)'Commensuration as a social process', *Annual Review of Sociology* 24(1): 313–43.

Ferlie, E., Lynn Jr., L.E. and Pollitt, C. (2009) 'Performance management', *The Oxford Handbook of Public Management*, New York NY: Oxford University Press.

Gov (2007) 'Budgetproposition 2007 Utgiftsområde 7: Internationellt Bistånd', 2007/08:1UO7.

Gov (2010) 'Ny myndighetsinstruktion för Sida', press release for Sida's new instruction on Government Offices of Sweden [website] <http://www.regeringen.se/sb/d/13350/a/149914> [accessed 16 June 2014].

Gov (2013) 'Nya riktlinjer för svenskt bistånd', introduction to new results strategy guidelines on Government Offices of Sweden [website] <http://www.regeringen.se/sb/d/17009/a/220825> [accessed 16 June 2014].

Gov (2014) 'Statement of government policy', 3 October, on Government Offices of Sweden [website] <http://www.government.se/sb/d/17662/a/250502> [accessed 16 June 2014].

Härdmark, E. (2010) 'Ministern och missnöjet', FOKUS, 24 May <http://www.fokus.se/2010/05/ministern-och-missnojet/> [accessed 26 August 2014].

Miller, P. and Rose, N.S. (2008) Governing the Present: Administering Economic, Social and Personal Life, Cambridge: Polity.

Natsios, A. (2010) The Clash of the Counter-bureaucracy and Development, London: Centre for Global Development <http://international.cgdev.org/publication/clash-counter-bureaucracy-and-development> [accessed 26 August 2014].

Petri Gornitzka, C. (2014) 'Vi är alltid villiga att pröva nya arbetssätt', Omvärlden, 16 June <http://www.omvarlden.se/Opinion/Debatt/Vi-ar-alltid-villiga-att-prova-nya-satt-att-arbeta/> [accessed 16 June 2014].

Proposition (1962) 'Kungl Maj:ts Proposition'. Angående svenskt utvecklingsbistånd. Regeringen.

Riksdagens Revisorer (1966) 'Riksdagens revisorers uttalande'.

RiksdagensRevisorer (1973)'Granskningspromemoria 10.Resultatvärderingi den svenskabiståndsverksamheten. 1973-11-30'.

Riksdagens Revisorer (1973) 'Granskningspromemoria 10. Resultatvärdering i den svenska biståndsverksamheten. 1973-11-30'.

Rosén (2013) 'Ministern: Jag bad attfåga', DagensNyheter, 17 September<http://www.dn.se/nyheter/politik/ministern-jag-bad-att-fa-ga/>[accessed 26 August 2014].

SIDA (1971) 'Resultatvärdering – ett programförslag (juni, 1971)'.

SIDA (1974) 'Program för SIDAs verksamhet på resultatvärderingsområdet'.

SIDA (1984) 'Project programme follow-up. With performance rating'.

Sida (2009a) 'Till biståndsminister Gunilla Carlsson', dnr 2009-002188 <http://www.sida.se/Svenska/Nyhetsarkiv/2009/December/Sida-chefernas-brev-till-ministern/> [accessed 13 September 2013].

Sida (2009b) 'God Jul Gunilla Carlsson, önskar vi som jobbar på Sida' <https://www.forumsyd.org/templates/FS_ArticleTypeA.aspx?id=11132> [accessed 13 September 2013].

Sida (2012a) 'Uppdragsbeskrivning: Indikatorer i biståndet', dnr 13/000211.

Sida (2012b) 'Attkommunicera resultat- på väg mot en modell', 2012-11-21. Kommunikationsavdelningen.

Sida (2012c) 'PM. Metodavdelningen 1/2012', 2012-000874.

Sida (2013a) 'Uppdragsbeskrivning: Indikatorer i biståndet', 2013-02-08, 13/000211 UTV/VU.

Sida (2013b) ' Revidering av Resultatsammanfattningen i IHS: Tre alternativ', internal paper, VU.

Sida (2013c) 'Protokoll Processrådet 2013-09-19', Ärendenummer 13/000141.

Sida (2013d) 'Resultatkommunikation Slutrapport', 2013-06-19, 13/000313.

Sida (2013e) 'Biståndsbarometern Hälsa', Stockholm: Sida <http://www.sida.se/Svenska/sa-arbetar-vi/Bistandets-resultat/Bistandsbarometern/Halsa/>.

Sida (2013f) 'Indikatorer i biståndet, Slutrapport 2013-12-21', 13/000211.

Statskontoret (2011) 'Styrning av svensk biståndspolitik, En utvärdering', 2011:25.

Statskontoret (2012) 'Utvärdering av svenskt bistånd, En översyn av utvärderings-verksamheten', 2012:17.

Sundström, G. (2007) 'Management by results: its origin and development in the case of the Swedish state', *International Public Management Journal* 9(4): 399–427.

Tarschys, D. and Lemne, M. (2013) *Vad staten vill: mål och ambitioner i svensk politik*, Möklinta: Gidlund.

Vähämäki, J., Schmidt, M. and Molander, J. (2011)Review: Results Based Management in Development Cooperation,Stockholm: RiksbankensJubi leumsfond.

Vollmer, H. (2007) 'How to do more with numbers: elementary stakes, framing, keying, and the three-dimensional character of numerical signs', *Accounting, Organisations and Society* 32(6): 577–600.

About the author

Janet Vähämäki has a background of 13 years with Sida, the Ministry for Foreign Affairs, civil society organizations and consultancies within development aid. Janet is now finalizing her PhD at the Stockholm Business School and Stockholm Center for Organisational Research. The topic of her PhD is 'The results agenda in Swedish development cooperation'.

CHAPTER 9

Valuing children's knowledge: the politics of listening

Vicky Johnson

Abstract

Children's voices matter and can help us to understand the complex realities of their lives, but for children and young people to be heard, people in positions of power need to be included in participatory processes with them to build their confidence in the value of children's evidence. Based on revisits to participatory evaluations in the UK and Nepal, I show how children and young people's evidence can lead to transformational change and that their evidence can be valued if local power dynamics, including those between adults and children, are recognized and addressed. Mechanisms for how this can be done are presented.

Keywords: children's rights, participatory evaluation, voice, evidence, Nepal

Although progress has been made to take into account the rights of children and young people to participate in decisions affecting their lives following the UN Convention on the Rights of the Child (UNCRC) in 1989, whether their evidence is actually listened to and acted upon in participatory evaluation processes varies depending on context and the capacity and experience of the adult and younger participants involved. In 1995, Save the Children called for 'A New Agenda for Children', suggesting that children and young people's evidence should be taken seriously and that their perspectives should inform services and resource allocation intended to improve their lives. Rights-based discourses over the past decade have also helped to recognize children and young people's voices as part of participatory processes that base decision-making on local people's realities. This has been exemplified by child-centred organizations and researchers working with some of the most marginalized children, such as street-connected children, child workers, and children in care (for example, see Ennew, 1994; Johnson et al., 1998). In broader international development practice, however, children and young people's perspectives have often been disregarded or ignored at worst and, even where their opinions are specifically sought, their evidence has been poorly understood or sidelined in comparison to adult perspectives (Bartlett, 2005; Chawla and Johnson, 2004; Theis, 2010).

In order to understand how children and young people's agency can be supported in participatory processes and their evidence taken more

http://dx.doi.org/10.3362/9781780448855.009

seriously by decision-makers, power dynamics in local cultural, political, and institutional contexts need to be acknowledged and explored so that interventions to improve their well-being are well informed. To translate a child's right to participate in decisions that affect their life into improved outcomes, it is necessary to move beyond the concept of voice and incorporate ideas of participatory spaces for children to build confidence and interact with adults, audiences who listen to children and young people's perspectives, and people in positions of power who are willing to act on their evidence (as also suggested by Lundy, 2007).

This chapter provides a brief overview of the methodology I used to revisit participatory evaluations to explore whether the perspectives of children and young people had been taken seriously in varying contexts. The analysis that follows will focus on the politics of evidence and power, and asks why, in the evaluations revisited, there were barriers to using children and young people's evidence and what made a difference to taking their perspectives more seriously. Examples will be provided to demonstrate what led to children's evidence being valued and acted on, drawing on case studies from the UK and Nepal. Finally, I present the 'Change-scape' framework that I developed to link children and young people to their contexts through mechanisms that helped to negotiate power and encourage decision-makers to start to see them as agents of change. These mechanisms or strategies include creating spaces for children and adults to interact and increasing communication and dialogue between children and young people and decision-makers.

Methodology and background to the research revisiting evaluations

When initially reflecting on evaluation processes with children and young people, I decided to explore the ways in which their evidence had been valued across a range of settings and political, cultural, and institutional contexts – hence the selection of case studies of participatory evaluations previously conducted with children and young people (described below). When revisiting the evaluations, I carried out a critical inquiry in which I interviewed participants who had been involved in the previous evaluation processes.

I firstly wanted to understand what staff, managers, commissioners, and the children and young people themselves thought about the different ways in which evidence had been collected, including what they thought about the use of participatory visual methods. This was discussed within a broader analysis of what participants thought about participatory approaches more generally and the type of evidence produced from evaluation processes, and also whether it made a difference when the evidence came from children and young people as opposed to adults. This aspect of the analysis is shared in a discussion of the politics and power of evidence with regard to voice and the use of participatory visuals with children.

The second aspect of my analysis examined changes at individual, organizational, and even societal levels that were linked to the evidence that had been collected with and by children and young people. This aspect of the research followed a critical realist approach, as articulated by Sayer (2000) and Robson (2002), in that it specifically examined the context in which the evaluations were being conducted and the mechanisms and strategies that had helped to shift power dynamics, including preconceptions about what children and young people can do and how their evidence can be valued in decision-making. I used a case study approach (based on Stake 2003) so that I could reflect on each of the evaluations that I revisited and compare similarities and differences across evaluations that were conducted in different contexts.

In the following sections I discuss the politics of evidence and reflect on how children's evidence was valued by participants who had been involved in the evaluations. I then present the transformational changes that occurred as a result of children's evidence being listened to and acted upon. In a final section of this chapter, I provide more detail on the mechanisms or strategies that were successful in shifting power dynamics and leading to children's evidence being valued so that these can inform practitioners and researchers in future evaluations with and by children and young people.

The analysis in this chapter is based on details from the following three evaluations that were previously conducted with the participation of children and young people. They were selected in order to provide a range of time frames and institutional, cultural, and political contexts for the case study analysis.

One evaluation revisited was located in Nepal, in the high hill villages of Nawalparassi in the Mahabarat range of mountains. I worked with a team of Nepalese researchers to evaluate integrated community development interventions of the Himalayan Community Development Forum (HICODEF), which included components to address school-based and informal education, local environment and energy (including water pumps and tree planting), and income generation. ActionAid Nepal and their local partner HICODEF were initially interested in involving children in the evaluation due to unintended negative consequences of some of their interventions. For example, one income-generation programme to assist village women had resulted in children dropping out of school to look after goats. The evaluation took place over a decade ago (Johnson et al., 2001) and involved the co-construction of innovative participatory visual assessment methods with children and young people in villages. Particularly active were some of the members of the child clubs supported by HICODEF and local village development committees.

Another process, conducted at around the same time in the UK, was carried out to evaluate Saying Power, a Save the Children programme of youth-led programmes (Johnson and Nurick, 2001). Young people designed and led their own interventions with peers and with the support of mentors who provided logistical and moral support, and host agencies that supported projects with resources and worked in partnership with the young people. Projects addressed a range of social inclusion issues facing young people, including social isolation, living in deprived areas, drug and alcohol use, sexual and racial discrimination, and activism in local political processes. The evaluation consisted of: 1) an external element involving interviews by the evaluators of young people, mentors, service providers, and policy-makers; and 2) an internal component that involved the evaluators training young people to carry out their own participatory evaluation with peers.

The third evaluation revisited was more recent, and rather than being commissioned or managed from within the voluntary or non-governmental sector, it was part of the UK government Children's Fund in Croydon (Johnson et al., 2005). The 19 funded projects were managed by Croydon Voluntary Action, but were located in government and non-government domains. The partnership board that made decisions about funding and resource allocation was a mix of statutory and voluntary sector representatives and included parents of children from several projects. Expectations of the representatives on the partnership board meant that evaluators needed to use a mix of participatory approaches and more quantitative monitoring methods so that decision-makers had a range of quantitative and qualitative evidence on which to base decisions.

This mix of time frames and institutional, cultural, and political contexts provided a rich foundation for examining what factors had led to decision-makers valuing evidence from children and young people. Comparing perspectives within the three case study settings, and then comparing mechanisms and strategies that were successful across the cases, provided the analysis presented in the rest of this chapter. The fact that I had previously carried out the evaluations could be seen as introducing bias. However, rather than examining the extent to which evaluations had been successful, my inquiry and interviewing of former participants (adults and children) sought to examine how evidence from children and young people had been listened to and acted upon. My intimate knowledge of the settings and processes gave me access to participants in case studies, as suggested by Stake (2003), making it possible to talk honestly and openly about power dynamics and what had not been successful when it came to taking children's perspectives seriously.

The politics and power of evidence

This section provides examples that illustrate issues of power and the politics of evidence that are relevant to this book and to the domain of children and young people.

Sharing children's visuals and voices

All too often, participation – and particularly children's participation – can be seen as a 'tick box' requirement of following a more rights-based approach to evaluation. Article 12 of the UNCRC specifies that a child has the right to participate in decisions affecting their life: in practice, this has often translated into an emphasis on 'voice' in rights discourses: that is, children and young people having the space to articulate their perspectives. Indeed, in participatory research I led with children in ActionAid over two decades ago, even the title implied the importance of this aspect of child rights: *Listening to Smaller Voices* (Johnson et al., 1995). All too often this has meant that processes have sought to raise the voices of children and young people as an end in itself, rather than a means to achieve positive transformational change. Simply signing up to a rights-based approach and gathering children's perspectives does not mean that their voices are heard. In this chapter I seek to move beyond the concept of voice and to go a stage further in analysing politics and power. What I examine is how evidence from children and young people, once generated, has actually been listened to or acted upon (or not), and whether their perspectives have been regarded as valuable knowledge and have resulted in transformational changes at individual, organizational, or societal level.

Voice, however, still remains an important aspect in children and young people's participation. How can processes genuinely obtain evidence from younger participants without falling into the classic trap of assuming that adults were once children and know what girls and boys need and want? Many participatory approaches and methods offer the opportunity for children and young people to express their perspectives and views in ways that are both enjoyable and rigorous. These methods can also provide mechanisms for children and young people to communicate their perspectives to decision-makers in evaluation processes, as I discuss below. The development of participatory methods with young people is widespread, and the development of visual methods within ethical research processes is well documented in the literature around participatory appraisal and participatory learning and action (for example, Johnson, 1996; Johnson et al., 1998; Chawla and Johnson, 2004).

Across the three evaluations, participatory methods used with children and young people were co-constructed with children and staff who were working on the projects that were being evaluated. This gave flexibility to accommodate cultural context and preferences expressed by the children in terms of what methods they enjoyed and found meaningful to express different aspects of their lives and the interventions being evaluated. The methods were piloted with children and the team allowed some flexibility in the design to respond to which methods the children enjoyed using. Each evaluation also included comparative analysis across different groups of children by gender, age, ethnicity, and caste, taking into account the fact that many different aspects of children's identity intersect, thus also making individual situations and stories an important aspect of the evaluations. In the UK cases, evaluators developed a coding system to enable collective analysis of quantitative scoring and qualitative information and quotes.[1]

Revisiting evaluations required careful interrogation of what decision-makers and managers felt about the evidence received from evaluators and children and young people, and what staff on the ground and children and young people themselves felt about the approaches used. When revisiting evaluations after so many years, children and young people involved had become young adults and needed to remember the participatory processes. Figures 9.1 and 9.2 show this aspect of the revisit in Nepal, reflecting with the young participants on evidence they had previously produced in order to remember the evaluations.

Figure 9.1 Children evaluating integrated community development interventions by the Himalayan Community Development Forum

Figure 9.2 Children 10 years later as young adults reviewing their original pictures

In Nepal and the UK, children and young people involved in the evaluations said that participatory methods had made it possible to communicate their important issues to the adults who were making decisions in their villages and projects. In my words, participatory methods gave them a mechanism for communication and gave them confidence to express their perspectives:

> I think they are good to use 'cause people can just pick them up and we can show them what we wanna say. (Boy, aged 11, Croydon)

> You are left with a visual that you can use and present...as young people we also directly see what we have achieved. (Young award-holder in the Saying Power scheme in Wales)

Valuing children's knowledge in decision-making

To create conditions for children's voices to be heard, I found it was important to understand adult attitudes to children's knowledge. In the revisits, managers and commissioners of evaluations generally said that children and young people's evidence showed 'soft outcomes'. The methods helped provide experiential evidence and demonstrated the perceptions of the children and young people about the programmes. This type of evidence had informed decision-making on programming and resource allocation more often in the voluntary sector than in the statutory or government sector. However, managers and staff said that, although they had previously been encouraged to explore 'different ways of knowing' during the 1990s when rights-based approaches were popular, they were now under pressure to provide more quantitative evidence in commissioned evaluations. Managers and commissioners referred to quantitative evidence as being 'more concrete' and 'more measurable'. Across the three evaluations, managers, commissioners, and staff suggested that evidence generated by participatory processes with children and young people, especially more recently and particularly in statutory or government institutions, required backing up with quantitative monitoring statistics, or what managers referred to as 'more structured qualitative data'. Examples they gave included numbers generated by using scoring or ranking on participatory visual methods accompanied by a coding system (as in the Croydon case study), longitudinal studies, distances travelled, and the use of proxy indicators.

The perceptions of managers, commissioners, and staff relating to the politics of evidence, however, had also changed during the evaluation processes. This depended on whether they had had the time and space to interact and become involved in dialogue with evaluators and with children and young people in order to build trust and relationships, and their understanding of children's evidence. They became convinced of the value of producing this kind of evidence in this way. One manager, for example, talked about how he had been unconvinced of the value of children's evidence at the beginning of the evaluation, simply fulfilling a government requirement to consider children's views. By the end of the process, however, he appreciated the importance of understanding the 'softer' outcomes of funded projects that had been illuminated by children's evidence about their lives. Another manager from the Croydon case said that she initially thought of children's evidence produced using participatory visual methods as 'pink and fluffy'. By the end of the five-year ongoing local evaluation process, she was convinced that their participation provided different and meaningful insights and so retrained staff and modified ongoing monitoring systems to ensure that the children and young people's perspectives were captured and informed the ongoing project. Some of the managers and commissioners who had been most sceptical at the beginning of the evaluation processes recognized the transformational changes that had occurred at individual and organizational levels as a result of children and young people's participation in the evaluations (see next section).

A manager, initially unconvinced by this way of working, ended up valuing the visual evidence generated by children:

> The value of the qualitative information is also in finding the linkages between issues. When a child is excluded from school this may link up with more than just the immediate problems in the school environment ... The problem comes when links are not acknowledged and the real issues that face children and young people are not found: then they may find another value system that they can relate to, for example in local gangs or in extended family or groups. (Manager in Croydon)

Children's evidence being acted on

Participants interviewed during the revisits to the evaluation sites discussed changes caused by involving children and young people in evaluations: transformation at individual, organizational, and societal levels.

Individual-level changes that were mentioned included children and young people increasing their confidence and staff and managers changing their attitudes to children's participation and their evidence. Young participants who had been children at the time of the evaluations in two of the cases and were young adults at the time of the revisit gave examples of more self-confidence and changed behaviour. In Nepal, young men reflected on how they had started to realize how much work girls did in the household and had started to wash some of the dishes and eat with the girls, who normally would eat after the rest of the family had eaten. Girls, especially from ethnic groups considered lower status, had only gradually been able to join in with the evaluation when field workers started to learn Magar, their local language. In the Save the Children example, one of the young people running his own project gave an example of how, although he thought at first it was a waste of time, being involved in the evaluation had gradually built his confidence; he was still running his own project with peers over a decade later. He felt that the evaluation evidence of project impact had helped him to maintain project funding. In Croydon, boys aged 9 to 11 years felt that, as a result of their evidence being listened to in the evaluation, adults seemed to better understand their lives and how the after-school project they attended could help them stay in school.

Different dimensions of power as expressed by Lukes (1974) and modified by Kabeer (1994), VeneKlasen and Miller (2002) and Chambers (2006) can help us understand how power is acted out in participatory processes – and can change these processes. These dimensions include: *power over; power to; power within;* and *power with.* Shifts in power and transformational change at the individual level arose as staff, researchers, and managers started to appreciate that children and young people's knowledge could inform their understanding of their complex lives. During the revisits, I found examples of adults increasing their awareness and confidence as they realized that children's evidence provided new insights. This shift happened as decision-makers recognized that children's evidence is part of the picture: they had the *power to* value children as agents of change and to create the conditions in which children's participation rights could be claimed. As children and young people became involved and interested in participatory evaluation, they too had the *power to* claim their rights. To a certain extent, when supported by adults, children and young people saw the opportunities to influence decision-making processes through their evidence – *power with* – and realized that their evidence could make a difference – *power within.* Some staff and managers talked about self-realization as the value of children's knowledge was established during participatory evaluations; in a sense, they became aware of their *power within* and some of the contradictions that children's evidence raised in their decision-making processes.

Staff and researchers from projects interviewed in both Nepal and the UK felt that training in participatory evaluation had helped them become more sensitive to the perspectives of children and young people throughout the project cycle, from planning to implementation and developing monitoring systems. In Nepal, researchers felt that the skills required to involve children and young people were transferred to other research programmes, such as in HICODEF's involvement in the UK government-funded Safer Motherhood programme, and that they were also embedded across their community development programmes. The scale of this influence varied in the two UK cases – from young people influencing policy and practice across the organization in Save the Children during the early 2000s; to staff and children feeling ownership of the evaluation process in individual funded projects in Croydon so that children and young people's views became increasingly integrated into the delivery of services.

People I interviewed gave many examples about how specific aspects of the interventions were changed as a result of children and young people's evidence eventually being acted upon. One example from Nepal is that of children who previously had to hang off the taps, which had been built too high for them to reach. When steps were built up to the taps, an idea initiated by children during the evaluation, they could better fulfil their household responsibility for collecting water. A second example is from a young woman in Wales who felt that she and her peers could more effectively lobby the Welsh Assembly through their youth organization, Funky Dragon, with the evaluation evidence that they had jointly planned and collected. A final example is from staff in the Youth Inclusion Support Project in Croydon. They changed the way in which they worked to ensure that they listened to young people and their families so that they could be effective in early intervention and identifying priority issues for children.

Achieving transformational change at an organizational level was helped by establishing new ways of working through the creation of different structures and spaces for participatory dialogue. HICODEF has rolled out children's participation in its programming and now always builds steps up to taps in its water programme (see above). In some cases, young people were recognized as a valuable resource and included in governance structures, for example including young people on boards and in broader decision-making in Save the Children. In Croydon, changes to ways of working were more limited to specific projects, which found innovative ways to include children in evaluation: the Xpress project ran child-led evaluation and the Willow project used drama to evaluate and communicate its work with children with life-threatening illnesses and complex disabilities.

In Nepal, transformations were possible by working through existing child clubs in villages, and finding new ways to encourage interaction between children and adults with responsibility for local decision-making. This process included finding enthusiastic children and young people who could help to sustain dialogue between children and adults. In one village, the level of change was on a broader societal level as dialogue was very much kept alive by one boy who organized his peers; now, many years later, he has become a local journalist. In this village, adults still listen to what children in the club say, unlike in other villages revisited. Creating space for children requires building adult capacity and creating opportunities for them to interact and dialogue with the younger people involved in the projects. When there was more sustained interaction between adults and children, those adults with decision-making power (*power over*) started to listen, value children's evidence, and act upon it. Shifting power dynamics by creating participatory spaces for dialogue between children and adults within organizations and between people in communities across generations could be seen as a strategy to foster the dimension of *power with*.

The 'Change-scape' framework: strategies for hearing children's voices

When I scrutinized the conditions under which children and young people's evidence had been listened to and acted upon,[2] I decided that a framework might help to disentangle and clarify evaluation contexts and to share strategies to address power imbalances between young participants and adults making decisions. I call the framework a 'Change-scape' to describe the landscape of change and the mechanisms that help turn evidence of outcomes into actions. Although similar to realist evaluation (Pawson and Tilly, 1997) in that the analysis of context is prioritized and the evaluation informed by critical realism, I have also stratified context by using Burawoy's (2003) analysis of realist revisits that takes into account 'external drivers' and 'internal processes'. 'External drivers' explain context and structural issues determined by political, cultural, physical, and institutional context, and 'internal processes' refer to those aspects that vary depending on the particular evaluation process, such as the capacity and confidence of individuals involved (young and old), their commitment to change, and whether there are 'champions for children'.

In addition, when considering children and young people as agents of change in development processes, I draw on socio- and cultural-ecological theories, following the later theories of Bronfenbrenner (2005) and Tudge (2008). These theories help to connect children and young people to their context. Particularly important in the Change-scape is the fact that the proximal processes are bidirectional: young participants are not only affected by their context, they can also influence and change their context (cf. Corsaro, 1992).

Figure 9.3 shows the mechanisms that link the agency of children and young people to context by shifting power dynamics. I have identified five key mechanisms or strategies that may be useful for practitioners and researchers who are thinking of involving children and young people in evaluation. These

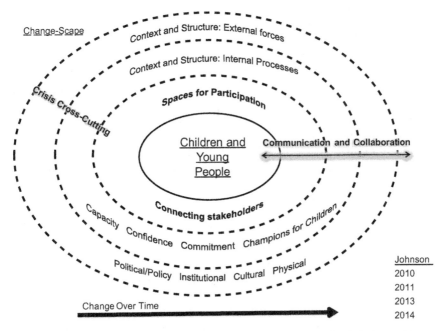

Figure 9.3 Change-scape: the landscape of change and mechanisms that help turn evidence of outcomes into actions

strategies have emerged as particularly helpful in making it more likely that evidence produced by young participants is listened to and potentially acted upon:

1. Capacity-building with evaluation participants.
2. Creating and strengthening participatory spaces.
3. Communicating and encouraging dialogue through different media.
4. Identifying champions for children.
5. Examining commitment to change as a result of children's participation.

The first mechanism relates to *capacity-building* carried out for managers, commissioners, and staff so that they become more aware of how children's knowledge can inform their decision-making. This capacity-building approach, relevant for any participatory evaluation process, can help key people appreciate the evidence generated based on a participatory approach, for example by using visual methods and giving marginalized people opportunities to share. In Nepal, staff piloted participatory visuals with girls and boys, for example, designing matrices with indicators developed by children to compare and score different interventions that had been implemented by HICODEF. They also drew project cycles – for example for designing, building, and evaluating water taps – to show at what stage and how children had been involved. In the evaluation of Save the Children's Saying Power, evaluators trained young people to lead their own evaluations with peers so that they could use their evidence to inform their projects and to influence policy and practice. Evaluators in Croydon worked over a five-year period with a partnership board of decision-makers to build their capacity to understand children's visual evidence, convincing them of the rigour of participatory approaches and the value of children's contributions.

The second mechanism relates to *creating and strengthening participatory spaces* as part of the evaluation process. This allows children and young people to interact with their peers, build confidence, and engage in dialogue with adults. An example in Nepal involved working with the village child club to provide girls and boys with the opportunity to analyse issues and work together prior to presenting their perspectives to local adults. In Saying Power, young people and mentors attended residential sessions that were an important and fun space for young people to develop skills and plan their participatory evaluations with their peers. Another example was 'networking lunches' for service providers; these were a space for them to interact informally and talk about the participatory evaluation processes with children across the 19 funded projects in Croydon. During these lunches, some structure was introduced in order to share successful strategies for involving children in a more meaningful way in ongoing programming and in monitoring and evaluation.

The third mechanism is to use *different forms of media* to communicate issues arising during and from the evaluation and to encourage dialogue between participants, therefore helping to shift perceptions and power dynamics. Children in Nepal communicated with adults using visuals that they had created with researchers, such as environmental and mobility mapping, preference ranking for their different household tasks, and diaries that showed how much time girls and boys spend working and going to school. In the Saying Power programme, appreciation of young people's evidence and roles in policy and practice grew as young people used drama, role play, quizzes, and visual evidence from their own peer evaluations to engage in dialogue with decision-makers. Children from some of the Croydon projects were also encouraged to communicate messages to the members of the partnership board using media with which they felt comfortable, such as pictures, video, and rap songs.

The fourth mechanism relates to *identifying champions for children*, either children or adults, who can motivate and inspire others to value the contributions of children and young people. I mentioned the example of the community journalist and activist from Nepal above, who, as a young boy, championed children's evidence by taking up the role of organizing his peers and encouraging them to present evidence to local adults. Mentors in Saying Power championed children's knowledge, supporting young people when they requested help on a range of issues of inclusion in running their peer projects. In Croydon, the voluntary sector manager convinced others on the partnership board to embark on participatory processes with children and allowed space and time for evaluators to set up an ongoing process to build the capacity of the adults who were receiving the evaluation evidence.

The fifth mechanism is about *examining the commitment to change* before embarking on the evaluation process, which involves understanding participants' expectations with regard to the politics of evidence and how the evaluation fits with broader theories of change. This also includes consideration of whether organizations have the flexibility to allocate resources and take decisions based on children's evidence. Insights about the commitment to change helps plan appropriate evaluation processes, including the other mechanisms that can shift power dynamics and perceptions towards children and young people's evidence. The ongoing dedication of staff – for example, Nepali researchers, Save the Children mentors, and service providers in Croydon – pays testament to their commitment on the ground to children and young people's participation. Even during times of conflict with the Maoist insurgency, Nepali researchers and HICODEF staff continued to listen to and act upon children's perspectives and incorporate their right to be heard into community development interventions. The evaluation, which included young people's evidence, generated commitment for a second phase of the Saying Power programme. In Croydon, the evaluator contract was renewed annually for five years, as it took time to convince decision-makers of the value of children's qualitative evidence, as opposed to relying solely on quantitative evidence that government-based services were expected to provide.

How these five mechanisms translate into practice is context-dependent and their development is based on analysing existing power dynamics and relationships between children and adults. Any capacity and commitment present at the beginning of an evaluation process may need fostering to overcome preconceptions about the roles of children and young people and to confront any resistance to valuing them as agents of change who are able to generate valuable evidence.

Conclusions: shifting power dynamics

In this chapter, I have presented evidence from three participatory evaluations that I revisited after a decade to show how mechanisms to shift power dynamics can help decision-makers value children and young people's evidence, and how this can result in transformational change. Organizational agreement to consider a child's right to participate in decisions affecting his or her life has unfortunately often resulted in tokenistic processes that serve to tick the boxes that require evidence that children's voices and perspectives have been gathered during evaluations. Whether this evidence is then listened to and acted upon depends on incorporating processes that build capacity, commitment, and spaces for communication and dialogue into the evaluation, and that identify champions for children. These mechanisms fit with recent discourses on participatory processes and child rights, such as encouraging a greater emphasis on listening to children, and the creation of participatory spaces and dialogue (see, for example, Percy-Smith, 2006; Lundy, 2007; Mannion, 2010). Actively engaging in dialogue between services and evaluation/research users, including children and young people and decision-makers, can help those involved to understand complexity and get services right for children (cf. Morton 2014).

Moving forward on children and young people's participation means moving beyond a token recognition of their voices to a more fundamental shift in attitudes with regard to the knowledge and evidence they provide in participatory processes that engage them in meaningful ways. Shifting local power dynamics, including between children and adults, will only happen when those making decisions about evaluations recognize that children and young people's perspectives matter. Simply gathering their voices is not enough: mechanisms that shift power and build confidence in children's knowledge need to engage adults in positions of power in dialogue. Listening to children and young people and co-constructing knowledge can inform transformational change at individual, organizational, and societal levels. A greater commitment to creating conditions in which children and young people can claim their participation rights therefore includes respecting children as agents of change and placing them at the centre of decisions that affect their lives.

References

Bartlett, S. (2001) 'Children and development assistance: the need to re-orientate priorities and programmes', *Development in Practice* 11(1): 62–72.
Bartlett, S. (2005) 'Good governance: making age part of the equation – an introduction', *Children, Youth and Environments* 15(2): 1–17.

Bronfenbrenner, U. (ed.) (2005) *On Making Human Beings Human: Bioecological Perspectives on Human Development*, Thousand Oaks CA: Sage.

Burawoy, M. (2003) 'Revisits: an outline of a theory of reflective ethnography', *American Sociological Review* 68: 645–79.

Burr, R. (2006) *Vietnam's Children in a Changing World*, New Brunswick NJ: Rutgers University Press.

Chambers, R. (2006) 'Transforming power: from zero-sum to win-win?', in R. Eyben et al. (eds) *Power: Exploring Power for Change*, pp. 99–110, IDS Bulletin, Brighton: Institute of Development Studies (IDS).

Chawla, L. and Johnson, V. (2004) 'Not for children only: lessons learnt from young people's participation', in *Participatory Learning and Action: Critical Reflections, Future Directions*, PLA Notes 50, London: International Institute of Environment and Development (IIED).

Cornwall, A. (2004) 'Spaces for transformation? reflections of power and difference in participation in development', in S. Hickey and G. Mohan (eds), *Participation: From Tyranny to Transformation? Exploring New Approaches to Participation in Development*, pp. 75–91, London: Zed Books.

Corsaro, W.A. (1992) 'Interpretive reproduction in children's peer cultures', *Social Psychology Quarterly* 55(2): 160–77.

Ennew, J. (1994) *Street and Working Children: A Guide to Planning*, Development Manual 4, London: Save the Children UK.

Harper, C., Marcus, R. and Moore, K. (2003) 'Enduring poverty and the conditions of childhood: lifecourse and intergenerational poverty transmissions', *World Development* 31(3): 535–54.

Hart, J. (2008) 'Business as usual? The global political economy of childhood poverty', Young Lives Technical Note 13, Oxford: Department of International Development, University of Oxford.

Johnson, V. (1996) 'Starting a dialogue on children's participation', PLA Notes 25: Special Issue on Children's Participation, London: International Institute of Environment and Development (IIED).

Johnson, V. (2010) 'Revisiting children and researchers in Nepal: what facilitates and hinders change in a context of conflict and the changing political economy', *Journal for International Development* 22(8): 1076–89.

Johnson, V. (2011) 'Conditions for change for children and young people's participation in evaluation: 'Change-scape', *Child Indicators Research* 4(4): 577–96.

Johnson, V. (2013) 'Changescape theory: applications in participatory practice, in participation' in J. Westwood, C. Larkins, D. Moxon, Y. Perry and N. Thomas (eds), *Citizenship and Intergenerational Relations in Children and Young People's Lives: Children and Adults in Conversation*, Basingstoke: Palgrave Pivot.

Johnson, V. and Nurick, R. (2001) *Young Voices Heard: Reflection and Review of the Saying Power Millennium Awards*, Birmingham: Save the Children <http://www.developmentfocus.org.uk/Development_Focus/Evaluation_files/youngvoicesheard.pdf>.

Johnson, V. and Nurick, R. (2003) 'Developing a coding system to analyse difference', PLA Notes 47, London: International Institute for Environment and Development (IIED).

Johnson, V., Hill, J. and Ivan-Smith, E. (1995) *Listening to Smaller Voices: Children in an Environment of Change*, London: ActionAid.

Johnson, V., Ivan-Smith, E., Gordon, G., Pridmore, P. and Scott, P. (eds) (1998) *Stepping Forward: Children and Young People's Participation in the Development Process*, London: IT Publications.

Johnson, V., Sapkota, P., Sthapit, S., Ghimire, K.P. and Mahatu, M. (2001) 'Rights through evaluation: main report', Hove: Development Focus Trust http://www.developmentfocus.org.uk/Development_Focus/Rights_files/DFID final report.pdf.

Johnson, V., with Pretzer, K., Drapkin, D. and Mendez, C. (2005) 'Croydon Children's Fund programme: full programme evaluation', Croydon: Croydon Voluntary Action.

Jones, N. and Sumner, A. (2009) 'Does mixed methods research matter to understand childhood well-being?', *Social Indicator Research* 9: 33–50.

Kabeer, N. (1994) *Reversed Realities: Gender Hierarchies in Development Thought*, London: Verso.

Kesby, M. (2005) 'Re-theorising empowerment through participation as a performance in space: beyond tyranny to transformation', *Signs: Journal of Women in Culture and Society* 30(4): 2037–65.

Lansdown, G. (2010) 'The realisation of children's participation rights: critical reflections', in B. Percy-Smith and N. Thomas (eds), *A Handbook of Children and Young People's Participation: Perspectives from Theory and Practice*, pp. 11–23, Oxford: Routledge.

Lukes, S. (1974) *Power: A Radical View*, London: Macmillan.

Lundy, L. (2007) 'Voice is not enough: conceptualising article 12 of the United Nations Convention on the Rights of the Child', *British Educational Research Journal* 33(6): 927–42.

Mannion, G. (2010) 'After participation: the socio-spatial performance of intergenerational becoming', in B. Percy-Smith and N. Thomas (eds), *A Handbook of Children and Young People's Participation: Perspectives from Theory and Practice*, pp. 330–42, Oxford: Routledge.

Morton, S. (2014) 'Creating research impact: the roles of research users in interactive research mobilization', *Evidence and Policy: A Journal of Research, Debate and Practice*, April [online], pp 1–21.

Nieuwenhuys, O. (1997) 'Spaces for the children of the urban poor: experiences with participatory action research', *Environment and Urbanisation* 9(1): 233–50.

Pattnaik, J. (2004) 'Introduction: rethinking children and childhood in South Asia', in J. Pattnaik (ed.), *Childhood in South Asia: A Critical Look at Issues, Policies and Programmes*, Charlotte NC: Information Age Publishing.

Pawson, R. and Tilley, N. (1997) *Realistic Evaluation*, London: Sage.

Percy-Smith, B. (2006) 'From consultation to social learning in community participation with young people', *Children, Youth and Environments* 16(2): 153–79 <http://www.colorado.edu.journals/cye> [accessed 12 March 2010].

Reynolds, P., Nieuwenhuys, O. and Hanson, K. (2006) 'Refractions of children's rights in development practice: a view from anthropology – introduction', *Childhood* 13: 291–302.

Robson, C. (2002) *Real World Research* (second edition), Oxford: Blackwell Publishing.

Save the Children (1995) *Towards a Children's Agenda: New Challenges for Social Development* (prepared by B. Bell, A. Chetley, M. Edwards, N. MacDonald and A. Penrose), London: Save the Children UK.

Sayer, A. (2000) *Realism and Social Science*, London: Sage.
Stake, R.E. (2003) 'Case studies', in N.K. Denzin and Y.S. Lincoln (eds), *Strategies for Qualitative Inquiry* (second edition), pp. 134–65, London: Sage.
Theis, J. (2010) 'Children as active citizens: an agenda for children's civil rights and civic engagement', in B. Percy-Smith and N. Thomas (eds), *A Handbook of Children and Young People's Participation: Perspectives from Theory and Practice*, pp. 343–55, Oxford: Routledge.
Thomas, N. (2007) 'Towards a theory of children's participation', *International Journal of Children's Rights* 16(3): 379–94.
Tisdall, K., Davis, J., Prout, A. and Hill, M. (2006) *Children, Young People and Social Inclusion: Participation for What?* Bristol: Policy Press.
Tudge, J. (2008) *The Everyday Lives of Young Children: Culture, Class and Child Rearing in Diverse Societies*, Cambridge: Cambridge University Press.
Van Beers, H., Invernizzi, A. and Milne, B. (2006) *Beyond Article 12: Essential Readings in Children's Participation*, Bangkok, Thailand: Black on White Publications, Knowing Children.
VeneKlasen, L. and Miller, V. (2002) *A New Weave of Power, People and Politics: The Action Guide for Advocacy and Citizen Participation*, Oklahoma City OK: World Neighbors.
White, S.C. and Choudhury, S.A. (2007) 'The politics of child participation in international development: the dilemma of agency', *European Journal of Development Research* 19(4): 529–50.
Williams, E. (2004) *Children's Participation and Policy Change in South Asia*, London: Save the Children and Chronic Poverty Research Centre (CHIP).

About the author

Vicky Johnson is a Principal Research Fellow in the Education Research Centre at the University of Brighton. She has been a practitioner researcher and manager in international non-governmental organizations and in the last 20 years has carried out research and training in collaboration with UN organizations, local and national government, and civil society in the UK and internationally.

Notes

1. Further details about the coding can be found in Johnson and Nurick (2003).
2. The research was informed by a critical realist perspective following Sayer (2000) and Robson (2002).

CHAPTER 10

Unwritten reports: lessons from an NGO collective[1]

Bernward Causemann and Eberhard Gohl

Abstract

This chapter concerns the difficulties of a reporting process for an NGO collective that worked across three continents. It describes how German civil society dealt with the results agenda, culminating in a project to develop participatory monitoring tools, how the project experimented with different forms of reporting, and why many partners did not provide written feedback. The reasons for these reporting difficulties (regarding utility, capacity, culture, and power) are explored. Alternatives to written reporting developed during the process are examined, and how such alternatives might be applied more widely is discussed.

Keywords: reports, participatory monitoring, German NGOs, results, learning

Much in the politics of evidence has to do with the requirement of written documentation and reporting. In practice, however, effective reporting can prove difficult, and may even become a barrier to satisfactory partnerships between NGO funders and their Southern counterparts. The process of reporting is often stressful and overly time-consuming for those who do it, and often does not contain the information required by report recipients. Further, how it is done may not encourage practitioners' reflection, many of whom do not judge reports to be beneficial for learning (Guijt, 2010).

This case study describes difficulties with the reporting process faced by an NGO collective working across three continents to develop and test participatory impact monitoring methods. The challenge of reporting this work to funding partners became a second, underlying theme for the collective and is the subject of the present chapter. The project experimented with different forms of reporting, and learned much about why partners did not provide feedback in a written form. The chapter explores the reasons for these difficulties and analyses the ensuing changes in cooperation between partners in the collective. We discuss learning from this experience, examine alternatives to reporting developed during the process, and discuss how these might be applied more widely.

The chapter's authors were project managers of the collective with programmatic and conceptual responsibility. We focus on issues of reporting in the Southern part of the collective as we consider this a neglected area of

http://dx.doi.org/10.3362/9781780448855.010

reflection. We only include insights into reporting within the Northern part of the collective when of direct relevance.[2]

The results agenda in German civil society

The 1990s saw an ongoing discussion between NGOs in Germany on how to manage and evaluate development projects (Misereor/AGKED, 1992; Dolzer et al., 1998), with consultations conducted with Southern partner organizations. VENRO, the umbrella body of German development NGOs, initiated a series of training workshops on how to improve monitoring and evaluation (M&E), and published what they saw to be core messages for NGOs in a book that emphasized the learning function of M&E (Gohl, 2003). Overall, the 1990s was a period of increased reflection by German organizations on the effects of their development interventions, partly driven by the introduction by Gesellschaft für technische Zusammenarbeit (GTZ) of ZOPP (Zielorientierte Projektplanung), or goal-oriented planning, which was similar to logframe thinking (GTZ, 1987).

Meanwhile, by the early 2000s NGOs were coming under increasing external pressure from funders. The German government introduced successive rounds of ever tighter regulations for ever more structured and detailed plans and reports based on a loose logic of results-based management; requirements from the European Union were even tighter and more restrictive. The German government particularly emphasized the need for NGOs and for government itself to have more information about the effects of development work. The notion of 'results chains' was introduced. NGOs themselves, many of which were financed through public donations or by foundation funds, also believed that the public had a results-based mindset, expecting greater accountability for predefined outcomes and impacts achieved with its money.

Over time, leadership as well as audit departments of many NGOs adopted this new 'accountability agenda'. NGO partners were increasingly required to report in standardized formats and against set objectives. While GTZ (now Gesellschaft für internationale Zusammenarbeit or GIZ) has long moved away from ZOPP,[3] and even from results chains, logical frameworks have become a common planning tool among German NGOs, with many demanding that partner organizations use them in project proposals – a development that we consider part of the increasing process of bureaucratization experienced by German NGOs during the 2000s.

Many NGOs in Germany felt that their space was shrinking, or even endangered, and that they needed to develop their own solutions for better accountability before the government imposed more restrictive requirements (see Chapter 5). NGOs were convinced that monitoring and reporting should focus on mutual learning and be designed in a way that benefited NGOs in the global South ('Southern NGOs') as much as they should serve for accountability to funders. At this stage, they came across the concept of Participatory Impact Monitoring (PIM) (Gohl and Germann, 1996). Thus NGO-IDEAs was born – NGO-Impact on Development, Empowerment and Actions.

NGO-IDEAs and the emerging issue of reporting

NGO-IDEAs as an NGO collective was a joint project between 14 NGOs in Germany (in future, 'German NGOs') and more than 30 of their partners in the global South ('Southern NGOs') in South Asia, the Philippines, and East Africa. The aim was to encourage self-monitoring by community groups whose activities were supported by Southern NGOs with funding from German NGOs. Southern NGOs were to develop and test participatory tools for impact-oriented management with the community groups they worked with to a point where these could be adopted by other organizations. Community groups set their own objectives and monitor their achievements themselves. Part of the information they generate feeds into the NGO-based monitoring systems. But some of the group objectives might not be linked to the NGO project at all. NGO-IDEAs, like PIM, facilitated autonomous but linked monitoring systems for groups and NGOs. The concept has been elaborated elsewhere (Brenner, 2011; Causemann et al., 2011, 2012c, 2013a, 2013b; Gohl et al., 2011a, 2011b; Rithaa, 2011). The NGO-IDEAs project described in this chapter ran from 2008 until 2011. It was a follow-up to a previous project in 2004–07 in South India with a similar number of participants. Both projects were 49 per cent funded by BMZ, the German Ministry for Development Cooperation, from its budget line for German civil society organizations.

German NGOs initiated the project, providing financial, capacity-building, and advocacy support for NGO development partners in the Global South. German NGOs, in cooperation with VENRO, invited a select number of their partner organizations to participate in the venture. All Southern NGOs were funded at least partly by their German NGO partners. Figure 10.1 shows NGO-IDEAs' structural set-up. Players involved in the venture included the following:

- The steering committee of eight members, representing the German NGOs and VENRO. Even though Southern NGOs were not represented on the steering committee, they had considerable influence through their practice and in regional workshops.
- Two project managers based in Germany, responsible to the steering committee and authors of this chapter. Our role was to manage the programme, supervise the regional coordinators, keep the network active, advise and mentor German and Southern NGOs, develop the tools together with the Southern NGOs and the regional coordinators, and finally publish project results We were contracted by one of the 14 German NGOs that had the administrative and financial responsibility for the programme.[4]
- Regional coordinators who came from and were based in the three regions in Africa and Asia. Their role was to advise and mentor Southern NGOs, conduct workshops, channel information, and contribute to the publications.
- The participating NGOs in Germany (funding the venture and selecting Southern partners) and the Global South (project implementation). All partners were involved in dialogue and in meetings that occurred at least twice a year for each region.

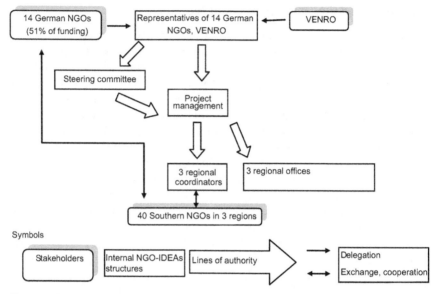

Figure 10.1 The structure of NGO-IDEAs

Over time, the issue of internal reporting on the progress of tool development came to have an unanticipated importance. The collective had relied on information flow through meetings and personal contact. There were no regular written reports. Southern NGOs had their regular communication with funding partners when they could also have written about their NGO-IDEAs experience. At this stage, we as project managers did not see reports that Southern NGOs sent to their funding partners.

In reality, field practitioners provided little written information about their experiences with the new tools, or, if they did, not the information felt necessary by German NGOs to develop the tools jointly. Often, heads of Southern NGOs who were responsible for overall reporting to their funding partners in Germany did not include much information about the NGO-IDEAs process. Either the persons writing the report lacked the information from the field staff required to satisfy funding partners, or they simply did not include such information in their reports. Some leaders of Southern NGOs told us that they experienced similar problems to those of funding organizations: their staff sent in reports that were of limited practical use. Nevertheless, we could see that staff spent a lot of time writing them. NGO managers were overwhelmed with paper that did not give them what they needed, but found it difficult to rely exclusively on verbal reports. In our view, specialized staff could have summarized these verbal reports, but there seemed to be a strong conviction that every staff member needed to write their own report, which in practice was often mostly about activities and had little analytical content.

In 2009, six months after Southern NGOs began developing and adapting the impact assessment tools, variations of satisfaction with the project's information flow became apparent at a workshop for Southern NGOs and their German partners. Staff of the Southern NGOs liked the project as they had benefited from the experience gained in trialling the tools. There had been ample opportunity to meet and share lessons with other Southern NGOs at NGO-IDEAs partner workshops. However, German NGO staff participated in these workshops at most once a year and felt that they had not been well informed about the experiences and the lessons their partners had learned during testing. Also, members of the steering committee considered that the level of information provided was insufficient to fulfil their role of guiding the process and ensuring accountability to all German NGOs, and to the donor government.

With hindsight, we conclude that one reason why partner organizations did not report in writing was because they were at an early testing stage. As such, they felt that they had not yet achieved results they themselves considered satisfactory; while they were prepared to talk about their experiences, they were not prepared to write them down. At the time, however, and following this workshop, we agreed to test ways to improve the information flow between all partners, but particularly from Southern NGOs to German NGOs.

As project managers working with the three regional coordinators in the global South, we had access to much of the required information. However, we were not free to share it as this would have eroded both loyalty and trust. We wanted to build a relationship with Southern partners in which they felt comfortable sharing their difficulties and challenges and discussing where they were prepared to invest, without the fear that we might report this to funders or even to their local managers. We wanted partners to see us as supportive. Similarly, regional coordinators needed to be able to report challenges and failures to us without the fear that this information would be passed on and then possibly damage the status or funding prospects of the organization. Given that loyalty and trust were crucial aspects of our cooperation, we felt that we could report to the steering committee and German NGOs only on overall project developments, and needed to be very careful about sharing information on specific partners. Also, having no power to make partners *do* anything, we could only coach and encourage.

German NGOs' dissatisfaction, and the demand for more information, put us project managers in a difficult situation. On the one hand, we considered it a reasonable expectation that Southern NGOs should write about their experiences as part of their regular reporting to the funding German NGOs, as the involvement of Southern NGOs was based on individual agreements with their German partner NGOs. As already noted, in reality, however, this rarely happened and was part of a broader issue in the relationships between funding and implementing NGOs with respect to poor written reporting and analysis of outcomes and impacts. Indeed, this had been a major reason why German NGOs started NGO-IDEAs in the first place.

German NGOs had started NGO-IDEAs on the assumption that Southern NGOs were not reporting about the effects of their work because they did not know enough about these effects, or because they often knew individual examples but did not have an overall picture. Part of the project's purpose was therefore that partners would become better able to plan and assess their effectiveness. It was assumed that improved reports would automatically flow from that.

Clearly, information needed to be shared with participating Southern NGOs, within and across the regions, as well as with German NGOs. Further, NGO-IDEAs was designed to produce a published output at the end of the project. Thus, after this workshop, German NGOs and the steering committee felt that verbal feedback was insufficient, and requested additional written reports from Southern NGOs so that all partners could be better informed about progress, as we now discuss.

Taking on the challenge: written reports

NGO-IDEAs developed a structure of reporting that respected NGO ownership of their reports. It was agreed that all partners would report quarterly on their activities and learning. In the spirit of mutual accountability, all 50 NGOs, including the German NGOs, would report to each other, starting with the German NGOs reporting on the effects of their learning from NGO-IDEAs within their own organizations. It was hoped that such 'reverse' reporting would show that this was a joint project, not one where one partner was more accountable to the other. It tried to take away the notion of Southern partners reporting only to their funding partners. We hoped that this openness about the challenges faced by German NGOs would encourage partners in the global South to report on their challenges. This system of reporting is shown in Figure 10.2.

A simple reporting template was introduced that contained the following questions:

- In terms of activities, what worked well and what did not work so well?
- What was achieved?
- Which challenges were encountered?
- Are there any suggestions for further action?
- Were there any other relevant experiences?

The format deliberately used questions, avoided technocratic terminology and made it clear that these reports were for sharing among all partners, but were not to be made public.

Reports were completed by individual organizations and then compiled regionally. In some cases, partners were also given the time and space to report during regional workshops. When reporting verbally or by PowerPoint, a workshop participant filled relevant information into the template, thus relieving people of the burden of producing reports at their desks. Where information was lacking, we asked for it during the workshop – this

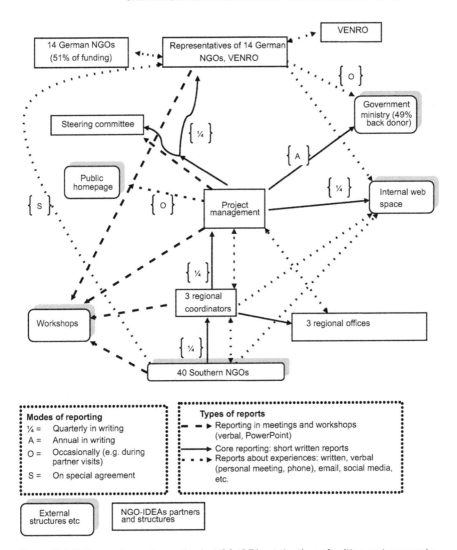

Figure 10.2 Written and verbal reporting in NGO-IDEAs at the time of written partner reports

way of reporting was highly appreciated by participants. Talking was so much easier to them than writing. Where the reports could not be constructed as part of the workshop process, regional coordinators had an arduous task in securing reports from Southern NGOs. Some partner organizations would send in their written reports quickly, but others had to be reminded repeatedly. Regional coordinators felt that they needed to send in complete reports and spent a lot of time in the follow-up and in compiling these reports into one document, although we repeatedly sent out the message to coordinators that we would prefer an incomplete but timely regional report.

We observed interesting differences between regions. At the outset, in two out of the three regions the number of participating organizations was small enough to allow for entirely verbal communication. Phoning, Skype and SMS played an important role. The introduction of written reporting therefore meant a lot of extra work for these regional coordinators. On the other hand, in the third region (where half the partners were located), direct contact with the coordinator was less frequent and from the start each partner sent regular written reports to their coordinator – but did not share them with any other Southern or Northern NGO staff. Reports often contained hints of difficulties and lessons learned. However, when it was suggested that the reports be shared with all partners, these suddenly became shorter, were more activity focused, and were much less enlightening. The reports contained hardly any difficulties or successes anymore. We concluded that Southern NGO staff were more prepared to share potentially sensitive information with one person they trusted than with a wider group.

Meanwhile, the quarterly mutual reporting by all partners introduced in late 2009 left the regional coordinators and us, the project managers, with less time for accompanying Southern NGOs or for conceptual work. We had not budgeted for this process. Making this new reporting system function risked absorbing a substantial amount of our time that we needed to support Southern NGOs to develop and test the impact assessment tools. It also changed relationships. Regional coordinators, who worked in a generally supportive mode with Southern NGOs, needed to spend more time pushing for information and compiling regional reports instead of focusing on creating value for the partner. Thus, the exchange between coordinators and partners became more extractive. On the other hand, the level of satisfaction of German NGO staff increased: they appeared to have more trust in us because the reports indicated that something meaningful was happening on the ground. Nevertheless, the new arrangements did not contribute to furthering mutual learning or conceptual development, nor did the reports produce practical hints on how to improve impact assessment, the main purpose of the project.

In addition to the quarterly reporting there was also regional coordinators' quarterly reporting to the project managers on their own activities and the situation of the NGOs in their region. This was partly done through standardized formats and partly by Skype. We observed that the verbal exchanges contained more relevant information than the written reports.

After about a year, the steering committee decided to discontinue partners' quarterly reports. This decision was probably facilitated by the German NGOs suggesting a change in the reporting period to a longer interval for all. They had realized the amount of work involved, and some of them possibly did not want to reveal that they had done little in terms of the project. Thereafter, we never heard of anyone complaining that they missed the quarterly reports.

Other approaches to written reporting tried out earlier had also failed. During the first project phase, we had provided a step-by-step guide to Southern

NGOs about how to analyse the findings from their application of the impact assessment tools, and how to briefly summarize these findings at each step. However, partners found it difficult to undertake such analysis, and this model was abandoned. Another attempt to improve reporting had been through a workshop at which German NGO staff defined two generic options for reporting with the help of guiding questions. This kind of reporting, however, overlapped to a great extent with existing mandatory reporting requirements to the funding agencies, so this attempt was subsequently deemed to be of no practical use to Southern NGO partners. All these experiences provided more insight into the question of why many Southern NGOs found it such a challenge to report in a way that would satisfy their donors

What makes it so difficult?

The NGO-IDEAs experience provided an opportunity to better understand why Southern NGOs found it so difficult to report according to the standards set by their donors. It allows us to make a number of observations about the usefulness of these reports, Southern NGOs' capacity and ability, cultural gaps, issues of power and fear of consequences. The following analysis is additionally informed by other experiences with NGOs outside the NGO-IDEAs project, and many of our observations apply likewise to other Southern NGOs that we have worked with in other processes.

Utility

Southern NGO staff told us that they had to write reports that they did not see being used. This was not directly related to the NGO-IDEAs project. Many staff members indicated that this was their general experience with project reports. We observed that many did not have a good understanding of what such reports could be used for and therefore could not write them in a way that would prove useful to whoever received the report, whether the recipient was in their own organizations or in the donor organizations. Many also perceived that the reports did not help to promote or improve their organizations' work, including with the poor or disadvantaged. Furthermore, many told us that funding partners hardly ever responded to reports beyond confirming receipt. This is perhaps due to the fact that German NGO staff members, as they themselves frequently told us, were already burdened with paperwork and lacked the time for real engagement.

From all this, we concluded that many organizations considered monitoring and reporting primarily as a tool for upward accountability. Reflection happened elsewhere in other processes not linked to reporting. In our view, merging reflection and reporting could increase both efficiency and the quality of the reports, but this approach was not considered by many organizations. Neither leadership nor staff emphasized using the time spent on reporting efficiently by making it useful for other purposes as well.

Capacity and ability

We realized that Southern NGO staff often had little understanding of the realities and needs of German NGOs. They had hardly ever travelled to Germany to meet NGO staff there, and thus did not have an opportunity to experience the realities of a donor desk officer. Southern NGO staff's experience of donor desk officers was that they did not explain what they did, how they thought, or why they had certain requirements. Donor desk officers told us that they lacked the time to provide such explanations, but we did not see any recognition of the need, nor any appreciation of how hard it was for Southern NGOs to put donor requirements in context. It was therefore difficult for Southern NGO staff to gear written reports to donor needs.

From our observations, we do not believe that the issue was rooted in a lack of capacity to observe or analyse. Possibly in some cases, analysis was not encouraged or people lacked external exposure that would have allowed comparative analysis. Nevertheless, we observed that, when they applied the NGO-IDEAs tools, many organizations were quite able to pick up and expand on the analysis that group members had developed, with many Southern NGOs changing their strategies and sending in adapted project proposals for the next funding phase.[5] The poor quality of reports could not be substantially explained by a lack of analytical capacity.

A cultural gap

We came to realize that much of the information that donors felt was missing in written reports in fact was contained implicitly within them. Donors are generally interested in the 'upstream' benefits and effects of 'activities' or 'outputs'. In the NGO-IDEAs project, for example, when groups applied the adapted tools it was hoped their members would understand their situation better, develop more initiative, and show practical solidarity with poorer members of the groups.[6] These benefits were becoming apparent to Southern NGO staff and could be clearly linked to activities. By reporting on activities or outputs, many of these upstream changes were implicitly contained in the reports – groups that meet are often groups that benefit. But the benefits were not explicitly described in writing, although staff members could name such changes verbally quite well. Either staff assumed that this was equally obvious to others, and therefore did not need to be written down, or they were unable to articulate this knowledge clearly until they were asked to explain verbally.

Staff from Southern NGOs were often required to write their reports in a second or third language. Many had a good understanding of the situation on the ground, but found it difficult to articulate this in written form. They lacked confidence and skill in the reporting language.

Meaningful communication for many staff members of the Southern NGOs was often through face-to-face exchange, short messages on SMS or email, or the use of PowerPoint at meetings; this is consistent with observations we made in other engagements in the global South. This style of communication, while helpful to build personal relationships, can make it difficult to write long reports. When discussing this with Southern NGO staff members, they often referred to experiences at school, where writing was not used for communication but rather as part of an assessment process. As a result, people became afraid to make mistakes. Staff members said that in schools and universities, good marks were often given for recounting learned facts, not for reflection and analysis. Innovation and flexibility were often not rewarded. This could also be a reason why report writing is such a burden to many people, and why it is also somewhat feared.

We also observed that Southern NGO staff tended either to give general descriptions, or to report only numbers that they could substantiate precisely. They were often unwilling to speculate, generalize, or estimate. Only occasionally were single experiences, or cases, exaggerated or generalized. If a particular impact was reported, we could not be sure that it occurred widely, although this was often the case; therefore much went under-reported. One of the authors of this chapter had a similar experience during a sector evaluation of Misereor's support to 260 local NGOs in rural development and food security on three continents. While the field studies found many spill-over effects and an online survey confirmed that these were widespread, the NGOs' written reports contained hardly any information about these (Causemann et al., 2012a; 2012b). Why is this under-reporting so common? We had the impression that many people did not want to be accused of making false claims; that is, they wanted to be absolutely sure that what they wrote was correct.

All these cultural forms of communication show a cultural gap that needs to be understood.

Power and fear of consequences

Sometimes we observed that organizations in the collective were hesitant to report externally on challenges, failures, and negative effects, and thus cautious about what they wrote. Reports often lacked significant content for fear of repercussions from donors, such as having to respond to difficult correspondence or even worrying about cuts in funding. For example, a staff member of one organization expressed happiness that he could report by speaking in a meeting, rather than writing a report with the same content, because he had to get permission from his director for anything written, a requirement that he considered cumbersome. The same was true for internal reporting within some Southern NGOs, which was made difficult by power relationships and hierarchies within organizations.

A year after the end of the project, we again realized this. In order to promote the NGO-IDEAs concept, we requested Southern and German NGOs to provide us with project reports that contained information from the

NGO-IDEAs tools. We knew they existed. In a 'raffle for reports' we offered a prize for those who made such reports available publicly. We received only one. There seems to be a high level of sensitivity towards project reports.

The experience with reporting confirms that the funding partners have a level of power (or are perceived to have such power) that causes people in the global South to be very careful when writing reports. Openness about this unequal power relationship was often lacking between German NGOs and Southern NGOs. Even though NGO-IDEAs was a joint project, German NGOs were in many ways still experienced as 'donors' by Southern NGOs. This exacerbated unequal power relations between partners, and caused Southern NGO partners to tread carefully. One observation hints at this: in practice, some German NGO staff behaved more as detached observers of the process rather than demonstrating active engagement. However, this behaviour and power relations were never discussed during the duration of the project: nobody brought these issues up.

The workshop experiment described in Box 10.1, like the general experience in NGO-IDEAs, led us to conclude that staff of Southern NGOs found it easier to gather and present information and insights if they did not have to produce a complete text. Reporting in manageable 'bite-sized' chunks and explaining processes verbally appeared easier than developing a consistent and analytical line of thought on paper. But a consistent text is what formal reporting often requires. Our experience with NGO-IDEAs' intranet, where participants could post information that was accessible only to partners but hardly ever did so, confirmed that participants preferred to engage directly rather than post something to a partly unknown audience without face-to-face engagement. This is not surprising: we could see that many people working in NGOs decide to pursue that career because they want to work with people, not paper. If their interests and skills lay in writing, many would pursue other careers that often

---

Box 10.1 What if there were no reports? An experiment

In order to explore the reasons why people had difficulties with reporting in writing, we conducted an exercise at a workshop in the Philippines in 2010. We told participants the imaginary story that the German auditor general had investigated reporting by development partners, found that it demanded a lot of time while generating little benefit, and thus was highly inefficient. The responsible ministry had therefore decided to abolish written reports, with the exception of financial and activity reports for accountability. But the ministry was still interested in knowing what the effects of its funding were. It would only fund organizations if they suggested alternative ways to inform the ministry of the effects of their work. We asked what they would suggest as alternatives. Participants suggested methods including audio-visual conferences, video documentaries, PowerPoint presentations and displays in face-to-face meetings, testimonials from target groups, visits to the field by ministry staff, postings on social media, and the creation of a website. From this, we concluded that participants preferred talking, direct engagement, and the use of visuals and short texts accompanied by explanation, rather than ordinary written reports. Nobody had suggested publishing booklets, journal articles, or books that involves much writing. Nor did anyone suggest photographs. Taking photographs of groups, Participatory Rural Appraisal visuals, or physical changes, and audio or video recording of verbal explanations either by project staff or community members would be other alternatives.

pay better. The increased bureaucratization is troublesome to many Southern NGO and German NGO staff because it is not their preferred way of working.

Alternative approaches to reporting

While writing reports was difficult for many of the Southern NGOs, NGO-IDEAs had numerous positive experiences with alternative forms of feedback and information flow that we had applied from the beginning; throughout the project, Southern and German NGOs communicated on many levels. Workshops, phone calls, personal meetings, and field visits were the main means of sharing information. PowerPoint presentations at workshops became a major medium of reporting. Here, the processes of implementing the tools were documented and made available to all involved. While the documentation of a workshop could take a lot of time before it was ready, a short one-page report on a workshop distributed to all partners immediately afterwards was always appreciated. It was actually read, unlike the lengthy workshop reports, and those German NGOs that had been unable to attend felt that they were informed. We replaced the unsuccessful attempts to introduce quarterly reports from all partners with quarterly reports that *we* wrote for German NGOs; these were based on our interaction with regional coordinators, partners, and staff on all levels, and on a synthesis of the information from the workshops, meetings, and even the web space. Perhaps this was one reason why German partners did not miss the quarterly reports from Southern NGOs when these were discontinued. Nevertheless, despite the relative success of our own quarterly reports, the most relevant transfer of information between the German NGOs and us happened at their half-yearly workshops. It was the spoken word that reached people.

What have we learned about alternative processes and forms of reporting? NGO-IDEAs has not abolished written reports as part of its internal procedures. However, it has reduced the number of reports required, and minimized the time spent on writing them by integrating reflection into the reporting process. This has also improved the usefulness of the reporting process for everybody involved and gave us – the project managers – more time to produce better written products. From that experience, some general lessons can be drawn. Flexibility of reporting is important, and so are regular interactions and trust in personal relationships. Simpler, more tailored, and more informal reporting requirements will be helpful and fear of failure should be overcome. This may require change not just in processes but in the organizational culture.

Some of the alternative forms of reporting that NGO-IDEAs used could also be used more widely. Here are some possibilities.

Talk to people and write it up yourself

Talking to NGO staff for reporting could involve interviews using a specific format and structure, or in and around meetings. This method may be particularly useful for M&E specialists to conduct. Those who have the skill and aptitude for writing, write the reports with greater efficiency, reflection and the depth of information gleaned can be enhanced simultaneously, if the interaction is more of an exchange and not just extractive. In NGO-IDEAs, the regional coordinators gathered much of the required information this way. In the project's practical advisory work, the regional coordinators frequently made phone calls to find out and discuss progress and challenges. This allowed them to stay on top of developments, with information subsequently shared with us project managers to become part of the quarterly reports that we produced.

Reduce the time spent writing and reading and do more reporting at face-to-face meetings

Drawing on our experience in facilitation, meetings became interactive, with as little time as possible spent on lectures and presentations. Exchanging experiences and seeking feedback were the major forms of exchange and reporting on project progress. Having short PowerPoint presentations helped focus the meeting (even if the presentations were sometimes rather long), and often led to helpful discussions. Such face-to-face meetings with staff can be a good solution for Southern NGO managers if further reporting is unnecessary. If a written report is required, a manager or even the head of the NGO engages staff in discussions, while an M&E specialist takes part and produces a report.[7]

Box 10.2 Merging reports and funding proposals in one meeting

While we searched for solutions to our reporting problems, we came across a programme that approached reporting in a particular variant of talking to people and writing it up oneself. Arbeitsgemeinschaft der Evangelischen Jugend (AEJ), a federation of Protestant youth organizations in Germany, runs an international youth exchange programme funded by the German Federal Ministry for Youth. Local affiliates of AEJ organize youth exchange programmes on an annual basis. Previously, affiliates had to write reports about each exchange, and send in an application for next year's exchange. AEJ gained little insight from these reports because they lacked content and because many local affiliates just recycled last year's reports. With consent from the ministry, they therefore changed the reporting routine: AEJ now organizes regional meetings during which applicants are engaged in individual interviews where they verbally present last year's exchange and next year's programme. All they have to bring in written form is the planned itinerary for next year. A staff member of AEJ or its affiliates conducts the interview, and another staff member enters the required information into a spreadsheet. Both AEJ and the ministry have a say in what information has to be collected. Often, an intensive discussion develops on how to conduct the exchange. For applicants, it is a mentoring process as well as a process of reporting and applying for funds. One applicant stated that he decided to apply for this programme because of the value of the interview, rather than applying for another one where his institution could get more money for the exchange but would not benefit from such a mentoring meeting. For AEJ, the procedure generates much better information about the exchange programme and about the local affiliates than they had previously obtained. Instead of each applicant writing a report, only one written report is provided to the ministry by AEJ, with more relevant content. Financial reporting is separate from this procedure (Causemann, 2014).

Use simple surveys

Towards the end of the project phase, NGO-IDEAs had a survey conducted by an internal programme assistant (Rithaa, 2011) on Southern NGOs' implementation of the tools developed. This survey quickly provided good-quality, standardized information on which tools had been applied by how many groups, and what benefits had been generated for Southern NGOs and for community groups. The regional coordinators who had a good understanding of the situation, having worked with partners for three years, completed part of the survey. Any missing information could be quickly gathered through email and by phone in a targeted manner. Thus, project managers came to the figure of about 15,000 households involved in activities initiated through NGO-IDEAs. Written reports alone could never have provided that information. The various processes of gathering this data made it more robust. The fact that the survey was conducted only once probably helped achieve a good return. We considered targeted surveys an efficient and easy means of gathering meaningful facts and figures that we could then integrate into our analysis for the final report.

Use standardized open questions

One option we used several times was a limited set of standardized questions that could be discussed by mail, phone, or even in individual and group meetings where people report verbally. We never used more than five fairly broad questions and therefore allowed different experiences to be captured, like in the simple reporting template described above. We avoided questions that 'boxed' participants into narrow interpretations of their work.

None of the suggestions above are one-size-fits-all solutions. In all contexts, appropriate ways for reporting on effectiveness need to be found. Written reports are often necessary, but there may be better ways of getting them done.

Conclusion

In this chapter, we have analysed our experience with internal reporting in an NGO collective working on three continents. As reflective practitioners, we have tried to understand the dynamics in Southern NGOs when they were required to report in writing. We have done this as consultants from Germany.

Box 10.3 Blogging by youth, not reporting by staff

The Big Lottery Fund in the United Kingdom supported the Neighbourhood Challenge Fund[8] to work with various community groups. Its monitoring approach in a youth programme was by means of blogs rather than reports. Youth participants had to blog regularly on their experiences in the programme. In turn, staff needed not write reports. The experience showed that blogs were often more detailed and more critical than typical reports in other programmes.[9]

While we made every effort to understand the views of partners we worked with, this is still a Northern perspective. We consider it important that the views of reflective practitioners in the global South on the difficulties with reporting are also heard.

Much of the politics of evidence centres on written documentation and reporting. Reports are often delayed and sometimes are not written at all – that is, they remain 'unwritten' – and many people prefer ways of reporting that do not require writing down their experiences: that is, they choose forms of 'unwritten' reporting. NGO staff currently spend a considerable amount of time on reporting, often to the detriment of their other responsibilities. Written reports do not deliver what they are meant to. As they are often not read, in a way reports can be considered idols: it is enough to have them, and their usefulness is not questioned. Furthermore, current reporting requirements often make people feel inadequate and send the message that external and upward accountability is more valued than reflection. All this reinforces an imbalance in power relations between partners. Reports are like other tools of the results agenda that perpetuate Northern dominance and make Southern organizations look weaker than they are.

Did NGO-IDEAs help to create more space for NGOs in a time of increasing bureaucratization? We contributed to a policy paper from VENRO that emphasized empowerment, learning, and steering as well as accountability as key purposes of impact monitoring (VENRO, 2010). However, the project has probably not significantly changed the increasing reporting demands that German NGOs pass on to their partners. On the other hand, participating Southern NGOs have integrated results from participatory monitoring into their reports. This was possible because much German NGO funding allows a lot of flexibility in changing indicators during a project phase, even within a logical framework (Gohl et al., 2011b: 32–3; Causemann et al., 2011: 11–26). The number of Southern NGOs using the NGO-IDEAs tools is increasing, but there is an interesting tension between a deeply participatory concept that NGOs apply in NGO-IDEAs, giving power to grass roots, and an approach to reporting that does not take into consideration the preferences of those who are required to report.

The NGO-IDEAs experience shows that, in order to overcome these difficulties and build on the competencies and preferences of NGO staff, reporting needs to be conducted in a way that promotes reflection.[10] This requires good facilitators and coaches so that the experience of participants is really explored, while at the same time their capacities, their motivation, and their ability to overcome challenges are strengthened. This increases the value of information provided and potentially creates new knowledge – and, in the end, it generates better reports too. With such an approach, written reports become a spin-off, and not the central purpose of the exercise. Reporting systems, like monitoring systems, need to be autonomous but linked. The current focus on reporting, and the way it is practised, leads to the paradoxical situation where those who demand reports get less of what they want than if they were to put more emphasis on the added value of exchange and learning for those involved. Changing this situation will probably require donors to deal more respectfully with the reality of those who receive their funds, and those organizations receiving funds will need to express their needs and cultural preferences more assertively.

References

Brenner, V. (2011) 'No development without self-effectiveness', minutes of the NGO-IDEAs International Symposium, Bonn <http://www.ngo-ideas. net/publications> [accessed 17 December 2014].Causemann, B. (2014) 'Berichten ohne Berichte, Tübingen' [online] <http://www.causemann.org/ aej> [accessed 17 December 2014].

Causemann, B. and Gohl, E. (2013b) 'Tools for measuring change: self-assessment by communities', PLA Notes 66, London: International Institute for Environment and Development (IIED), pp. 113–22 <http://pubs.iied. org/G03665.html> [accessed 17 December 2014].

Causemann, B., Gohl, E., Cottina, G., Limotlimot, G. and Rajathi, C. (2011) '"How do they do it?" – civil society monitoring self-effectiveness: an NGO-IDEAs documentation of field experience' on NGO-IDEAs [website] <http:// www.ngo-ideas.net/field_experiences> [accessed 17 December 2014].

Causemann, B., Currle, J., Horneber, G., Huber, A. and Pres, A. (2012a) *Rural Development Sector Evaluation With Special Focus on Food Security*, Stuttgart/ Aachen: FAKT/Misereor <http://www.misereor.org/en/cooperation-and-service/evaluation.html> [accessed 17 December 2014].

Causemann, B., Currle, J., Horneber, G., Huber, A. and Pres, A. (2012b) *Evaluierung des Förderbereichs Ländliche Entwicklung. Schwerpunkt Ernährungssicherheit. Synthesebericht*, Stuttgart/Aachen: FAKT/Misereor <http://www.misereor. de/fileadmin/redaktion/Misereor_Bericht_FBEvaluierung_LE_2011.pdf> [accessed 17 December 2014].

Causemann, B., Brenner, V., Cottina, G., Gohl, E., Limotlimot, G. and Rajathi, C. (2012c) *'Tiny Tools': Measuring Change in Communities and Groups. An Overview*, Bensheim: NGO-IDEAs <http://www.ngo-ideas.net/tiny_tools> [accessed 17 December 2014].

Causemann, B., Gohl, E., Rajathi, C., Susairaj, A., Tantry, G. and Tantry, S. (2013a) 'Community groups monitoring impact with participatory statistics in India: reflections from an international NGO collective', in J. Holland (ed.) *Who Counts? The Power of Participatory Statistics*, pp: 113–23, Rugby: Practical Action Publishing.

Dolzer, H. et al. (1998) *Wirkungen und Nebenwirkungen. Ein Beitrag von Misereor zur Diskussion über Wirkungsverständnis und Wirkungserfassung in der Entwicklungszusammenarbeit*, Aachen: Misereor.

Gohl, E. (2003 [German ed. 2000]) *Checking and Learning. Impact Monitoring and Evaluation – A Practical Guide*, Bonn: VENRO <http://impact-plus.de/ index.php/publikationen> [accessed 17 December 2014].

Gohl, E. and Germann, D. (1996) *Participatory Impact Monitoring*, Eschborn: GTZ/ Vieweg <http://www.fakt-consult.de/content/publications-participatory-impact-monitoring-pim> [accessed 17 December 2014].

Gohl, E., Causemann, B. and Brenner, V. (2011a) *Monitoring Self-Effectiveness: A Manual to Strengthen Outcome and Impact Oriented Project Management*, Bonn: VENRO/NGO-IDEAs <http://www.ngo-ideas.net/monitoring_self_effectiveness> [accessed 17 December 2014].

Gohl, E., Causemann, B., Cottina, G., Limotlimot, G., Rajathi, C. and Rithaa, M. (2011b) *NGO-IDEAs Impact Toolbox: Participatory Monitoring of Outcome and Impact*, Bonn: VENRO/NGO-IDEAs <http://www.ngo-ideas.net/impact_toolbox> [accessed 17 December 2014].

GTZ (1987) *Management der Projektdurchführung im Partnerland. Ein Leitfaden*, Eschborn: Gesellschaft für technische Zusammenarbeit (GTZ).

GTZ (2008) *Capacity Works: The Management Model for Sustainable Development*, Eschborn: Gesellschaft für technische Zusammenarbeit (GTZ).

Guijt, I. (2010) 'Accountability and learning', in J. Ubels, N.-A. Acquaye-Baddoo and A. Fowler (eds), *Capacity Development in Practice*, pp. 277–91, London: Earthscan.

Misereor/AGKED (1992) *Evaluierung in der kirchlichen Entwicklungsarbeit. Ein Arbeitsbuch*, Aachen/Stuttgart: Misereor/AGKED.

Rithaa, M. (2011) *Review of NGO-IDEAs: Survey of Partners from the Global South. Opinions on Utility, Effects and Suggestions for Follow-up*, Bensheim: NGO-IDEAs <http://www.ngo-ideas.net/publications> [accessed 17 December 2014].

VENRO (2010) *Quality before Proof: Policy Paper on Impact Monitoring*, Bonn: VENRO <http://venro.org/uploads/tx_igpublikationen/Positionspapier_QualityBeforeProof_v03.pdf> [accessed 19 December 2014].

About the authors

Bernward Causemann is a sociologist and works as a development consultant and coach with 15 years experience in evaluation, monitoring, and impact assessment for government and non-government agencies and international networks. He is an administrator of the NGO-IDEAs yahoogroup.

Eberhard Gohl is a consultant sociologist and economist specializing in outcome/impact monitoring and evaluation. He has extensive experience in using qualitative research methods such as surveys with participatory approaches and the set-up of grass-roots-based systems for monitoring self-effectiveness.

Notes

1. The authors would like to thank Fiona Deppeler, Rosalind Eyben, Chris Roche and the anonymous reviewer for valuable feedback on earlier drafts of this chapter. We would also like to express our appreciation to the members of the steering committee, the regional coordinators, and NGO-IDEAs' partner organizations for all the insights that we gained.

2. We are limited in disclosing discussions and experiences with reporting in the German section of the NGO collective as we had been contracted by German NGOs.

3. GTZ has adopted another management model, Capacity Works (GTZ, 2008). This model is widely implemented within GIZ now, but is not as well known and has not been adopted by other actors as widely as ZOPP has.

4. The financial and administrative functions were performed by one of the German NGOs that also contracted the project managers on behalf of all German NGOs. Likewise, the regional coordinators were contracted by one Southern NGO per region, which also conducted administration and finance. In this chapter, the difference between the conceptual work of the project managers and the administrative function is not further elaborated.

5. Capacity to analyse quantitative data, on the other hand, was limited (Causemann et al., 2011: 77–82).

6. For a description of benefits from applying NGO-IDEAs' participatory impact assessment tools, see Causemann et al. (2011). Our observations suggest that these benefits occurred particularly when NGO staff encouraged groups to actually reflect on findings. Many staff members initially applied the tools mechanically and later improved their application, adopting a reflective use.

7. We are aware of one small project fund in Latin America that works in this way and gives participants time at the workshop to write up their verbal reports in a few sentences. At NGO-IDEAs, workshop time was so precious that we did not want to spend it on such writing. Instead, we documented what people said on flipcharts, took photographs, and documented these post-workshop.

8. See <http://www.nesta.org.uk/project/neighbourhood-challenge>.

9. Personal information from Sarah Mistry.

10. For some ideas on how to organize meaningful internal and external reporting, combined with reflection and reconciling participatory impact assessments with logical frameworks, see Gohl and Germann (1996: Booklet 2) and Gohl et al. (2011a, 2011b).

CHAPTER 11

Playing the rules of the game and other strategies

Irene Guijt

Abstract

This concluding chapter takes a forward-looking perspective. It identifies how those seeking to create or maintain space for transformational development can use the results and evidence agenda to better advantage, while minimizing problematic consequences. Given that the politics around results and evidence are inevitable, what strategies can lead to a practice of generating and using results and evidence that supports transformational development?

Keywords: Big Push Forward, change strategies, results, practices, evidence

The argument that power and 'politics' matter and have implications for how we think about and pursue development is now increasingly accepted by academics and practitioners, at least at a rhetorical level, and arguably by some policy-makers (cf. Booth and Unsworth, 2014; Carothers and De Gramont, 2013). This book adds to the body of evidence that the politics surrounding results and evidence also matter.

No one disputes the need to seek evidence and understand results. Everyone wants to see clear signs of less poverty, less inequity, less conflict, and more sustainability, and to understand what has made this possible. Development organizations increasingly seek to understand better what works for who and why – or why not. However, disputes arise around the power dynamics that determine who decides what gets measured, how, and why. The cases in this book bear witness to the experiences of development practitioners who have felt frustrated by the results and evidence protocols and practices that have constrained their ability to pursue transformational development. Such development seeks to change power relations and structures that create and reproduce inequality, injustice, and the non-fulfilment of human rights.

And yet some of these cases also recognize that the results agenda can, in theory, open up opportunities for people-centred accountability processes (Chapter 5) or promote useful debates about value for money (VFM) (Chapter 4), or shed light on power dynamics using theory of change approaches (Chapter 6). Some participants at the Big Push Forward (BPF) conference shared the view that greater emphasis on evidence has led

http://dx.doi.org/10.3362/9781780448855.011

to more intelligent consumption of data and use of protocols, methods, and approaches, more knowledgeably challenging those that are imposed inappropriately (Guijt, 2013). This book is an advocate of such critical use of artefacts – the protocols and methods used to assess and report on changes, to select interventions, and to evaluate impact (Chapter 2).

In this chapter, I draw on the cases in this book and on the discussions at the BPF conference to examine two questions:

1. What results and evidence practices support transformational development?
2. What strategies can help achieve or work towards such practices?

Results and evidence practices that support transformational development

The authors in this book are not alone in making the observation that results and evidence practices can advance but also hinder or harm social change efforts:

> significant aspects of current practice undermine iterative, local problem-solving. These include a focus on achieving direct, short-term results based on project designs that over-specify inputs and expected outputs; pressure to spend that makes relationships with partners aid-centric and allows insufficient time for iterative learning.

Thus conclude Booth and Unsworth (2014: v) after analysing seven successful cases in which donor-funded programmes appear to have contributed to change in complex and difficult settings. But Booth and Unsworth also noted factors that they found facilitated success:

> In all the cases, flexible funding arrangements facilitated iterative approaches to project design and implementation, and aid was deployed strategically as funding requirements emerged. Donors made long-term commitments, with good continuity of staffing. (ibid.)

Understanding such enabling factors can help organizations take stock of their own ways of working and assess whether their results and evidence practices are 'benign environments', to use a Booth and Unsworth phrase, or are hindering the thinking and working politically that is so critical for transformational development.

The authors in this book suggest their own set of six success factors, which, although hardly surprising, merit restating: results and evidence practices must be feasible, useful, and rigorous, be accompanied by autonomy and fairness, generate time and space for reflection on evidence of results, and be agile.

Evidence-seeking processes, sense-making, and reporting must be *feasible*, which is much easier said than done, as the chapters in this book illustrate. Vähämäki's account of cycle after cycle of results initiatives that staff and funding recipients simply did not know how to implement points to the need for a realistic design, one that might benefit from consultation with those expected to implement changes. The prevalent reporting formats in the

German development sector impeded reflection and led Causemann and Gohl to experiment, with limited success, with formats and processes of reporting that matched the more oral cultures of German-funded partner organizations. Oxfam Australia struggled, Roche reflects, to communicate existing good ideas about being accountable in ways other than those dictated by contracts:

> I now wonder if a greater focus on the exposure to, as well as analysis and communication of, the *practice* of transformative development and associated forms of accountability might be a more strategic way of... supporting those who are attempting to promote this agenda. [emphasis in the original]

Particularly detrimental is the wasted effort invested in collecting incorrect and unused results data, as highlighted by Whitty, van Es and Guijt, and Vähämäki. Using protocols and methods to generate *non-trivial and timely information* is clearly more likely to be sustained than using them to trap people into narrow interpretations of their own work (Chapter 10). Johnson's case highlights the dawning appreciation of initially sceptical programme managers when confronted with so-called 'soft' data. Having a personal experience of the information shared by children and young people – information that had been missing – led one programme manager to build it into ongoing monitoring (Chapter 9). Abu Alghaib fought for inclusion of results data that field realities had shown mattered (Chapter 7). However, those results did not fit within the donor's results framework; locally relevant results data were not accepted by the donor.

Rigour, which leads to trustworthy data, is critical for the kind of results and evidence practice advocated in this book. While much of the rigour debate in development and evaluation circles focuses on whether data is rigorous, the chapters focus on seeking more rigorous thought processes and method selection and use, as well as more rigour about including those voices that matter. Oxfam Australia sought to be more rigorous about being socially accountable, for example by linking reporting to reflection processes at different levels (including with the board), clarifying complaint and redress mechanisms for communities and partners, and opening diverse channels for staff and senior management to question and debate (Chapter 5). Hivos' monitoring and evaluation (M&E) unit worked for several years to develop a theory of change approach, one that was rooted in reflexive practice and recognized the diversity of Hivos initiatives (Chapter 6). In Chapter 4, Shutt describes how Christian Aid's rigorous engagement with VFM led it to define VFM in terms of its social justice values, and to require 'deep understandings of context'. Johnson details how being rigorous about 'the right to be heard' requires, for example, serious action around safe spaces for children and the time and willingness to listen (Chapter 9). These examples show how the term 'rigour' needs to be reclaimed beyond narrow method-bound definitions to encompass better inclusion of less powerful voices and improved analysis of power, politics, assumptions, and resource allocation.

Autonomy and fairness are qualities highlighted by Abu Alghaib, whose account of donor-driven non-negotiable requirements led to a project feeling alien to staff in the community-based organization (CBO), who, as a result, were no longer motivated to implement the initiative. She reflects on the importance of freedom to formulate goals and measure success within the realities, interpretative lenses, and paradigms of her own organization, run by and for citizens. Results or evidence requirements unable to do justice to the messy reality of progressive social change also stand out in Vähämäki's account of decades of results reforms in Sida (Chapter 8). Staff objected, rebelling and refusing to comply with what they considered to be unfair ratings systems based on submitted data: 'How was Sida going to validate what was a poor- or a well-performing project? And what would happen to projects rated 'bad'?' Van Es and Guijt (Chapter 6) mention the apprehension of Hivos partners when first confronted with the need to provide pre-selected indicators, even if on their own terms. Was this the beginning of constrained room to manoeuvre that would impinge on their agility to respond? Roche's account of Oxfam Australia summarizes the tension for the agency as it sought to be more responsive to feedback (Chapter 5):

> field staff ... expressed the view that the head office did not always achieve the right balance between managing risk and allowing field offices to respond to the specific factors they faced in their own countries.

A fifth feature evident in the cases is the need for results and evidence approaches that *strongly emphasize reflection* about what is known and what needs further inquiry. Asking people to transcribe results data rather than making sense of that data is increasingly seen as an entrenched problem of bureaucratizing aid: 'insufficient time remains for making wise assessments' (Chapter 8). The complex nature of development points to the need to support problem-driven iterative adaption (Andrews et al., 2012). Some approaches – such as theories of change, systematic reviews, and VFM – potentially invite this type of reflection by those with direct experiences and those with the power to decide strategies and resource allocation.

Finally, results and evidence practices need to be *agile*. Progressive social change may have clear goals. However, intermediate outcomes less easily quantifiable and multiple pathways of change are likely, enmeshed in ways that blur explanatory variables (cf. Carothers and De Gramont, 2013). Agility is therefore needed to respond to both diversity and unexpected opportunities. This brings me to more positive options for riding the waves of the results agenda.

Strategies for making the most of the results and evidence agenda

If these are the conditions needed for results protocols and practices to keep open or expand operational space for social change, then the authors also suggest strategies for how these conditions can be created. As outlined in Chapter 1, six 'power practices' are common in international development that push towards a results and evidence agenda that does not serve the best interests of those working towards societal transformations. Creating distance between field realities and those making resource and strategy decisions, keeping people so busy they have no time to think, and referring to the value-free nature of methods and approaches are some of those practices. In response, people have resisted, complied, or simply walked away.

We created the BPF as an explicit strategy of resistance – a space for discussion, debate, and the exploration of appropriate approaches for assessing transformational developments. In those discussions, the diversity of cases, contexts, and relationships brought to the surface an equally wide diversity of strategies. Participants had sometimes successfully adopted diametrically opposed strategies to tackle similar issues in different organizational settings. Thus, there is no consensus about guarantees for success, simply options that may be worth exploring.

Strategy 1: Develop political astuteness and personal agency

'The politically alert are subtly playing the game to change the rules' (Chapter 2). But how can 'political alertness' be cultivated if one is not, by nature, a keen observer of opportunities or a skilled negotiator? And how do you know which rules to follow and which rules to challenge?

Personal agency, individual personal power to decide how to respond to the way in which artefacts are framed and imposed, was the most mentioned strategy by participants at the BPF conference. People's ability to use the results and evidence agendas positively makes them activists within their organizations, and with funding agencies and partner organizations. Shutt (Chapter 4) looks at how 'politically astute individuals' in intermediary agencies influence their organizations to act with authority in order to avoid passing on ambiguous reporting requirements to small NGOs that are still struggling to develop functioning M&E systems. Vähämäki (Chapter 8) refers to letters to senior staff initiated by individuals, agency-wide calls to colleagues to ignore results protocols, and staff who resigned. When it came to partner organizations, van Es and her colleagues at Hivos chose to be a buffer between back donor demands for particular frameworks and partner organizations. As an M&E unit, they exercised their power to not simply pass on results demands.

Those who constitute what Eyben (Chapter 2) calls 'the squeezed middle' are potentially effective brokers because their position provides them with more than one perspective. Initially, Causemann and Gohl felt powerless – unable to persuade the Southern partners of German NGOs to submit quarterly reports, an example of how partners resisted what was perceived as an imposition. They eventually brokered an agreement for alternative reporting methods that the Southern partners found more useful and less burdensome. This case illustrates a creative response that emerged out of resistance to pressure that was viewed as unhelpful. On the other hand, organizations and individuals may see advantages in that same pressure when it provides the opportunity to reform organizational practices judged as slack or casual – brokering change in another direction

(Chapter 3). Shutt's account (Chapter 4) of how British development NGOs responded to the Department for International Development's (DFID's) VfM requirements reveals a variety of perspectives and responses to such pressure. It helped reformist staff secure greater transparency of financial decision-making, enabling serious consideration of how an organization understood and promoted efficiency and effectiveness, while 'small but sophisticated' organizations have been able to use VfM approaches to demonstrate how they deliver greater value than multilateral behemoths.

At the BPF conference, one participant's case study showed how an aid agency's country office in Tanzania was able to effectively protect a project from head office interference. It was 'able to answer parliamentary questions from results evidence without further reference to us' and organized visits from senior headquarters staff so that they came away impressed and did not create VFM difficulties. 'Where delegates don't behave as emissaries but act as authorities able to exercise discretion, then central plans can be sabotaged' (Clegg et al., 2006: 177).

Organizational response depends on personal political savvy. The BPF conference organizers are personally familiar with a case of two similar organizations receiving an identical grant from a common donor and with identical results and reporting requirements, and yet they responded very differently. The leadership in the first organization initiated a conversation with the donor's senior staff, securing greater flexibility in programme design, results specifications, and reporting protocols, and largely managing to protect their staff from negative effects of the donor's requirements. Leadership in the second organization made sweeping changes to organizational ways of working, creating a hierarchical and oppressive culture. In this case, the grant was perceived as having an overall negative effect on staff morale.

Personal agency extends to using knowledge about methods and approaches, which some have gained as a consequence of the results agenda, to question interpretations. For example, so-called objective evidence can be contested on the grounds of its subjective interpretation. Researchers looking at social accountability have reinterpreted the evidence from randomized control trials and concluded that 'field experiments tend to study bounded, tactical interventions that rely on optimistic assumptions' (Fox, 2014: 5). The reinterpretation has led to new propositions, beyond the power of information alone, that focus on 'sandwich strategies through which "voice" and "teeth" can become mutually empowering' (ibid.).

However, shifting the results agenda only through personal agency has limits, as evident from Vähämäki's story of ongoing reforms as resistance slowly evaporated. Hence the need for other strategies.

Strategy 2: Understand dynamic political context and use organizational values

As people have been confronted with the demands of the results and evidence agenda, they have become smarter about the comparative strengths and weaknesses of protocols and procedures, methods and approaches. The chapters in this book offer insights that can also make development practitioners smarter about the political context from which and in which the artefacts generate and spread. Eyben recounts her sense of powerlessness when asked to produce a number to show that her work contributed to 'policy influence'. The feeling that she had no choice about inventing spurious numbers 'provoked [her] investigation of these artefacts as "techniques of power"' (Chapter 2). Eyben complied in that instance, not knowing where or how to challenge the required number. However, it did contribute to the genesis of the BPF as part of her inquiry into the politics surrounding such results requests.

Shutt's account of British NGOs dealing with the need to show 'value for money' illustrates a donor, DFID, that was frank about the challenges it was experiencing (Chapter 4). One NGO in particular, Christian Aid, seized the political opportunity of this public uncertainty to interpret the VfM concept in line with its organizational values. The example Shutt gives illustrates how this results concept was not 'inherently empowering or disempowering'. Her experiences show the potential benefits of being astute about how to use the VFM concept: to encourage more transparency, increase accountability, or even in 'highlighting the significant costs associated with servicing DFID's never-ending demands for evidence of results and proper compliance!'

Many of the chapters were written as personal journeys of discovery relating to the political processes surrounding artefacts and their use. Vähämäki's PhD – of which Chapter 8 in this book is one part –focuses on the dynamic history of management technologies to understand whether the intended reform goals can help achieve actual results for transformative development. Her account of Sida illustrates the paradoxical mix of dynamism with ever new initiatives and stagnation with the 'new' being mere tweaking of the old. She discusses the political journey of push and pull around results initiatives and how, in the end, new forces at play have led to less contestation about results protocols now than ever before within Sida. In Chapter 7, Abu Alghaib describes how she came to realize how strongly the donor's theory of change diverged from that of her community-supported organization. She knew exactly who had the power but requests to change requirements fell on deaf ears.

For van Es and myself (Chapter 6), writing the chapter on Hivos entailed a slow unravelling and clarification of the context-specific tensions within which approaches to strategic accountability evolved. Our story illustrates how the political context within Hivos, in relation to the back donor and the dominant discourse in the development sector, influenced the potential and limits of our personal agency. We discussed multiple possible explanations for the persistent challenges of how we could promote critical reflection. With hindsight, we identified some effective strategies upon which we inadvertently stumbled, such as using external legitimacy for the concept of theory of change to help leverage internal interest.

In her account about understanding the influence of children and young people's voices, Johnson (Chapter 9) concludes that participatory evaluation is not enough. It requires political clarity about how to leverage the principle of children's right to be heard to make decision-makers actually listen. She also encourages an assessment of the organizational commitment to act on evidence when designing an appropriate participatory evaluation.

The politics of results are as much about internal politics as external pressures. In his conclusions about why progress towards social accountability was never truly 'mission critical' for Oxfam Australia, Roche highlights ongoing internal disagreements about the role of planning, performance management, and accountability that were never resolved:

> Some – especially those responsible for marketing and fundraising, as well as human resources and finances – consistently articulated the need for uniform, standardized approaches across the agency...it was hard if not impossible to see why others, and in particular programme staff, could not and should not all be held to account in the same way.

At the BPF conference, some participants used their understanding of organizational values that formally drive priorities as a strategy to make certain protocols or methods work for them. Understanding how organizational values are – or are not – reflected in proposed or imposed protocols or practices allows one to question anomalies and to discuss possible adverse effects of certain artefacts. Knowing an organization's readiness to align protocols or methods with its values and what room to manoeuvre exists can help to reframe artefacts, or to guide (more) intelligent adoption of aspects of the results and evidence agenda.

Strategy 3: Identify and work with what is positive about the results and evidence agenda

Artefacts can be made one's own by complying and playing by the rules or by playing the game to change the rules. Collectively, the case studies reveal great variation in organizational responses to the demands of the results and evidence agenda. Some of this variance is down to individuals, as both Shutt (Chapter 4) and Johnson (Chapter 9) make clear. Endogenous organizational dynamics and quality of leadership undoubtedly also contribute to the manner in which the agency responds and 'whether they stand up for what they believe' (Chapter 3), or instead pass on and emphasize back donor requirements. These responses have meant that the same protocols and methods have helped as much as hindered.

To make the results agenda contribute to progressive social change, the authors in this book suggest that people need to be aware of the potential – and limits – of their personal power (Strategy 1) and develop a political understanding of how the results agenda is playing out in their organization, sector, and relationships (Strategy 2). Shutt's VFM tales of woe and triumph are a prime example of the 'make it your own' strategy. As well as developing a definition of VFM shaped by key organizational principles (Strategy 2 above), one NGO she mentions is also committed to ensuring that its implementation aligns with the organization's social justice agenda.

Creative compliance was mentioned at the 2013 conference in two ways: adapting the rules of the game and playing the game, in order to create space in which other, more useful results work is possible. One participant coined the phrase 'organizational t'ai chi': the practice of engaging with a problematic protocol or method and redirecting it towards making a positive contribution. One strategy suggested repeatedly was 'use the label' but focus the content on critical reflection rather than on the formulaic. Van Es and Guijt (Chapter 6) illustrate this well with the Hivos theory of change process. Hivos colleagues became interested, creating an opportunity for van Es in which she had to keep theory of change approaches focused on politically critical strategy assessment, and not on 'tick the box' exercises. A focus on what and how artefacts can be changed might mean accepting some ideas and requirements, even if they are ineffective. At the conference, those involved in organizational change in particular noted that, to make the most of 'tipping points for opportunity', they had to work in nuanced ways that did not, at least initially, threaten staff who were critical about decisions to roll out protocols or methods.

Strategy 4: Facilitate front-line staff to speak for themselves

Keeping the voices of front-line staff far from decision-makers is an example of what Clegg refers to as the division of labour 'in complex chains of power that enable elites [heads of development agencies in our case] to maintain a distance from power's effects' (Clegg et al., 2006: 178). Conscious agency ('power to') is required for senior managers to make themselves available to listen and be prepared to act upon what they hear from those at the coalface. Equally, it requires concerted action and courage from front-line workers to circumvent the hierarchy and go straight to the top.

One of the cases presented at the conference illustrates this strategy for shifting results and evidence practice. A multi-country international NGO (INGO) project funded by a bilateral agency had a diverse set of partner organizations supporting sex workers, with a key 'success indicator' required by the back donor being 'people withdrawing from sex work'. Two years after the project started, the INGO brought together the nine partner organizations. Despite their extreme diversity, all the partners agreed that attempting to stop people working as sex workers was senseless. What was needed was to support them in making their work safer. Representatives from the organizations asked for and got an audience with the minister whose agency was funding the work. They told him that they would continue to be part of this project only if he agreed to allow each partner to choose its own locally appropriate success indicators. Faced with this unanimity of multiple groups speaking directly from their experience, the minister agreed to a revision of the results framework for the organizations involved. We infer that an insistence by those working on the front line to represent their concerns collectively and directly with the politicians responsible led to a heightened understanding of the realities and complexities of the context by the minister.

Facilitating front-line staff and partners to speak for themselves is one of the power strategies discussed by Johnson (Chapter 9). In her cases about the influence of children's voices in evaluations, bringing senior managers together with children bridged the gap that had hitherto kept this evidence from decision-makers' ears. This, in turn, had required capacity-building efforts to make senior managers more aware of how children's knowledge can inform their decision-making, making them willing to listen. Causemann and Gohl (Chapter 10) provide details about how the Southern partners 'often had little understanding of the realities and needs of German NGOs', making it difficult for them to focus written reports to meet donor needs. The face-to-face exchanges valued by Southern partners clashed with the required reports written at a distance from where decisions were made. One of their concluding suggestions concerns facilitating reflections by front-line staff as part of reporting protocols, to generate more in-depth and useful information about results.

Strategy 5: Create spaces for learning and influence

The BPF started as an attempt to create space for learning and potentially for influence. We initially focused on creating an online space for sharing ideas and resources and for debating issues. The conference was a facilitated face-to-face space.

Getting to and holding these BPF spaces was not easy. At the outset, while clear about the frustration and confusion with the results agenda, we as conveners were less clear about our objectives. Our initial ideas were more ambitious than funding, time, and energy permitted. Our objectives became more realistic: 'creating the space for discussion, debate, and the exploration of appropriate approaches for assessing transformative development processes'. We then struggled to find an effective structure. Our first experiment with thematic clusters and cluster leaders proved too time-consuming and had stimulated little external interest. In the meantime, our blogs had started generating conversations that gave the topic more space and gave the BPF forum some street credibility. We were asked to comment on documents, to attend meetings, and to come and hold events (see Chapter 1).

We, as conveners, navigated our own differences, with some more positive and less strident about the consequences of the results agenda and others more vocal on perverse effects. This variation perhaps related to a personal appetite for risk – early versus later in one's career – as well as differences in personal style and position, consultant versus NGO staff member versus academic, and so on. Our own varying stances echoed Whitty's survey observations about a range of views from development practitioners (Chapter 3).

We learned how to use different mechanisms to develop our own understanding of the issues involved: the BPF website blogs became a mechanism for learning and clarifying our own doubts, for example about how to define transformational development and the potential to use humour as strategy (see Chapter 5; Roche, 2011). The BPF became better known, making it possible to undertake a crowdsourcing effort which gave us much food for thought (see Chapter 3). Our continual strategizing over the course of 12 months about how to make the BPF space more effective led us to organizing a conference, the Politics of Evidence (Guijt, 2013).

Planning the conference greatly helped give BPF an achievable focus, helping us as conveners to concentrate our limited time and energy. A conference was more amenable for funding, although this remained difficult due to the contested nature of the topic. The conference itself was a face-to-face opportunity to gather and share concrete examples of how politics were imbued in results and evidence practices. It was a practical space in which learning occurred and strategies were articulated, shared, and created. It was also a political space for learning and strategizing, as evident from the conference evaluation: many participants reported leaving with greater clarity on key terms such as 'the results agenda' and the politics and drivers of the agenda, and with actionable ideas for their own spheres of influence. In the end, we were surprised how the BPF was referred to by some as the 'go-to' place on the topic of results agenda consequences (see, for example, Valters, 2014; Wallace and Porter, 2013).

The authors of several chapters share their own versions of 'space', each with its own purpose. Van Es felt the need for a space within Hivos to facilitate sharing and strategizing about how best to further theory of change approaches for critical reflection (Chapter 6). She created an action learning group of colleagues and trusted consultants, who organized regular collaborations, joint articles, collective training experiences, and systematic assessments that helped them stay realistic and hopeful. Johnson noted that the regular convening of children and young people helped to build the confidence they needed for engaging with adults in evaluations – spaces for learning how to engage effectively with the protocol of an evaluation. Causemann and Gohl (Chapter 10) talk about the importance of workshop spaces that facilitate learning while creatively meeting reporting requirements. Even certain methods or protocols can be 'spaces of influence', such as a theory of change audit (Chapter 6) or a mid-term review. When combined with clarity about organizational principles and values, they can foster discussions on how to do justice to assessments of progressive social change.

Some spaces remain wishful thinking – as with Roche (Chapter 5), who was keen to pursue a sector-wide process to experiment with more radical reforms to accountability processes (see Strategy 6). Arguably, growing funding pressure and narrower results thinking have created more unfavourable circumstances for this kind of collaborative space among NGOs in Australia. Perhaps the lesson here is to strategize carefully about which spaces need fostering most – in this case the wider NGO space or the learning space within Oxfam.

Strategy 6: Advocate for collective action

So, what happens when personal agency hits a wall and when the spaces for learning do not lead to action, as several case studies illustrate? Strength in numbers is an age-old political strategy for taking action. The successful lobbying by nine organizations working with sex workers (Strategy 4) illustrates the power of collective action. It combines enabling front-line staff (Strategy 4) to convene in a space in which to learn and seek influence (Strategy 5), and to take action collectively for themselves (this strategy).

Several authors touch on this strategy for challenging unhelpful protocols or methods, and for proposing alternatives that align better with social change. Collective action can also take place within an organization; for example, the case of Sida demonstrates several instances of staff objecting publicly in large numbers to what they experienced as unhelpful and harmful management technologies (Chapter 8).

Collective action can also be across organizations. Shutt (Chapter 4) describes how British NGOs used their collective organization, BOND, to respond critically and constructively to the new VfM requirements of DFID. In Chapter 10, Causemann and Gohl speak about the merits of collectively reflecting on and generating reporting alternatives with a larger group of German NGOs and the organizations they fund. Oxfam Australia tried to convene other Australian NGOs to take action around social accountability (Chapter 5), and this is the strategy that Abu Alghaib will now promote among disabled people's organizations (Chapter 7). The BPF itself offered a platform across organizations that helped make the topic of the politics of results and evidence discussable.

But collective action, while an obvious option to overcome the limits of personal influence, is discussed by the authors in this book in more hesitating terms than other strategies. Although the non-compliance call by senior managers with the Sida internal rating system won that particular battle, the war could arguably be said to have been lost. New results frameworks and protocols continue to be proposed, tested, and institutionalized with limited reflection on past failures. Roche speaks of another unsuccessful effort to rally Australian NGOs to seek radical reforms to accountability processes (Chapter 5). Despite disappointment that the conveners of the BPF were ending the initiative in December 2013, no one has taken up the baton.

So why is this seemingly obvious, tried and tested strategy so little mentioned? And why does it seem to be limited in its effect? Some spaces, such as that of the BPF, may be temporary, despite the ongoing needs and urgency of dealing with the results agenda. The chapters hint at other possible reasons. Not all development practitioners can sustain the appetite for dissent in the face of problematic protocols and methods (Chapter 8). Some organizations do not have the financial luxury to opt out of accepting funding from donors with problematic results demands (Chapters 6 and 7). The competitive nature of the sector, for example between NGOs all receiving funding from the same back donor (Chapters 5 and 6), may inhibit concerted efforts to change that donor's results and evidence demands.

It could also be that collective action strategies are not based on robust enough political analysis or driven by assumptions of 'quick wins' for more appropriate results and evidence practices. Perhaps the theories of change that drive so much short-term donor-funded governance programmes also apply to this agenda. If organizations in the development sector are trapped in the same system, albeit with different levels of power over resource allocation and strategic direction, then is it right to target the organization higher up in the decision hierarchy? Many other non-development sector agencies are subject to similar trends, including universities, schools, and hospitals (see Chapter 5). Perhaps certain collective action strategies have been too confrontational or not confrontational enough. Perhaps individuals are too strapped for time (one of Clegg's power practices) to invest in non-obligatory efforts.

The collective action problem might require different, more imaginative coalitions in order to address systemic perversions of the results agenda. But it might also require more self-awareness about how agencies contribute to the deeper drivers of the politics of results and evidence (also see Chapter 2). Research has suggested that NGOs have been part of the problem due to their transactional approach to raising funds (Darnton and Kirk, 2011) and with the uncritical doubling of aid budgets in Australia and the UK (NAO, 2015).

Strategy 7: Take advantage of emerging opportunities

The diversity of cases discussed in this book suggests the potential for exploiting the heterogeneity and dynamism of the sector, or countervailing trends (Chapter 2), taking advantage of what is on offer or being mainstreamed. Take the current surge of effort on working and thinking politically (cf. Faustino and Booth, 2014; Booth and Unsworth, 2014; Halloran, 2014, Andrews, 2014; Marquette, 2014). Some may grumble about this recent discovery by mainstream academics, policy-makers, and organizations of a perspective long held by feminists and other development activists and practitioners. But recognition by the likes of Harvard, DFID, the Australian Department of Foreign Affairs and Trade, renowned economists, and even the World Bank to some extent arguably give it greater credence. Such attention, of course, needs to be treated with some caution, as along with opportunities for more political ways of working come the risks of co-optation (cf. Baur and Schmitz, 2011).

Which opportunities offer potential for bolstering results and evidence practices that help progressive social change? Another discourse that has led to organizational experiments, besides that of thinking and working politically, relates to the complexity of development, with its many ramifications for management and evaluative practices (Mowles, 2010; Mowles et al., 2008; Stern et al., 2012; Roche and Kelly, 2012; Forss et al., 2011; Ramalingam, 2013). USAID is undertaking action learning on complexity-aware monitoring that ticks all the boxes of emergent, non-linear, locally grounded, and reflective use of promising results practices (Britt, 2013). Growing understanding of the limitations of evidence based on randomized control trials (RCT) has made RCT debates less polarized, and mixed methods presentations are no longer a sideshow at evaluation conferences. DFID's civil society department, Comic

Relief, and the Lottery Fund meet regularly to share ideas on how to reduce or even avoid perverse effects of the results agenda. The International Fund for Agricultural Development and the Bill and Melinda Gates Foundation are funding piloting of a participatory approach to impact assessment and learning explicitly to gain insights into how people experience poverty and change in their own terms.

However, plenty of problematic experiences exist. The 'glass half full' list can be matched with an equally long list of detrimental results and evidence practices that are prioritized, funded, and implemented (cf. Chapters 2, 7, and 8). While the tone of global RCT debates might feel less polarized in development conferences, has this translated to more methodological freedom for research programmes or for CSOs to choose relevant approaches that do justice to transformational efforts? Have organizational bureaucracies adjusted their data entry to give development practitioners such as Abu Alghaib the freedom she needs to define and share results in her terms and at a pace dictated by her realities – and those of the people she works with – rather than by contractual milestones? Perhaps the trends are contradictory, with new threats and opportunities emerging as a result. Is it possible to identify worthwhile opportunities while being aware of potential pitfalls?

One such opportunity is the latest development fascination with prioritizing citizen or client 'feedback' (Guijt, 2014). Where development efforts have become about procedures and protocols rather than relationships, feedback can re-humanize efforts by saying 'your voice matters'. From an effectiveness perspective, feedback makes sense to develop a better product or service. And feedback can empower. It is, however, interpreted in many different ways – feedback by people of their experience of 'aid', feedback to people to help them make informed choices and advocate for change, or feedback as a dialogue loop involving the collection, acknowledgement, analysis, and response to feedback received. The discussion is uncomfortably silent on power dynamics in the feedback processes, and so it could become another inappropriately used artefact – even though, paradoxically, the core idea is to create platforms to deal with the current voicelessness of many. Fox's analysis (2014) suggests that initiatives that consider power as opposed to just information are much more effective.

Final thoughts

Carothers and De Gramont describe the proving of results as 'perhaps the most challenging element of current debates around aid effectiveness for the politics agenda' (2013: 271). The greatly intensified preoccupation of many donors to justify efforts could be used to 'craft more politically informed interventions' (ibid.: 272). However, few donors seem to have an appetite for the results and evidence practices needed to make this possible. The authors in this book propose that such practices must have six critical qualities: feasibility, utility, rigour, a basis in autonomy and fairness, the ability to generate reflection on the evidence of results, and agility.

Given the limited appetite – to date – for such ways of working, efforts are needed to make this possible. The chapters suggest seven strategies – used with varying degrees of success by those working in CBOs, NGOs, donor agencies, consultancies, and research – to challenge 'inappropriate means for designing and assessing development programmes with multiple pathways of change' (Chapter 2) and to create alternatives.

All experiences mentioned the recognition of one's personal power to question, create, and act. Individuals tackle their particular set of planning protocols, results frameworks, and reporting requirements to create more workable options. Being an astute political actor requires understanding the political context and organizational histories and leveraging organizational values. Several chapters describe working with what is positive about the results and evidence agenda, using certain protocols or methods to advance social justice ideals and to be self-critical about what is worth doing or not. A fourth strategy, though less mentioned, is that of helping front-line staff to speak up and be heard by those making decisions about strategies, priorities, and resources. Such local experiences need spaces in which learning about what works and does not can take place, and where ideas for influencing can be developed. This can then lead to collective action, although the chapters are cautious about how effective that strategy has been for them. The final strategy is about being politically opportunistic about results-related concepts or methods on everyone's lips that can help challenge power relations that cause inequality rather than reinforce them. VFM, theory of change, social accountability, and working politically are four examples.

The chapters show how strategies were combined in the different experiences. Shutt (Chapter 4) describes how some UK NGOs prioritized social justice values, grabbed the VFM bull by the horns, and cemented ideas through sector-wide discussions. Roche (Chapter 5) used a similar strategic mix for furthering social accountability. Johnson (Chapter 9) discusses five mechanisms, including creating space for learning. Van Es and Guijt (Chapter 6) refer to their particular combination as a benign virus, although, in the end, other drivers – both internal and external to Hivos – may erase theory of change approaches from the list of options.

Politics influence the many manifestations of the results and evidence agenda. Success with results and evidence practice that does justice to the messy reality of social change has varied and, where evident, is tenuous. Development practitioners have two options: they can learn how to reconcile their understanding of messy, unpredictable, and risky pathways of societal transformation with bureaucracy-driven protocols, or they can persist in the pursuit of space and time for more appropriate protocols and methods. The politically astute might do both, and in the process use political analysis to scrutinize the development sector itself and its practices and procedures.

References

Andrews, M. (2014) *The Limits of Institutional Reform in Development: Changing Rules for Realistic Solutions*, Cambridge: Cambridge University Press.

Andrews, M., Pritchett, L. and Woolcock, M. (2012) 'Escaping capability traps through problem-driven iterative adaptation (PDIA)', Working Paper 299, Washington DC: Centre for Global Development.

Baur, D. and Schmitz, H.-P. (2011) 'Corporations and NGOs: when accountability leads to co-optation', *Journal of Business Ethics* 106(1): 9–21.

Booth, D. and Unsworth, S. (2014) 'Politically smart, locally led development', ODI Discussion Paper, London: Overseas Development Institute (ODI).

Britt, H. (2013) 'Complexity-aware monitoring', USAID Discussion Note Version 2.0, Washington DC: USAID <http://usaidlearninglab.org/sites/default/files/resource/files/Complexity%20Aware%20Monitoring%20 2013-12-11%20FINAL.pdf> [accessed 19 January 2015].

Carothers, T. and De Gramont, D. (2013) *Development Aid Confronts Politics: The Almost Revolution*, Washington DC: Carnegie Endowment for International Peace.

Clegg, S., Courpasson, D. and Phillips, N. (2006) *Power and Organizations*, London: Sage.

Darnton, A. with Kirk, M. (2011) *Finding Frames: New Ways to Engage the UK Public in Global Poverty*, London: BOND <http://www.findingframes. org/Finding%20Frames%20New%20ways%20to%20engage%20the%20 UK%20public%20in%20global%20poverty%20Bond%202011.pdf> [accessed 19 January 2015].

Faustino, J. and Booth, D. (2014) *Development Entrepreneurship: How Donors and Leaders Can Foster Institutional Change*, San Francisco CA/London:Asia Foundation/Overseas Development Institute <http://www.asiafoundation. org/resources/pdfs/DEODITAFWPIP2.pdf> [accessed 19 January 2015].

Forss, K., Mara, M. and Schwartz, R. (eds) (2011) *Evaluating the Complex: Attri- bution, Contribution and Beyond*, New Brunswick NJ: Transaction Books.

Fox, J. (2014) 'Social accountability: what does the evidence really say?', GPSA Working Paper 1, Washington DC: Global Partnership for Social Accountability (GPSA)/World Bank <http://gpsaknowledge.org/wp-content/uploads/2014/09/ Social-Accountability-What-Does-Evidence-Really-Say-GPSA-Working-Paper-11. pdf> [accessed 19 January 2015].

Guijt, I. (2013) 'The Politics of Evidence conference report', Institute of Develop- ment Studies, Brighton, 23–24 April <http://bigpushforward.net/wp-content/ uploads/2013/09/BPF-PoE-conference-report.pdf> [accessed 19 January 2015].

Guijt, I. (2014) 'Feedback loops – new buzzword, old practice?' on BetterEvaluation [blog] <http://betterevaluation.org/blog/feedback_loops_new_buzzword_ old_practice> [accessed 19 January 2015].

Halloran, B. (2014) 'Thinking and working politically in the transparency and accountability field', London: Transparency and Accountability Initiative <http://transparencyinitiative.theideabureau.netdna-cdn.com/wp-content/ uploads/2014/05/Thinking-and-Working-Politically.May-2014.pdf> [accessed 19 January 2015].

Marquette, H. (2014) *The Research of the Developmental Leadership Program: Findings and Future Directions*, Birmingham: Developmental Leadership Program, University of Birmingham <http://www.dlprog.org/publications/dlp-research- findings-and-future-directions.php> [accessed 19 January 2015].

Mowles, C. (2010) 'Post-foundational development management: power, politics and complexity', *Public Administration and Development* 20(1): 149–58.

Mowles, C., Stacey, G. and Griffin, D. (2008) 'What contribution can insights from the complexity sciences make to the theory and practice of development management?', *Journal of International Development* 20(6): 804–20.

NAO (2015) *Department for International Development: Managing the Official Development Assistance Target*, London: National Audit Office <http://www. nao.org.uk/wp-content/uploads/2015/01/Managing-the-official-development-assistance-target.pdf> [accessed 19 January 2015].

Ramalingam, B. (2013) *Aid on the Edge of Chaos: Rethinking International Cooperation in a Complex World*, Oxford: Oxford University Press.

Roche, C. (2011) 'Humour, rude accountability and the results agenda' on Big Push Forward [website] <http://bigpushforward.net/archives/1773> [accessed 19 January 2015].

Roche, C. and Kelly, L. (2012) 'The evaluation of politics and the politics of evaluation', DLP Background Paper 11, Birmingham: Developmental Leadership Program (DLP), University of Birmingham <http://www.gsdrc. org/go/display&type=Document&id=4340> [accessed 19 January 2015].

Stern, E., Stame, N., Mayne, J., Forss, K., Davies, R. and Befani, B. (2012) *Broadening the Range of Designs and Methods for Impact Evaluations*, Working Paper 38, London: Department for International Development <https:// www.gov.uk/government/uploads/system/uploads/attachment_data/ file/67427/design-method-impact-eval.pdf> [accessed 19 January 2015].

Valters, C. (2014) *Theories of Change in International Development: Communication, Learning, or Accountability?*, JSRP Paper 17, London: Justice and Security Research Programme (JSRP), London School of Economics <http://www.lse. ac.uk/internationalDevelopment/research/JSRP/downloads/JSRP17.Valters. pdf> [accessed 19 January 2015].

Wallace, T. and Porter, F. with Bowman, R. (eds) (2013) *Aid, NGOs and the Realities of Women's Lives: A Perfect Storm*, Rugby: Practical Action Publishing

About the author

Irene Guijt is a rural development specialist with 25 years' experience in participatory processes in planning and monitoring and evaluation. She is particularly curious about how to understand what we do not know we need to know that is critical for transformative change. She is a research associate for the Overseas Development Institute on impact evaluation. She is active in global evaluation capacity-building through BetterEvaluation and on theory of change with Hivos. She was a Big Push Forward convener.

Index

CPSIA information can be obtained at www.ICGtesting.com
Printed in the USA
BVOW06s0023301015

424878BV00002B/4/P